The
Hidden Mind

To
my wife
Esther
and my children
Arik, Rachel and Tamar

The Hidden Mind

Psychology, Psychotherapy
and
Unconscious Processes

Israel Orbach
Bar-Ilan University, Israel

JOHN WILEY & SONS
Chichester · New York · Brisbane · Toronto · Singapore

Copyright © 1995 by John Wiley & Sons Ltd,
Baffins Lane, Chichester,
West Sussex PO19 1UD, England

National   01243 779777
International (+44) 1243 779777

Other Wiley Editorial Offices

John Wiley & Sons, Inc., 605 Third Avenue,
New York, NY 10158-0012, USA

Jacaranda Wiley Ltd, 33 Park Road, Milton,
Queensland 4064, Australia

John Wiley & Sons (Canada) Ltd, 22 Worcester Road,
Rexdale, Ontario M9W 1L1, Canada

John Wiley & Sons (SEA) Pte Ltd, 37 Jalan Pemimpin #05-04,
Block B, Union Industrial Building, Singapore 2057

British Library Cataloguing in Publication Data

A catalogue record for this book is available from the British Library

ISBN 0-471-95578-7

Typeset in 10/12pt Palatino by MHL Typesetting Ltd, Coventry
Printed and bound in Great Britain by Bookcraft (Bath) Ltd

This book is printed on acid-free paper responsibly manufactured from sustainable
forestation, for which at least two trees are planted for each one used for paper
production.

Contents

About the Author

Israel Orbach is a clinical psychologist and Chairman of the Psychology Department at Bar-Ilan University, Israel. His research and practice span unconscious processes, cognitive style, learned helplessness, psycho-therapy, and, particularly, suicidal behaviour in children and adults. Dr Orbach received his PhD from Yeshiva University. He has been affiliated as a Visiting Professor at UCLA and at the Albert Einstein School of Medicine. Presently he is engaged in extensive research projects in collaboration with the Child Study Center at Yale and with the Neuropsychiatric Institute at UCLA. His first book, *Children Who Don't Want to Live*, has been published in five languages.

Preface

This book is a study of the hidden worlds of the unconscious. Its aim is to expose the supposed mystery which clouds both the concept and the processes that it represents. Usually the concept of the unconscious triggers associations of the hidden soul pulling strings and controlling the overt soul. These associations arise in the wake of theories such as psychoanalysis and even more so those of Jung. In this book there is an attempt at clarifying unconscious processes, not adding to their mysterious and obscure nature.

Research into unconscious processes in the last two decades has contributed to the clarification of these same processes. Concepts such as subliminal perception, repressive style, dichotic listening, the hidden observer, divided attention, automatic information processing, parallel distribution processes, unintentional learning, and many more have enriched the understanding of unconscious functions and how they influence behavior.

Today there is no theory in psychology which explains behavior without taking into account unconscious processes and their influence. Psychoanalysis is no longer criticized for its speculative assumption of the existence of a hidden mind. Rather there is a continuous and fruitful effort to examine the hidden mind by means of modern research.

Yet the versatility and diversity of theoretical concepts, formulated processes and theories are quite confusing at times. An attempt is made in this book to clarify the various processes involved as the unconscious influences on behavior, to define precisely the theoretical concepts, and to distinguish as clearly as possible between different theoretical models of the unconscious. These different views allow the unconscious to be discussed within the wider context of the specific theory of personality upon which each view of the unconscious is based.

The approach found in this book is that the unconscious is not a physical or physiological entity but the conceptualization of (or even metaphor of) mental processes, an approach which seeks to explain human behavior in the clearest and best way. As a result, there exist many concepts of the unconscious in psychology. Every concept of the unconscious grows from within the theoretical principles on which it is based. A number of theoretical models of the unconscious are explored in this book: the psychoanalytic model; the humanistic model; the dissociation model; the cognitive model; and the inner incongruence model. For each model there is an introduction to the general principles of the theory, a definition of the essence of repressive and unconscious processes, the connection between the unconscious and the pathology, and the therapeutic principles which have arisen from the particular perspective of the essence of the unconscious in each model. The last chapter makes an attempt to examine how the different models relate to one another and form an integrated perspective.

CHAPTER 1

Introduction

Anyone attempting to explore the mystery of the unconscious immediately comes face to face with a wealth of definitions, processes, theories, attitudes, and questions. These encompass concepts such as instincts, wishes, energy, dual control of personality, memory, forgetting, repression, information processing, subliminal perception, splits, etc. These theoretical concepts give rise to the basic question: Is the unconscious a real mental process, or is it merely a metaphorical idea? In other words, can one say that particular behavior expresses an unconscious process, or is the latter a purely theoretical notion, whose existence is unproved, and whose purpose is to help us better understand behavior? This question leads on to others: Do the different theories offer different explanations for the same unconscious behavior, or do they indicate different processes and describe different coexisting unconscious worlds? What is the relationship between the unconscious and the conscious? Do they represent different, contradictory facets of personality? How do they divide behavioral control between them? What is the extent of the link between them and their mutual recognition?

These are only a few of the many questions related to the concept of both the mysterious and the day-to-day unconscious. The purpose of this book is to attempt some answers.

PARADOXES OF THE UNCONSCIOUS

A surprising paradox has developed in the field of psychology: Freudian and cognitive theories, traditionally diametrically opposed, are finding common ground in the realm of the unconscious.

Cognitive psychologists, who generally analyze human psychology in the light of conscious behavior, have come to recognize that unconscious factors do in fact influence human behavior and conscious experience, an assertion taken directly from Freud's theory (see Eagle, 1984, 1987).

This assertion immediately raises the question of the duality of two minds within the same psychological entity and what the ultimate control tower is that regulates the two minds. One of the paradoxical solutions to this question is that the existence of the unconscious mind does not just reflect innocent non-awareness, but positive self-deception.

Another paradox relates to the subtle power of the unconscious. According to some theories, repressed material wields great power precisely because it exists on an unconscious level. The moment a thought enters the conscious mind, its power dissipates. Repressed material can have a major influence as long as it is hidden from consciousness. Only when it has been brought to the level of conscious thought can the repressed material be erased and its power neutralized and forgotten.

An additional paradox of the unconscious involves the concept of knowledge, generally defined as a rational awareness. While the forces that are active in the unconscious are characterized as essentially irrational, sometimes they can absorb knowledge where rational, intellectual processes fail.

The story of the German chemist Kekule is a well-known example of this (see Wortman and Laftus, 1988, p. 187). Initially one of many in a long line of chemists striving to discover the chemical formula of benzene, Kekule was hampered by his conscious conception of molecular chains, based on the traditional principles of chemistry. Ultimately, his brilliant realization that the molecular structure of benzene is circular came not through intellectual efforts, but through an unconscious activity: dreaming. One day while trying to solve the problem, he fell asleep and had a dream of squirming snakes. Suddenly, one snake swallowed its tail, thus forming a circle. On awakening, Kekule immediately understood the molecular structure of benzene, which had so long eluded him. The dream state is considered to be a manifestation of the unconscious which, uninhibited by the rules of logic, is free to fill cognitive voids left by the conscious mind.

Yet another paradox is that the very concept of the unconscious is defined by the concept of the conscious, and that all knowing creates a level of not knowing. The flash of light in the darkness enables us to see one thing, but at the same time everything else remains in deep shadow. Basically, the knowledge or understanding of a phenomenon according to one set of principles implicitly precludes the ability to see it from a different perspective. Thus, the extent to which one focuses on a particular aspect of an idea is the extent to which its other aspects are out of focus, or unconscious. According to this approach, the unconscious is an end result of conscious processes. Humans' limited attention span, and their tendency to restrict themselves to one particular angle of perception instead of looking at things in different ways, creates the unconscious.

This special relationship between the conscious and the unconscious, in which the latter is an inevitable result of the former, is described in French psychologist Merleau-Ponty's (1962) phenomenological perception of the unconscious. Merleau-Ponty views the relationship between consciousness and unconsciousness as that between the self and the world, in a horizontal plane, in contrast with the psychoanalytic approach, which sees this relationship as in a vertical plane, the unconscious representing life beneath consciousness. Human nature, according to Merleau-Ponty, functions so that man can focus on only one given area of the horizontal plane at a time. The self and the world have a figure—background relationship: when the self is the figure the world fades into the background, i.e., the unconscious, and vice versa. Focusing on the external world, claims Merleau-Ponty, requires forgetting the self, and in order to focus on the self one must forget the world. The unconscious is thus a necessary condition for consciousness — yet another paradox.

Different psychological theories view the nature of the unconscious in different ways, each explaining the paradoxes we have presented in its own terms. This book aims at presenting various models of the unconscious and exploring their theoretical and practical contributions to understanding behavior, pathology, and therapy. Before describing these models, we will follow in the footsteps of Klein (1977) and describe the many meanings attributed to the unconscious.

THE DIFFERENT CONCEPTS OF THE UNCONSCIOUS

The various views of the unconscious reflect different theoretical approaches. To enable us to compare them, we must first define the terms we will encounter.

Repression, Forgetting, and Unconscious Remembering

The best-known facet of the unconscious is repression, a form of selective memory featured in the psychoanalytic approach. Repression causes one to forget unpleasant and anxiety-provoking events. Such forgetting is not the result of memory decay, but rather an unconsciously motivated psychological event. While individuals are oblivious to the forgotten content, they are nevertheless influenced in their behavior by the very same repressed content. The repressed content is ever ready to break into consciousness, given the right conditions. Psychoanalysts believe that neurotics try to forget their past, yet precisely because of this, they are constantly forced to relive their past experiences.

A good example is the case of a patient who complained of difficulties in concentration and of perpetual tension, both symptoms dating back to her childhood. After a few sessions, she recalled an event that had occurred when she was seven years old, which turned out to be central in her life and the focal point of the therapy. She could remember only a small fragment of the event, in which she was sitting curled up in the corner of an unfamiliar room, and an older man dressed in a pair of jeans and a checked shirt was approaching her. She could visualize the man only from the neck down. This type of scene is a typical prelude to a sexual assault by a family member. The therapy consisted mostly of reconstructing this traumatic experience, a long and frightening seesaw process of progress alternating with setbacks. While consciously the young woman made every effort to remember the event, she blocked the memory with equal intensity. At the same time, she could easily reconstruct other, unrelated events from the same period. Since the traumatic episode, she had undergone happy and meaningful experiences, such as marriage, pregnancies, and births, yet the repressed memory of her sexual abuse remained as powerful as ever.

The repressed memory of the trauma found expression in certain clear symptoms and behaviors, such as avoiding certain men in the family and refraining from staying alone with another male. In fact, she was unaware that she remembered the traumatic event. The prevailing symptoms were an unconscious reminder that she constantly lived through the so-called forgotten memory. Only as a result of consciously reconstructing the whole scene was she able eventually to forget it and escape from her perpetual tension and anxiety.

Evidence for the impact and activity of unconscious memories comes not only from the therapy room but also from the neurological laboratory. Warrington (1971) showed that people with a specific type of brain damage interfering with short-term memory can, after a while, recall material that they did not remember immediately after learning it. In other words, for some time these people were not conscious of the fact that they had successfully learned the material, only to discover later that they had.

The Unconscious as Lack of Rational Control

The unconscious is also viewed, primarily by the psychoanalytic schools, as a lack of control over emotions and drives. Consciousness can be defined as mental processes and behaviors regulated by rationality, while the unconscious is described as a reservoir of uncontrollable forces, an irrational system controlled by drives and impulses. From this perspective, behavior guided by unconscious forces is thought to be impulsive, driven incomprehensibly, disorganized, and lacking in intentional monitoring. The irrational and strange behavior of a person suffering from psychotic symptoms or of people showing uncontrollable compulsive habits or irrational fears is thought to reflect uncontrollable unconscious energies. However, the psychoanalytic approach assumes that the seemingly uncontrollable behavior is actually the end result of a carefully executed plan by hidden forces which, when uncovered, reveals an inner logical and meaningful sequence of wishes, plans, and actions.

Subliminal Perception, Unconscious Processing, and Perceptual Defense

Subliminal perception is a perception of stimuli presented at a lower intensity than that at which people are able to register consciously. Nevertheless, it has been repeatedly demonstrated that such perception, although not registered consciously, can dramatically influence overt behavior. The influence of subliminal stimulation on behavior was anecdotally demonstrated on an American television program some years ago. A film was shown about the use of subliminal perception to prevent shoplifting. In the drug store chosen for the demonstration the background music was masked by a voice reading the Ten Commandments, but at a frequency below the human hearing threshold. A hidden camera in the store focused on a customer who seemed to be taking merchandise from the shelves and putting it into his pocket, apparently intending to steal it. Suddenly, for no apparent reason, he turned around and replaced the items he had pocketed. The suspected thief was seen to repeat this behavior in an almost ritualistic fashion. The fear of God seemed to have fallen upon this individual without his conscious awareness.

Psychoanalytic researchers believe that subliminal perception can be used effectively to access and manipulate the unconscious, because it bypasses the defenses that block the way to the unconscious. These researchers triggered unconscious conflicts by presenting subliminal messages to subjects. The result, which will be discussed later at greater length, was that the subjects' behavior was influenced without their being conscious of this effect. Unlike the psychoanalytic psychologists, cognitively oriented psychologists identify subliminal perception with the unconscious. Subliminal perception is not a process that reflects other unconscious activity, such as wishes, conflicts, or drives which can be manipulated by means of a subliminally induced stimulus. Rather the processing of the subliminal stimuli is in itself the unconscious.

The cognitive approach expands unconscious activity to include information processing, relating it to the way we perceive stimuli, filter them, categorize and interpret them, connect them to other material, store them in our short- and long-term memory, express them in our behavior, and retrieve them. Information processing, through most of its stages, is an unconscious process. In contrast to the psychoanalytic approach, which views unconscious activities as working from the deepest layers of the personality toward the surface, information processing reflects unconscious activities working from the outside in, from the external stimuli to the internal processing.

Another closely related phenomenon, perceptual defense, was an early focus of research in the systematic investigation of the unconscious. These studies tried to show that unconscious anxiety and taboos interfere with the perception of external stimuli. Some studies showed that rude or emotionally charged words projected above a perception threshold were perceived more slowly than neutral words. The assumption was that this slowing of perception is caused by anxiety, unconscious attitudes, and emotions. (See Almgren, 1971.)

Inability to Discriminate or Notice Internal and External Events

A fourth approach to the subject of the unconscious relates to processes of attention or inattention. Here, one is concerned with the inability to recognize a given stimulus. The inability to discriminate a stimulus may pertain to an external event, internal mental event, or even one's own behavior (movements, facial expression, gestures).

The attentional avoidance of unpleasant stimuli is a normal phenomenon of daily life which sometimes attests to the fact that not noticing may have an ulterior motive. A woman participating in couple therapy complained that her husband never complimented her on anything. Yet just a few minutes earlier the husband had told the therapist how much he liked his wife's looks. The woman was unconsciously avoiding the compliment she longed for. The fact that the stimulus — the compliment itself — was definitely within the normal range of perception shows that this issue is not as simple as it may appear, and that complex processes play a part.

Similarly, there are situations in which a person is not aware of his or her own response. In a family therapy session, a mother shook one of her legs each time her young daughter was asked about her feelings about her parents' quarrels. The daughter would begin to answer and then stop immediately as the mother started to shake her leg. Neither the mother nor the daughter noticed her own or the other's behavior.

When internal mental events, such as thinking or imagining, have been diverted to the unconscious, they cannot always be reconstructed consciously. Bowers (1987) claims that individuals can think or meditate but be unaware that they have been thinking. For example, sometimes while reading a book, a person suddenly realizes that he has not retained any of what he has read on the previous page; in fact, he realizes he was not actually reading at all, but was immersed in imaginative and meditative thoughts that also escape him as soon as he tries to focus on them. Likewise, a person can drive for great distances and then be unable to recall how she arrived at her destination. More complex processes, such as learning, can also occur without awareness. In all these examples we are concerned with the inability to notice, recall, reconstruct, or account for unintentional behavior and mental events.

Inability to Identify Patterns of Behavior and Principles of Action

The inability to identify principles of action and behavior patterns according to which an individual functions is yet another facet of unconsciousness.

Cognitive theories view behavior as a result of an individual's system of beliefs and appraisals about the world and about him- or herself. These direct behavior, regulate interpersonal relationships, and define goals.

Some theorists speak of internal scripts and narratives that people develop and change during their lifetime and according to which they live. Others refer to constructs, hidden views, and concepts they have about life that motivate and direct their behavior and regulate their experiences. Thus, for example, the script or construct can contain a system of laws that govern male—female relationships, the main motifs and themes that determine the nature of their relations, their emotions, and their common goals. Eagle (1987) even revised the traditional psychoanalytic instinct theory, describing it as a set of fundamental inner laws and scripts that regulate the individual's life, rather than using instinctual terms. For example, he turns the fear of castration, interpreted by the classical psychoanalytic school as anxiety and guilt related to hidden sexual fantasies about one's mother, into a framework of internal notions or an unconscious belief that assertiveness, independence, or rebellion against authority will result in harsh counteraction.

These systems of beliefs and laws are not usually conscious, in the sense that they cannot be captured and clearly verbalized. Even though individuals live according to consistent principles and patterns of behavior, they are unable to identify or define them. The unconscious, according to these theories, is the realm in which these covert laws exist.

The concept of intentionality, taken from the existential—phenomenological theories (see Jennis, 1986), can be included in this aspect of the unconscious. Intentionality is described as the individual's conscious focus on some aspect of the world or him- or herself. Intentionality is an essential part of an individual's experiences, and to understand individuals one must see them from the perspective of their intentions. However, it is possible for the individual to live his or her life in a state of non-directedness and unintentionality. In this sense going through life unintentionally is like living unconsciously.

The Unconscious From the Perspective of Thought, Understanding, and Language Processes

Yet another approach to the unconscious deals with high-level mental processes: thought, understanding, and language.

Freud (1915a,b) described the functioning of the unconscious in terms of a particular mode of thinking which he termed primary thought processes. This mode of thinking is apparent in dreams, artistic creativity, and slips of the tongue, and they are vastly different from logical thinking. Thus, Freud equates unconsciousness with primary thought processes.

Matte-Blanco (1975) expands and clarifies Freud's conception of unconscious thought by describing and elaborating on the special rules and forms of unconscious thought. Likewise, Epstein (1983) sees the conscious and the unconscious as using different methods to acquire and express knowledge and feelings. While conscious thought is principally rational, unconscious thought is more associative—symbolic. These two forms of thought express similar ideas and arrive at the same goal, but by different paths.

Bowers (1987) sees the absence of thought or, more precisely, lack of understanding, as the essence of the unconscious process. When people do not have a clear notion about the causal relationship between phenomena, internal or external, they are in effect unaware of this relationship. Bowers differentiates between two levels of understanding. On the first level, understanding relates basically to the ability to discern that a relationship between phenomena exists. Second-level understanding reflects the essence of this relationship.

Another aspect of the major role played by thought processes in the unconscious relates to language. Here one can define the unconscious in two opposing ways by reference to language. The more traditional approach is represented by Sartre (1943) who identifies consciousness with language and the ability to use concepts, and the absence of verbal conceptualization with the unconscious. In his opinion, emotions and intuitions that cannot be defined in words are unconscious, even though they may be experienced consciously. Verbal conceptualization turns these mental processes into conscious ones. Consciousness is thus equated with conceptualization. ¹(special?)

Lacan (1966, 1973), the modern psychoanalyst (see also Stewart, 1982, 1986), completely disagrees with Sartre's view. He claims that the unconscious is the mental state in which inner realities (wishes, instincts) are experienced directly and deeply. When individuals verbalize an inner experience in words, they lose the essence and depth of the experience itself. A conceptual label reduces the instinct or wish to a dull reflection of the original intensity. The yearning of a child for his mother is strongest and most complete when he cannot express his feelings in words. When he learns the word 'mommy,' the real yearning in the unconscious is lost and the child is left with a reduced, limited verbal shell of the experience, compressed into the word. The unconscious is thus exposed in the transformation of experience into words.

The Unconscious and Dissociation

The psychoanalytic view of the unconscious emphasizes repression as a central process by which conscious contents are transformed into the unconscious and by which the contents and instincts are kept there. Pierre Janet (1889), Freud's contemporary, has described a different process for the very same functions — the process of dissociation. According to the dissociation approach, the unconscious is a mental state in which a particular part of personality or psychological function — cognitive, emotional, or behavioral — splits off from the rest of the personality, from the central control system, and becomes independent. In this definition, the unconscious is once again associated with a lack of control over behavior, as opposed to a lack of awareness. Lack of awareness may be one characteristic of the dissociative condition, but it is not the essence of the unconscious. For example, compulsive and automatic hand washing is considered unconscious behavior because it has broken away from central control, not because of the lack of awareness of its causes.

The Unconscious as Inhibition

Some theories of psychology reject the concept of the unconscious. For example, the behaviorist approach views mental processes only in terms of observable behavior, thus not allowing for unconsciousness to be an explanatory concept of behavior. Nevertheless, a way of relating to the unconscious can be found even within the principles of this approach. Behaviorists Dollard and Miller (1950) use the concept of the unconscious, but define it in their own terms. The unconscious, in their view, manifests itself in the absence of behavior, whereas repression is the inhibition of behavior; both are conditional responses. All conditioned responses — thought, perception, memory, or learning — can be inhibited, since they are considered behaviors like any others. This concise definition of the unconscious attempts to bridge the gap between psychoanalysis and behaviorism.

Surprisingly, the concept of the unconscious as a lack of response and as inhibition of behavior is also used as a theoretical basis in some humanist theories. According to these, inhibition of inner potential in the broad sense of the word is the essence of repression.

The Unconscious as a Lack of Inner Congruence

Finally, I propose one more way of viewing the difference between the conscious and the unconscious. Conscious functioning is defined as congruence of the inner experience or of different mental systems, such as perception, interpretation (appraisal), and emotion. Unconscious functioning, in contrast, lacks such internal congruence. Incongruence can be expressed as incompatibility or inappropriateness between the various aspects of an experience; for example, sorrowful thoughts accompanied by happy or neutral emotional responses constitute an incongruent experience. Another form of inner inconsistency is a lack of association, a dissociation between different aspects of the experience perception, appraisal, and feelings. Incongruence can also be considered as a lack of compatibility between one's internal world and the external environment.

The essence of this conceptualization is that consciousness or awareness is not defined merely by self-knowledge or self-understanding, but by the characteristics of self-experience. A complete self-experience, i.e., self-awareness, reflects a harmony between all aspects of the experience perceptions, memory, interpretation, and appropriate feelings. The greater the inner connections and congruence between these aspects, the fuller and richer the self-awareness. Basically this approach represents an integration between dynamic and cognitive approaches.

Some aspects of inner inconsistency can be exemplified in the case of 16-year-old Aron. Aron was referred to his school psychologist because of a recent deterioration in his conduct in class. Friendly in nature, he started to exhibit uncharacteristically provocative and aggressive behavior, especially toward his teacher. In several therapeutic meetings it was revealed that this behavior came about following the recent death of his father. He related to the therapist that in the few months prior to his father's death his relationship with his father was characterized by many power struggles. Aron felt that his father was trying to 'break him.' He described this as a recent deterioration in an otherwise good and close father–son relationship. But at the same time he could not feel any sadness following the death of his father. Instead he felt angry all the time.

In the course of the therapeutic sessions he was able to express feelings of guilt, remorse, sadness, and pain over his loss, and that in some ways he felt responsible for his father's death. Yet his misconduct reflected an inner inconsistency between living through the loss, the way he interpreted this loss, and the feelings of anger. The short therapeutic intervention helped to create a new inner consistency between the various parts of his experience. According to the incongruence approach to the unconscious, it was not the lack of knowledge or lack of awareness that motivated Aron in his provocative behavior, but rather the lack of inner consistency of his experience.

MODELS OF THE UNCONSCIOUS

The many definitions of the unconscious presented above belong to different theoretical models which are explored in this book. These models relate to some of the issues, questions, and paradoxes presented earlier in this chapter.

Five principal models and their variations are described. The first and best known is the psychoanalytical model, which we refer to as the substitution model. In this model we concentrate on the process of substitution — of one emotion for another, of one idea for another, or of one behavior for another — as the main feature of repression and as essential processes of the unconscious. This is not a new idea, but it is one that is usually considered of only marginal importance. In this book substitution is presented as a fundamental process. In explaining this model and its evolution, we describe, in detail and in ordered stages, the process of repression and its reverse, the raising of unconscious content to consciousness.

The second model belongs to the humanist school, whose means of understanding the unconscious are not encompassed by one comprehensive formula. The humanists, with all their differences, identify repression as the inhibition of the inner potential of personal expression. Special conditions are needed to lift inhibition to allow free expression. Rogers, Laing, the Gestalt, and others are the main proponents of this approach.

The third model of the unconscious is the dissociation model. Founded on the definition of the unconscious as a lack of control over behavior, this is built principally on the ideas of Janet, who claims that the unconscious is actually based on internal dissociation of some parts of the personality.

The fourth model described is that of the cognitive school. A collection of approaches, observations, delineated processes, and research on the subject of the unconscious from a cognitive perspective will be described. Although there is some overlap between the different cognitive approaches, one cannot speak of a unified cognitive model which encompasses them all. Each version is presented with its central ideas concerning the essence of the unconscious, its formation, and its implications for pathology and therapy.

The fifth approach is that of internal congruence or inner consistencies. Its central idea, as stated above, declares that consciousness is a revelation of congruence between the different aspects of experience (perception, meaning or interpretation, and feeling), whereas a lack of congruence produces a partial and incomplete experience, namely, unconsciousness.

The last chapter is devoted to a comparative evaluation of the different theoretical models and how they relate to one another. Similarities and differences between these models are discussed, and the question is posed as to whether they represent different theories on the essence of the unconscious or whether different unconscious processes may exist side by side.

Each of the five models is presented from the perspective of a specific theory of personality upon which it is based. The specific mechanisms and conditions needed for the unconscious process to take place are described for each model. The implications for the understanding of pathology as well as therapy stemming directly from the theory are delineated.

but who decided what is normal, unconscious?

CHAPTER 2

The Psychoanalytic Approach: The Substitution Model

Ira Levin's riveting novel *Compulsion* (1958) can exemplify the psychoanalytic approach to the unconscious. Two exceptionally bright, wealthy, young college students, Artie Strauss and Judd Steiner, growing up in Chicago in the 1930s, set out to commit the perfect crime. The two enter into a symbiotic relationship with homosexual overtones based on a grandiose Nietzschean fantasy in which they consider themselves supermen, and above the laws that govern ordinary mortals. They commit a number of small crimes, including smashing store windows, petty theft, and arson, but none of these satisfies their inflated aspirations, so they plan and carry out the horrendous and apparently unmotivated murder of a young boy.

The novel is based on an extremely disturbing real-life incident, of which Levin attempted to make sense by means of psychoanalytic theory. From the outset, Levin involves his readers in the boys' psychological states. We learn that Artie has psychopathic tendencies, and he is described as seething with uncontrollable hatred, stemming from feelings of being unloved and rejected by his family. Judd suffers from a perverted sense of identity; his personality was twisted by a long series of childhood traumas, which started almost immediately after his birth. His mother, who had wanted a girl, set out to rectify nature's error by various means, including keeping his hair long, demanding passive, feminine behavior, and even sending him to a girls' school dressed up as a girl. He suffered another trauma when his caretaker introduced him to the realities of adult sex while he was still a small child, by sexually abusing him. He experienced yet another trauma when his mother died during his early adolescence. As a result of these traumas, we are informed, he grew up totally confused as to his personal and sexual identity. The reader is told that Judd's identification with his friend and hero, Artie, on whom he became highly dependent, provided partial compensation for his early deprivations, while their homosexual relationship ameliorated his sexual traumatization, and comforted his badly damaged sexual identity.

Thus Levin paints the backdrop for the youths' 'perfect crime,' and furnishes them with motives that are not immediately apparent. The point relevant to our discussion is that the motives were unconscious, as they often are in psychoanalytic theory. The advocate of this theory in the novel is a Dr. Weiss, who attends the trial and pieces together the data, and constructs an eye-opening psychoanalytic explanation of the criminal and apparently incomprehensible conduct of the two youths.

In addition to the motive for the murder, the major mystery that Levin attempts to unravel via Dr. Weiss is the botched nature of the crime itself. Here were two intelligent young men who carefully planned the perfect crime, yet just about everything they did from the moment they enticed the boy into their car and killed him led to their getting caught as surely as if that had been their aim.

They stripped the body and poured acid over the boy's face, supposedly to obscure his identity, and over his genitals, and then pushed him into a sewage pipe under a bridge, screened by bushes. This spot had been selected at Judd's insistence. Then they sent a ransom note to the victim's parents, trying to make them believe that their son was still alive, and demanded $10 000.

They were soon caught. The ransom attempt was transparent; the body was soon discovered, and the killers identified and captured, all with remarkable ease. The burial location the youths had chosen turned out to be by a popular footpath, where one of the many passers-by spotted the corpse at the mouth of the pipe, since the killers had failed to push it in deep enough. To add to the string of avoidable errors, Judd had dropped his glasses at the site, and since they were recently purchased prescription lenses, they led straight to him.

Far from being a perfect crime committed to prove the protagonists' superiority over the inferior human beings around them, the cruel murder turned out to be one long series of blunders that led to their apprehension and punishment. In the psychoanalytic view which Dr. Weiss propounds quite faithfully, such errors were not accidental, but derived from psychological motives, among them the desire to be caught and punished, as actually happened. As Dr. Weiss explains, the apparently senseless and incomprehensible actions make sense only if we take into consideration the workings of the unconscious mind.

The murder, Dr. Weiss suggests, represented a compulsive return to the youths' childhood traumas. For Artie, it was the expression of the urge to murder his younger brother, who was the same age as the victim, and who he believed had stolen his parents' love. For Judd, it was a continuation of the process, started by his mother, of rectifying his sexual identity. In committing the murder, Dr. Weiss suggests, Judd wanted to kill the female part of himself, and to be reborn as a male. At the same time, he wanted to kill the male part of his identity and to be reborn a female. Pouring acid on the boy's penis (it should have been clear that this would not obliterate the victim's identity) was a means of fulfilling the second of these desires. The choice of a fluid-filled pipe screened by bushes as the dumping ground for the body, i.e., symbolic of female genitals, represented the return to the embryonic state. Pouring acid on the victim's face satisfied Judd's own death wish; the victim, unidentifiable, was himself.

That these wishes contradicted one another was irrelevant to the unconscious. In the psychoanalytic view, internal contradictions are a characteristic feature of the unconscious, so behavior aimed at satisfying particular unconscious motives can simultaneously satisfy opposing needs. Dr. Weiss's point, drawn from psychoanalytic theory, is that the youngsters were driven by powerful unconscious wishes. Their actions were forced on them, as people cannot consciously restrain their unconscious drives. In this view, Artie and Judd can be understood as victims of strong forces rooted in powerful unconscious wishes — aggression in Artie's case, sexual identity in Judd's. According to psychoanalytic theory, these drives force their way into expression. They overcome moral and social conventions, and play a larger role in behavior than do conscious motives.

Moreover, whereas the drives are wild and uncontrolled, the unconscious itself operates in a planned and precise manner. If we consider the various unconscious motives, it is clear that nothing was left to chance, and that the choice of victim, the location and positioning of the body, the pouring of acid on the victim's genitals and face, and Judd's dropping his glasses were all carefully selected by unconscious forces.

These are just a few of the ways in which Levin uses the psychoanalytic conception of the unconscious to obtain a coherent view of an event which, on a solely rational level, is so full of anomalies that it seems utterly senseless. To make sense of the apparently inexplicable sequence of events and the choices made by the two youths, and to explain the internal contradictions, requires the psychoanalytic approach to assume two minds, the conscious and the unconscious, exercising dual control over behavior, or perhaps one mind working in separate but parallel ways. In *Compulsion*, the series of events can be understood once we accept the idea of simultaneous operation of the conscious mind with its fantasy of the Nietzschean superman committing the perfect crime, and the ultimately more decisive unconscious mind, pushing on with its own drives.

We now turn from literature to a more systematic analysis of the unconscious from the point of view of the psychoanalytic school. In the more than half a century since he formulated his views, many interpretations have been offered of Freud's theory of the unconscious as reflected in everyday life, dreams, and pathology. Yet there is still a great deal of ambiguity regarding the precise mechanisms and processes of the unconscious, as well as its very nature.

This chapter tries to address the mystery of the two minds in the psychoanalytic approach, how they operate, and how they relate to each other. It tries to reemphasize the position that the essential mental process accounting for the so-called two minds is a process of substitution of one mental activity by another. This process is characteristic, according to psychoanalysis, to the unconscious, to repression and in fact to all mental life. From this perspective the so-called two minds are none other than two aspects of the same psychological entity.

The unconscious cannot be observed directly. It is an abstract concept based on extrapolations from observed behavior. These form a concept that explains and predicts behavior in a manner better than that achieved without it. Freud (1915a) explains the necessity of the concept in terms of continuity and discontinuity in subjective experience and behavior. We often find gaps in logic or breaks in continuity in observed behavior. The book *Compulsion* abounds with examples of these logical gaps. Judd's burying the corpse where it was likely to be found is one such example. Why would a person possessing Judd's exceptional analytic abilities insist on burying his victim's body near a well-trodden path? This discontinuity, this logical hiatus, calls for explanation. The psychoanalytic explanation is that the sewage pipe filled with fluid and screened by bushes is symbolic of the vagina and the womb. Judd, driven by an unconscious need to be reborn, selected a hiding place which, while highly unsuitable in terms of his conscious aim of committing the perfect crime, was ideal in terms of his unconscious motive. Thus the unconscious provides the missing logic and continuity in Judd's conduct.

According to Rapaport (1967), the psychoanalytic approach is historio-biological: the psyche is not an airy concept, but is firmly anchored in biology and in biological determinism. Psychoanalytic theory, in line with the classic scientific method, claims that every mental phenomenon is the result of some prior psychological or physical event. To understand a psychological phenomenon, we must examine the occurrence that preceded it, and then the occurrence prior to that one, and so on. When the earliest conscious phenomenon is reached, we turn to biology to explain behavior. That chain of events creates a continuum of psychological phenomena.

Freud, Rapaport points out, coined the term 'instinct' as an unconscious entity, an explanatory concept connecting the psychological to the biological. The biological explanation of behavior closes the chain, and we achieve continuity. This brings us to one of the basic problems of psychoanalysis, even before we reach the core of the concept of the unconscious, i.e., the confusion between two completely different theoretical systems of explaining conduct, the biological and the psychological. This is also known as the mind/body problem.

There is a lack of clarity regarding the unconscious throughout Freud's works. According to Freud, at least part of the unconscious is composed of instincts that have a biological basis. This biological reality, somehow or other, becomes an unconscious wish, which is a psychological or mental phenomenon, not a physical one. Freud does not explain how the biological process of an instinct is transformed into a psychological, unconscious wish. The biological aspect of the unconscious generally explains behavior in physical terms. The experiential—psychological explanation, on the other hand, assigns meaning and significance to behavior. Freud takes it for granted that the unconscious wish derives from the biology of the instinct, but he never describes the process by which that development occurs.

The confusion in psychoanalysis between physical and psychological systems (cause vs. meaning) pertains also to the concept of the unconscious. The interaction between the physical and the psychological which, according to Freud, takes place in the (unconscious) instinct, is not clear; nor did Freud describe how it is supposed to occur. Nevertheless, the notions of the unconscious and of unconscious motives bridge the hiatuses in our behavioral continuum, and this alone provides ample justification for them.

CHARACTERISTICS OF UNCONSCIOUS BEHAVIOR

In a comprehensive article, Shevrin and Dickman (1980) tried to formulate the features that define a given behavior as unconscious. Although these apply to the unconscious in general, they are particularly relevant to the psychoanalytic approach. The authors propose three characteristics of unconscious processes:

1. They must be psychological, not physiological.
2. They must be active and dynamic.
3. They must differ from conscious processes in their mode of operation.

Psychological behavior refers to mental activity such as cognition, emotion, perceptions, expectations, appraisal, and learning. On the surface, there is an innate contradiction between some mental activities such as perception, cognition, and appraisal, on the one hand, and unconscious processes, on the other. However, the psychoanalytic approach stresses that these functions exist in the unconscious.

The second characteristic of the unconscious is its activity and dynamism. While Freud initially viewed the unconscious as having both a passive (descriptive) and an active (dynamic) aspect, ultimately he emphasized the latter. The passive aspect is seen in such things as latent memories. At any given moment, memories, beliefs, etc. are not the center of attention; they are stored or organized in a passive form until attention is focused on them, at which point they become conscious. While Freud noted this feature of the unconscious in the early stages of his theory, in the later stages he saw the unconscious as an active network of motives which constantly influences conscious behavior without the individual realizing it, just as the villains of *Compulsion* were driven by unconscious motives without being aware of them.

Like motives, memory can also be active and dynamic, and can act selectively. The pathological state known as fugue illustrates this. People in this state may leave their home, family and familiar environment; they forget their identity, their past, and their family ties, and adopt a new identity, profession and home. However, they may remember some or all details unrelated to their former identity and history. They forget only those aspects of their past that are associated with the conflict causing the fugue reaction. Selective memory points to an unconscious force which dynamically organizes and regulates the acts of remembering and forgetting.

The third characteristic of unconscious behavior is its method of organization and functioning, which, although parallel to that of conscious behavior, differs from it. Conscious thought is governed by the secondary processes reflecting rules of logic and based on the reality principle. Unconscious thought is characterized by alogical, primary thought processes. However, it also contains cognitive activities such as analogies, symbolizations, generalizations, distinctions, conclusions, etc., but these are organized by what Freud termed the primary thought processes guided by the pleasure principle reflecting the unconscious wishes and fantasies.

Recently, Giora (1988) refuted this tenet, and gathered a long list of studies invalidating the differentiation. The differences between the conscious and unconscious modes of mental activity, he claims, merely reflect the different cognitive styles of different individuals. Thus, Giora claims, there is no difference between conscious and unconscious processes, and furthermore, no foundation for Freud's theory of the unconscious. Nevertheless, even if Giora is right, Freud's theory does not necessarily have to be dismissed. The fact that the modes of operation of the conscious and unconscious minds are not entirely distinct does not disprove their separate existence.

Instead of the difference between conscious and unconscious processes, we propose a different characteristic as being definitive of unconscious activity: the principle of substitution. Substituting one idea for another, one emotional expression for another, or one behavior for another, is the essence of the unconscious. Despite the fact that Freud himself emphasizes this aspect of the functioning of the unconscious, it has not, until now, been widely considered an essential or even major defining characteristic. The one exception is the work of Klein (1977), which will be discussed later in this chapter.

THE DETERMINANTS OF THE UNCONSCIOUS

In his essay on the unconscious, Freud (1915b) asserts that all repressed contents remain in the unconscious. However, the unconscious comprises more than this. The following pages outline the various components of the unconscious: instincts and wishes, memories and complexes, censorship, primary thought processes and defense mechanisms.

Instincts and Wishes

According to Freud, the most basic component of the unconscious is the id, which comprises sexual and aggressive instincts. Unlike repressed memories and traumas, these instincts are an integral part of the unconscious from birth. They are not merely part of unconsciousness, they are the essence of the unconscious. They fuel all our actions and all the manifestations of our personality. They can be said to be uncontrolled primeval drive energies which propel themselves towards any weak point through which they can find relief.

The instincts are responsible for the 'nervous' and conflictual character of the human being and for the cyclical swing from quiet to storm in human behavior. Above all else, since they work as hidden forces, they leave the individual oblivious to his or her real nature. Although we experience their influence, we are unable to grasp their essence or their real nature.

In his early works, Freud spoke of one basic unconscious instinct, the sexual instinct, as opposed to the powers of the ego, which he termed the instincts of existence. Later, he changed his formulation to include two basic contradictory instincts: the sexual instinct (Eros), which he also called the life instinct, and the instinct of aggression, also called the death instinct (Thanatos). The two would seem to be in conflict. The life instinct represents a constructive force, creative, aiming at synthesis, enhancing life and personal and human existence; whereas the death instinct is destructive, tending to a static, passive state and to annihilation. It is the latter which also sustains the yearning for Nirvana experienced inside the mother's womb.

Each instinct can branch out and manifest itself in many diverse forms. The sexual or life instinct can assume the form of heterosexual or homosexual attraction, a longing for love, narcissism, an urge for nourishment, or artistic creativity. The death instinct can manifest itself in aggression towards others or oneself, assertiveness, a tendency to thwart oneself, sadism, masochism, a fear of close interpersonal relationships, etc.

As different from one another as these manifestations may be, they are all nourished by the same source of energy and aim to satisfy one or both of the two basic instincts. Despite their apparent contradiction, the two instincts can combine in order to achieve an objective of the life instinct. For example, aggression, expressing (the death instinct), and love (the life instinct), can join forces in a very positive way in the matter of children's education where love and limit-setting are combined. Sado-masochistic sexual relations are another example of the opposing life and death instincts combining to serve the purpose of self-destruction.

Instincts are the biological expression of human action; however, they also have psychological ramifications, these being unconscious wishes. The wish is the psychological translation of the basic energy of total desire, accompanied by excitation. The life instinct can be expressed as a desire for sexual relations with a person of the opposite sex, attraction to one's opposite sex parent, a desire for food, etc. Some of these wishes are permitted to enter consciousness, while others are not.

From another perspective it can be said that the instincts comprise emotional—energetic aspects and cognitive—ideational aspects. A sexual instinct, for example, is composed of the emotional component (the instinctive desire), and the conceptualization of the specific desire as sexual attraction to someone. Thus, we can speak of a boy in the Oedipal phase, who feels sexual arousal (energy, emotion) for his mother (the idea). These expressions of the instincts are also unconscious, and appear in consciousness only in disguised form. An unconscious wish may occasionally burst into consciousness, at which point the process of repression comes into play.

Freud often refers to the concept of 'cathexis.' Cathexis is the instinctive charge of energy that is directed at and invested in another person, object, idea, or wish. It represents the force in behavior directed towards external objects, which arises from unconscious motives. Freud sees the relation between the conscious and the unconscious as a struggle between opposing forces. The unconscious force is the cathexis, while the conscious force is the anticathexis. Unconscious content, motivated by cathexis, constantly tries to break into consciousness. When the ideational element of a wish enters consciousness, it is recharged with energy from the conscious (anticathexis).

Anticathexis manifests itself in the form of a defense mechanism, or as a symptom which represents an instinctual wish in a naked form or other obstacle blocking the path of the wish into the conscious. (This matter will be explained in greater detail in the discussion of the dynamic aspects of the unconscious.)

Traumatic Memories

Traumatic memories comprise another component of the unconscious. There are two ways of defining a trauma; one is as a dramatic, unusual, life-threatening occurrence; the other as a sudden, uncontrollable arousal of instinctual energy, for instance an outburst of sexual passion or murderous aggression. Such an outburst causes great anxiety. The combination of the lack of control and the anxiety results in the worst mental state, a feeling of helplessness. Most traumas consist of both types, i.e., external and internal, and they give rise to anxiety and conflict not only when they actually occur, but also later, when they surface in conscious memory. One method of avoiding the anxiety in a trauma is to repress it into the unconscious. These traumatic, repressed memories are not originally part of the unconscious, but are mental contents transferred from the conscious during one's life. They may be organized in the unconscious in one of two ways: they may be forgotten, far away from conscious memory, but still organized realistically and logically by secondary thought processes (realistic—logical thinking); or, as is usually the case, organized according to primary thought processes, an organizational system unique to unconscious activity.

Repressed memories of traumatic events may re-enter consciousness in a variety of forms: as more or less accurate recollections of traumatic events, or in a disguised form, as a symptom, as parapraxes, or in a dream. Repressed childhood memories are likely to return, suddenly and powerfully, in a changed form, at a later stage of development. Thus, for instance, a repressed Oedipal conflict expressed as hostility towards the father may resurface with greater force in adolescence, either indirectly, or in the disguised form of extreme rebelliousness. Freud calls this eventual reappearance of repressed material, in all its varied forms, 'the return of the repressed.'

Complexes

Repressed memories and instinctual wishes provide the basis for the different types of unconscious complexes. Complexes, such as the Oedipus complex or castration complex, are made up of biological instincts, and their psychological representations are the wishes and repressed memories of traumatic experiences. These isolated elements combine to form a broad outline of personality. Systems of complexes are likely to interconnect.

FUNCTIONS OF THE UNCONSCIOUS

The unconscious is responsible for several mental functions. These include censorship, primary thought processes, and defense mechanisms. These functions are aimed at regulating by various means emotional excitation and anxiety.

Censorship

The censor or censorship acts as a control valve regulating the passage between the conscious and the unconscious minds. When unconscious wishes try to reach consciousness they undergo a process of adaptation in order to comply with the rules and standards of consciousness. Thus, a morally unacceptable sexual or aggressive wish is altered to suit the individual's value system. This alteration is essentially a process of disguise. For example, a child jealous of a younger sibling may wish the younger child dead. After being selectively altered by the censor, this wish may appear in the child's conscious mind in the disguised form of excessive concern that the younger sibling gets plenty of sleep, ostensibly for the younger child's health, but in fact finding a way to secure the mother's attention for the older child.

Freud draws an analogy between the conscious – unconscious relationship and two neighboring states, with the censor as the border guard. The wishes and desires are illegal immigrants, who are faced with two possibilities: to disguise or camouflage themselves so that the guard will not recognize them, or to obtain a disguise from the guard himself. The censor's cooperation in providing a disguise is seen most clearly in dreams. In dreams, unrestrained threatening instinctual wishes are disguised to such an extent that their original meaning is unrecognizable. Freud hinted that there may be several censors, but essentially focused on two: one mediating between the unconscious and the subconscious (the transition stage between the conscious and the unconscious), and the other between the subconscious and the conscious. These censors' work is carried out, for the most part, using two mechanisms, condensation and displacement, which are among the functions of the unconscious.

Erdelyi (1985) provides a more detailed picture of the censor's work, and identifies three of its tasks. The first is to destroy and erase certain unconscious contents, just as a censor may delete certain lines in a letter (Freud, 1917, p. 125). The second is to alter the original content. This happens in dreams, for example, by substituting an unknown figure wearing a father's hat for the father himself. The third is to alter emphases and values, for example by having important persons, events, or issues show up in a dream only briefly or incidentally, or, conversely, by over-emphasizing the insignificant. All these are operational methods for diverting attention.

Hence, Freud (1915b) assigns great importance to the censor, which, as described above, acts as an omniscient mediator in allowing transfer of contents between the levels, disguising unconscious material *en route*, thus enabling the conscious to accept it without causing anxiety. The process of transfer of material from the unconscious to the conscious is a complex one, involving many stages and censors, each one contributing another layer to the disguise of the wandering idea. In the course of transfer of an idea from the unconscious to the conscious it changes from irrational primary thought processes to rational secondary thought processes, and vice versa.

The question thus arises: Did Freud mean that contents passing between the conscious and unconscious (in either direction) are present simultaneously in the two different levels? Must material be eliminated from the unconscious in order to enter consciousness? In other words, are there two parallel systems of awareness, with every item being registered in both, but in a different form (according to primary or secondary thought processes)? Or does the creation of a new impression in one level delete its previous version in the other level? Freud never makes his position clear, offering different views on different occasions. It seems that on balance he favored the view that a particular psychological identity passes from one system to another, changing its form while it does so, rather than the alternative 'double-entry' theory.

At this point we are faced with a fundamental problem, which was defined by Sartre (1943): the censor is only a part of the personality, but it acts as if it were an all-knowing entity. It is aware of the true meaning of the unconscious wish. At the same time, it represents the conscious mind, blocks the entry of the wish into consciousness, and furnishes it with the appropriate disguise. Sartre points out that this scenario is illogical and inconsistent: the censor must deceive itself. It is as if it serves two masters simultaneously, the conscious and the unconscious, but it also controls them. Thus the question arises: Who is this censor really? Sartre further objects to Freud's personification of a psychological process, when he refers to the censor as a personality within a personality; Sartre maintains that this has no place in a serious theory.

Primary Thought Processes

My girlfriend and I were climbing up a mountain, and suddenly we fell into two barrels of water and rolled down into a house full of water. From the foot of the mountain, we saw John, my army commander, standing on the peak, then suddenly he was standing next to us and said, 'Well done! Mission accomplished!' Then he handed me the phone and said, 'Jane is on the line.' I didn't know who Jane was.

This description of part of a young patient's dream is characterized by primary thought processes. Most dreams are based on primary thought processes, and this example illustrates the main characteristics: the strangeness, the surrealistic atmosphere, lack of continuity, odd combinations and strange images, and being divorced from time — all these are the work of the primary thought processes. Freud referred to the primary processes as 'pure thought,' i.e., thought not based on sensory images. Basically these are principles of organizing contents, and are not the contents or images themselves. These principles, which will be elaborated later, include condensation, displacement, lack of negation, ignoring reality, and symbolization. However, it is not clear from Freud's writings if primary thought processes represent the principles of organization of the energy and contents within the unconscious, or whether they reflect the way the disguised contents appear in the conscious. Thus, it is not clear if the dream represents unconscious activity or the work of the censor before the contents reach the conscious mind. In effect, Freud combines both these alternative formulations into one.

A third quandary is that Freud did not indicate how these primary thought processes develop, nor whether they appear before or after the secondary thought process which is based on logic (Archard, 1984).

Defense Mechanisms

When we do not discern the anger of a loved one, we are using the defense mechanism of denial. When we ascribe our own faults to others, we are using the mechanism of projection. We are using displacement when we are afraid to be angry at someone, and vent our anger on someone else. When we tend to analyze a phenomenon or experience which arouses strong feelings, in a logical, philosophical manner, we are overcoming anxiety by means of intellectualization. When we forget unpleasant memories or disregard unacceptable urges, we are using repression.

The defense mechanisms, with a primary emphasis on repression, are themselves unconscious processes aimed at rejecting unpleasant ideas, unacceptable urges, and other threatening content from consciousness. In the same vein the defenses restrain unconscious, instinctual urges and wishes as well as threatening memories from being expressed overtly or being remembered. The defenses are triggered by an inner signal, a minimal degree of anxiety in order to protect the individual from even greater anxiety, should the unpleasant content persist in consciousness or should the forbidden impulses be acted out. Thus, the defenses operate unconsciously against other unconscious mental activity and are triggered by anxiety in order to prevent greater anxiety. The operation of the defense mechanism, especially that of repression, is responsible for keeping the two human minds (conscious and unconscious) split and for further enhancing this split.

However, Erdelyi and Goldberg (1979) point out that from the start, Freud considered repression to be a conscious, voluntary process of defense, a willful rejection of unacceptable ideas from consciousness, although later on it may become unconscious. Moreover, Erdelyi and Goldberg emphasize that in his initial formulations, Freud used the terms 'defense mechanism' and 'repression' interchangeably, and defined their function as pushing undesirable ideas out of the conscious and storing them (Freud, 1894). Only later on, in his description and analysis of the cases of the 'Rat Man' and of Dr. Schreber (1909, 1918), he broadened the concept of repression to include a large number of mechanisms: omission, ellipsis, symbolization, isolation, displacement, doubt, regression, undoing, reaction formation, rationalization, denial, and projection (see Erdelyi, 1985). Only the post-Freudians, Erdelyi and Goldberg claim, have formalized the concept of defense mechanisms, especially repression, as operating unconsciously, directed at warding off anxiety, inhibiting sexual and aggressive drives and wishes at the expense of great energetic efforts.

It is worth pointing out that Erdelyi and Goldberg apparently missed Freud's distinction between suppression, which he describes as a willful and conscious process of rejecting contents from the conscious, and repression, which he says is essentially an unconscious process (see Mackinnon and Dukes, 1964).

POINTS OF VIEW ON THE UNCONSCIOUS

In every topic he dealt with, Freud consistently employed a dynamic, research-oriented approach, and his views developed over time, with the result that today they sometimes seem inconsistent and full of contradictions. Moreover, he approached the unconscious from many different angles, and sometimes rejected his own earlier views. His first model of personality and of the unconscious was the topographical model (the unconscious, subconscious, and conscious). After 1923, he presented the structural approach to personality (the id, ego, and superego). He wrote about the unconscious from different points of view — the descriptive (topographical), the dynamic, and the economic. We will focus mostly on the economic and dynamic points of view, since these are most relevant to the theme of the present chapter.

The Economic Viewpoint

Freud brings the economic outlook to bear in unraveling issues relating to the flow of material between the conscious and unconscious. What prompts the movement of contents from one to the other? How does the transfer occur? What are the psychological processes involved in repression and in the operation of the unconscious? Freud couches the answers in terms of energy, and the concept of economy here is synonymous with energy. Thought, feeling, defense, anxiety, symptoms, imagination, dreams, all these require energy in the course of their realization.

Freud, influenced by contemporary developments in physics, viewed every mental activity from a physical point of view. He drew a parallel between the psyche and a machine. As he saw it, every mental activity requires mental energy. Moreover, the law of conservation of energy, according to which matter and energy do not disappear but merely change form, applies in the mental realm too. Thus, energy that has charged a particular mental activity can change form and charge another activity, even one that is the very opposite of the first. For example, the energy that activates anxiety and the flight mechanism can be altered and used to inhibit that anxiety or flight. Freud uses many terms relating to energy processes: energy charging, energy discharge, energy change, bound and unbound energy, cathexis, anticathexis, and libido.

Freud also described the unconscious in mechanical terms. Before introducing his complicated and confusing mechanistic formulations, we will use simpler terminology to explain his meaning. According to Freud, repression of material, bringing it back to the conscious realm, resisting its acceptance by the conscious, and its renewed repression, are processes which require energy. Each passage from one stage to another requires a different kind of energy. In other words, when an idea or wish passes from the unconscious to the conscious, it alters its energy, or exchanges it for a different type. Let us take as an example a person who represses his anger at his mother. When his anger and his thoughts about it were conscious, they were fuelled by conscious energy, but when repressed and passed to the unconscious, this energy was replaced by unconscious energy. If the original concept and thoughts try to return to the conscious, and succeed in doing so in a disguised form (e.g., by transferring the anger onto someone else), the disguised idea will release the unconscious energy, and will again be charged by conscious energy.

We may now restate this idea in Freud's more technical terms. As Freud puts it, every conscious idea or wish is charged with conscious energy, which is neutralized by instinctual energy. When a conscious idea causes anxiety, its conscious energy is emptied and is repressed into the unconscious. When the idea enters the unconscious, it is recharged with unconscious or instinctual energy. In Freud's terms of mechanical energy, the idea is emptied of conscious energy and recharged with unconscious energy. Analogously, material entering the conscious realm is emptied of instinctual (unconscious) energy and charged with conscious energy.

Energy is also involved in keeping an idea, impulse, or wish confined to the unconscious. Freud used the term 'anticathectic energy' to denote this energy, which is conscious. In his complex formulation (Freud, 1915c), it is the same (surplus) energy that was created when energy was emptied from a conscious idea which passed to the unconscious. In other words, when an idea leaves the conscious realm for the unconscious, conscious energy is expended, which converts into a force which prevents subsequent re-entry into the conscious of a (now unconscious) thought.

Freud tried to clarify this merging of mechanistic and mental concepts by using a clinical example, which he termed 'hysterical anxiety,' a phobia of animals. The source of the phobic reaction, which in its initial phases consists of vague, undefined anxiety, is the intrusion into consciousness of an impulse or idea from the unconscious. This impulse is likely to consist of a strong aggressive urge towards the father stemming from an Oedipus complex. When the undefined anxiety is experienced, it causes the conscious cathexis to be emptied from the aggressive urge. It is as if the conscious mind is deterred and flees from the urge (Freud, 1915c) or diverts its attention from the urge. Put differently, the aggressive urge towards the father is rejected and is returned to the unconscious, where it is recharged with unconscious energy, and remains repressed. The now conscious energy, which was emptied from the urge during the passage from the conscious to the unconscious (i.e., the same energy which was needed to divert attention from the erupting urge and to reject it from the conscious and redirect it to the unconscious), has now become anticathectic, opposing and preventing the return of the urge into the conscious.

In this example, the anticathexis takes the form of a symptom, the animal phobia. The initially vague anxiety assumes a new and more specific form. The anxiety and feelings of aggression towards the father are replaced by the fear of animals.

The phobia constitutes the anticathexis which, by its very existence, prevents the re-eruption into consciousness of the patient's aggressive feelings towards his father. The phobia is conscious; the aggression is not. The phobia can be seen as a disguised form of the aggression. The process may be considered as a dialogue between the conscious and unconscious minds. The unconscious asserts aggression towards the father, while the conscious rejects this assertion, loudly proclaiming the animal phobia, thus silencing the unconscious declaration. Alternatively, the process may be viewed as a struggle for control of an area. The anticathexis, a phobia, substitute idea, defense mechanism, etc., occupies the conscious mind's total space, leaving no room for unconscious material, which is thus left out of the conscious.

Freud (1915c) added yet another dimension to his explanation of the flow of materials from the unconscious to the conscious. An unconscious wish or idea, charged with unconscious energy, can reach consciousness only when it is disguised or replaced by an idea that provokes less anxiety. The process of substitution proposed by Freud is gradual, consisting of a number of stages; at each stage the idea is modified, until a version approved by the censor is found. This process is accompanied by changes in the energies. The instinctual energy in the original unconscious thought changes with each change in the idea, until in its final form it enters consciousness, changing the final version of the modified idea. This procedure of energy changes is at the heart of free association, which works back from the disguised version to the original idea.

The Dynamic Viewpoint

How do unconscious processes affect the conscious mind and behavior? The dynamic aspect of the unconscious provides answers to this question, focusing on the causes of conscious and unconscious behaviors. While the dynamic outlook is very similar to the economic one, it differs in emphasis, and gives meaning to conduct which may appear inexplicable, as in the case of Levin's *Compulsion*.

A case presented by Nemiah (1984) illustrates this approach. A 27-year-old married woman, mother of three young children, was hospitalized suffering from symptoms of anxiety, depression, feelings of worthlessness, and self-destructive thoughts. In the course of therapy she was found to be a devoted mother, whose concern about her children was exceptional and exaggerated. Later, she confessed that she occasionally had thoughts of hurting them. From this stage it was a simple matter to explain the anxiety and depression. The greater her feeling of anger at her children, the more worried she became about their safety. In terms of the dynamic perspective, her anxiety and subsequent depression could be understood as simultaneously being reactions to and against her unconscious urges, which threatened to burst into her conscious mind as well as a defense against their eruption. Thus, she repressed the anger she felt against her children, and when it appeared in her conscious mind, she was assailed by feelings of anxiety, and hence, by depression as a substitution for the dangerous urges.

Another defense mechanism, reaction formation, is illustrated by the patient's transformation of feelings of anger and aggression towards her children into excessive worry. An additional factor involved in the formation of the symptom is the guilt feelings stemming from the superego. Some of these guilt feelings were unconscious, and others conscious. In this case, the complex, dynamic impact of the unconscious on the conscious leads to the creation of pathology. Unconscious aggressive drives threaten to break into the conscious mind, which responds with defense mechanisms and repression; yet even so, the drives find expression through reaction formation, anxiety, depression, and guilt feelings.

According to Freud, the dynamics of the unconscious system are the very essence and nature of a human. Drives, which are the basis of personality, constantly try to use their energy to force their way into consciousness. By its very nature, drive energy constantly strives to find an outlet, just as blocked physical energy does in the physical world. The surfacing of drive energy in the conscious causes anxiety. Anxiety thus becomes an opposing force, pushing the drive energy back into the unconscious, and the cycle continues. Other drive energy is tolerated in the conscious in a well-disguised, more acceptable form. In our current example, the anger at the children could only surface in the form of depression, anxiety, and exaggerated care for the children.

THE PROCESSES OF REPRESSION

Repression and the unconscious are not synonymous: repression is the process by which conscious material is transferred to the unconscious and stored there. We will describe repression by breaking it down into three processes: first, the transfer of material from the conscious to the unconscious; second, the storage of material and instincts in the unconscious; third, emergence of repressed material from the unconscious.

Operation of Repression: Transfer of Material from the Conscious to the Unconscious

Preliminary Step: Rejection of Ideas from Consciousness

Repression begins as a result of anxiety, arising from an internal trauma, from continuous conflict, or from an external threat. Anxiety has many forms: fear of castration, of death, of abandonment, guilt, etc. The extreme expression of all these anxieties is a feeling of utter helplessness.

The preliminary stage of repression is the rejection of a threatening idea from the conscious realm. This may take the form of hampering the idea from reaching the conscious mind, diverting attention from it, purposefully forgetting or rationally condemning the idea, wish, or impulse, as morally or normatively inappropriate (Breuer and Freud, 1893; Freud, 1915b). Freud called these the 'withdrawal of cathexis.' In his descriptive, mechanistic style, Freud describes the emptying of energy as the flight of the conscious from an unacceptable idea or from a forbidden, intrusive impulse. On other occasions Freud called this whole preliminary stage suppression, as opposed to repression. In the early stages of the formulation of his theory (Freud, 1894), he claims that following the emptying of the various energy forms, the next stage of repression is the separation of the ideational from the emotional components of the drive, and the repression of each one independently. Afterwards, however, (Freud, 1911, 1915c) he assigns this separation to a later stage in the repression process, the storage stage.

Primary Repression

The next step in the process of actual repression is what Freud termed 'primary repression' (Freud, 1915b). Several definitions of this term appear in the writings of Freud and other psychoanalysts. The most common is a first step or stage in the process of actual repression. A second definition relates to the historical aspect, and views primary repression as the childhood repression responsible for the first barrier between the conscious and the unconscious. Subsequent repressions are considered more mature (Madison, 1961). A third definition links primary repression to certain specific kinds of events, such as extreme traumas (Kingston and Cohen, 1986). A fourth sense of the term repression refers to the prevention of unconscious wishes and instincts which never were conscious from erupting into consciousness (Frank, 1969, 1984). We will consider here primary repression in its first meaning only as the first step of repression.

The preliminary step of rejecting an idea from consciousness is not efficient enough to keep the repressed idea permanently in the unconscious, since it is charged with unconscious instinctive energy which repeatedly tries to burst into consciousness. Thus, another mechanism is needed to make the repression permanent. This function is fulfilled by anticathexis; i.e., the forces opposing eruption of repressed ideas from the unconscious. These can include forces of the superego, defense mechanisms, anxiety, and a variety of symptoms. As we have seen, the very appearance of the symptom, defense mechanism, anxiety or guilt, which captures and occupies the conscious space, serves to confine the unconscious contents to their proper place, i.e., in the unconscious.

Thus, one of the main expressions of the anticathectic process is the creation of substitute behaviors for the unconscious, instinctive ones, or alternatives for repressed ideas. As in the example cited above, an animal phobia may be an alternative behavior to the instinctive outburst of aggression towards the father; instead of feeling this aggression, the child experiences fear of animals. In so doing, she is substituting one expression of an instinct for another. Similarly, other anticathectic expressions are also merely substitute behaviors.

The substitution of a particular ideational emotional aspect of the instinct or unconscious content tends to broaden and be generalized to other areas of life. For example, animal phobia may extend to anything connected, by any type of association, to the feared animal, e.g., where it lives, the food it eats, or a word which reminds the child of it, even if by association only. In this way the anxiety distances itself from its original instinctual source to increasingly distant associations. This procedure strengthens the repression procedure itself, and the chances of discovering the original anxiety-arousing stimulus decrease progressively. Clearly, this procedure requires a great deal of energy.

Secondary Repression (Repression Proper)

The next stage in the process of repression is secondary repression, also called repression proper or after-pressure. Like primary repression, secondary repression also has a number of overlapping definitions, but we will focus on one only.

Secondary repression, following primary repression, is based on withdrawal cathexis, and to some extent also on the process of anticathexis by creating opposing forces which ensure the stability of the repression. Freud is not entirely clear about exactly how primary and secondary repression differ if both entail similar processes. He does, however, claim that the main activity of secondary repression is the attraction of conscious material into the unconscious by virtue of its similarity to material repressed in the primary repression stage. In other words, the contents which were subject to primary repression drag after them any other contents which are related by association.

Freud never clearly explains how and what material is removed from consciousness in secondary repression. However, in the context of a discussion of the verbal basis of the unconscious, he describes a process which may be relevant (Freud, 1915b) through a case study. The case is that of a patient who suffered from facial acne, and who drew an analogy between the acne and the scars it caused, and castration anxiety and symbolic self-castration (the scars) as a result of masturbation. Symbolically the patient castrated himself. Freud observes that in the process, the object or action is distinct from the word representing it. While breaking out in pimples and masturbation are very different, they are connected, for German-speakers, by a common word: ejaculation. The similarity does not lie in the actions or the objects, but rather in their names. While in the conscious mind an action is always associated with the word that represents it, in the unconscious, objects are also associated on the basis of their verbal similarity. This is just one of the ways in which associations are created. They also occur on the basis of similarity of symbols, contiguity in time and space, similarity of form, etc.

To summarize: the process of repression begins with the preliminary phase of purposefully suppressing an idea or wish from consciousness. Then comes primary repression, the first stage of the process, which transfers the contents to the unconscious, and immediately erects barriers in the form of defense mechanisms, symptoms or conscious substitutes for a wish, to prevent possible outbursts of repressed contents. The next phase is secondary repression, also based on diverting attention and on opposing forces. Secondary repression is characterized by the attraction of new material, similar to previously repressed contents, into the unconscious. It acts mainly on current material and experiences. Two main forces can be identified in the act of repression: the push (diverting of attention), which rejects the material from the conscious, and the pull (association) which attracts conscious content to the unconscious and absorbs it.

Storage of Material in the Unconscious

The next stage in the process of repression is the storage of material in the unconscious, where it can appear in different and changing forms. According to one version of Freud (1915b, p. 152), in storage the two components of the instinct or repressed experience separate from each other, i.e., the ideational and the emotional aspects split. The timing of the split does not emerge clearly from Freud's writing. The separation of the ideational and the emotional components, and the changes they undergo, occur via a variety of mechanisms. This process is seen clearly in the above example of the woman whose depression was the result of her anger and aggression towards her children. According to Freud, there was a split between her knowledge of her anger, and the actual feeling of anger. Each component adopted a different form.

The emotional component, once it is divorced from the idea, can undergo three types of change. The first is a complete destruction of an instinctual expression, or total elimination of the emotion connected with it, particularly a negative one. The second is the alteration of one form of emotional energy (e.g., anger) into another (e.g., love). The third is the transformation of the drive energy into generalized, undefined anxiety. The second and third changes differ only in the form of the substitute, and not in the process itself. All three changes entail the substitution of forms of expression and the nature of the energy. The first change can be seen in the example of a surgeon. The surgeon's choice of career may have been originally based on the aggressive impulse which has been eradicated in time and turned into an altruistic behavior.

The second type of alteration in the unconscious content takes on the form of substitution. While the original unconscious idea may remain unchanged in the unconscious, it must take on a disguised form in order to re-enter the conscious. For example, the child's fear (emotion) toward his father (idea) may take on the form of phobia (emotion) of a particular animal (disguised idea). The child is now aware that he is afraid of an animal and is unaware of the fact that he is afraid of his father.

A third type of transformation is the change of a specific wish into a more generalized anxiety reaction. The roots of this reaction may lie, for example, in a child's aggression towards his or her father. This drive is first expressed consciously, and subsequently repressed, to be transformed into anxiety, whose focus may then shift from the father to an unspecified object, namely, generalized anxiety.

In his description of the process of repression of the emotional component, Freud makes the surprising claim that there are no unconscious emotions (Freud, 1915c, pp. 177–8). They are always experienced consciously. When a psychoanalyst speaks of unconscious love, hatred, guilt, or anxiety, these terms are used only for convenience. Emotions, Freud states definitively, cannot be repressed.

It would appear that this contradicts the concept of the various transformations of emotional energy in the unconscious as part of the process of repression. No contradiction exists, however. Freud means, simply, that the expression of emotions cannot be held back or forgotten, as words or ideas may be denied expression. Emotions are manifestations of energy and as such must be expressed, or, in technical terms, discharged. Only the form or the meaning can be changed, but the emotional element cannot be blocked. On the subject of blocking emotions, Nichols and Efran's view (1985) is of interest. They claim that it is wrong to consider, as many psychologists do, that emotions are an entity which can be stored in some psychological space, and that a human is an emotional warehouse. In this fallacious view, the emotions are seen as an independent part or component of personality, distinct from other experiential components such as thoughts, memories, and actions. Emotions are not separate, storable entities, but an integral part of experience, which express a position, relationship, or behavioral attitude to reality or to the self.

When individuals express or feel anger, they are relating to, or expressing, a specific relationship with reality, and not merely emptying emotional content. Anger expresses an attitude towards an obstacle in the path of achieving a goal. Grief expresses yearning and search for a lost object or person. Fear occurs with the realization that the only solution to a critical problem is action. Gilbert (1989) proposes a similar idea that emotions are not storable.

Re-emergence of Repressed Material from the Unconscious

When a repressed idea powered by drive energy tries to reach the conscious, it is encountered by resistance until it takes on a substitutive form. If the first substitute in turn encounters resistance, the instinctive drive continues to wander through different substitutions until one is found that is sufficiently disguised for the original drive to be indiscernible.

The task of the psychoanalyst is to retrace this chain of transformations, the repressed wanderings, by means of free associations formed by the patient, in order to reveal the original unconscious idea. Freud's account of the case of the Rat Man (1909) provides a vivid example of retracing the substitution to the original unconscious via free associations. One day when he was on holiday, the patient, Dick, suddenly decided that he was too fat and had to lose weight. He imposed a rigorous regimen on himself, including a strict diet, running in the hot sun, and mountain climbing to the point of exhaustion. He could not understand his own compulsive behavior until he associated freely and recalled that his girlfriend had vacationed in the same place with a companion, an English cousin named Richard (Dick), of whom he had been jealous. Freud claimed that the patient was unconsciously trying to kill his competitor and namesake, Dick.

In Freud's interpretation, the patient's extreme weight loss was an expression of his aggressive drive, whose energy was transformed into a self-destructive drive (rigorous diet and exercise). The aggression was directed away from the competing Dick and towards the self, and was disguised further into the form of dieting, a nonviolent and unconventional form of doing harm. Furthermore, the hatred of Dick, the man, was transformed into a hatred of 'fat' (*dick* in German). It is this verbal overlap that suggested the direction of the patient's disguise, and served as the clue to break the code of the associative connection.

THE ESSENCE OF REPRESSION: SUBSTITUTION

The process of substitution of an original idea by a disguise is in my opinion the essence of repression in the psychoanalytic view. If this is indeed so, then the unconscious is better understood as a psychological process, rather than as a topographical concept referring to a hidden place where 'psychological content' is stored, and from which it is removed.

The two minds, conscious and unconscious, do not represent a special compartmentalization of the personality forming two different mental worlds with a barrier between them. Rather consciousness and unconsciousness represent two different forms of organization of thought and experience. Individuals who are unaware of the special rules by which they organize their experience are unconscious to themselves.

Klein (1977) interprets repression in a similar manner. He claims that the term refers to the unique organization of psychological material, not to its location. Secondary thought processes represent one type of organization, while primary thought processes represent another; and the process of repression involves the translation of one type of thought into the other. A person employs these forms of organization, each with its own rules, without being aware of doing so. According to Klein, in therapy individuals learn the rules they use in the process of transferring material from the unconscious to the conscious. In learning these rules, they acquire new tools for understanding themselves, just as an art enthusiast may obtain skills necessary for analyzing and understanding works of art, or a historian, history, or an economist, economics.

To show the importance of substitution in the unconscious, we will re-examine primary thought processes, instincts, and defense mechanisms, and will try to clarify the role of substitution and camouflage in each of these processes.

Primary thought process can be defined as the principles that characterize the nature of the mental and energetic activities of the unconscious, i.e., a form of organization of thought and energy flow in the unconscious. They include a number of mental mechanisms: ignoring reality, lack of negation, condensation, displacement, timelessness, and symbolization.

- *Ignoring reality.* In general, primary thought processes do not acknowledge the laws and restrictions of reality. Thus, in a dream, in which this mechanism is seen clearly, the hero may change forms, be in several locations at one time, and be simultaneously male and female, young and old, object and idea, tangible and abstract symbol. A child may demand that her wishes be realized immediately, and may be incapable of restraining her needs, or of adapting herself to the constraints imposed by reality, law, or morality. A man driven by momentary aggression does not take into account the fact that his outburst may result in severe punishment.

- *Lack of negation (indifference to contradictions).* In primary thought processes, seemingly opposing drives may exist side by side without difficulty. They may also be expressed in a single behavior without one weakening the impact of the other. For example, love and hate can both be fully expressed in the same behavior, such as in overprotective behavior of parents towards their children, in which the opposing drives of love and aggression come together, undiminished.

- *Condensation.* Condensation involves the merging of energy from two or more drive representations in a single idea or action. In a dream, a single image may be a combination of several ideas, events, or people. A patient dreamt that he was imprisoned in a fortress guarded by a patrol. Through analysis, it became clear that the patrol consisted of his parents, whose names were Patricia and Oliver. Freud applies condensation to the anxiety and hysteria reactions, which are expressed in the form of physical symptoms (conversion). He claims that the energy (cathexis) of the unconscious drive merges with physical energy in the form of physical action, to create a physical symptom.

- *Displacement.* In displacement, the energy of one ideational or drive element is transferred to a different one; alternatively, one part of the context represents the entire context. Displacement occurs when individuals transfer their anger from one object/person to another, with whom it is easier to be angry. In a dream, for example, a father's hat may represent the father. Displacement also appears in the dream about the patrol guarding the fortress in which the dreamer is held prisoner. Patr is cut off from Patricia, and Ol from Oliver, and these two fragments, via condensation, create 'patrol'. The transfer of emotion from a loved one to a pet is also a form of displacement.

- *Timelessness.* The components of the unconscious and its contents in all its forms know no chronological order and make no distinction between early and late; material can converge without reference to past, present, and future.

- *Symbolization.* Unconscious material is not expressed directly, but through real, tangible symbols. Cameron (1963) cites a patient's dream in which a woman appears in the form of a Greek goddess and gives him a bow and arrow with which to wound her. The dreamer shoots an arrow but misses. The woman then offers to enlarge herself, so that he will not miss her. In analysis, the act of shooting an arrow turns out to be a symbol for sexual intercourse. This symbolization becomes meaningful within the specific dream context. Freud also wrote of primitive symbolization (Freud, 1900), which involves the use of universal symbols, such as houses (symbolizing the body), kings and queens (parents and parenting), small animals (children), water (birth), setting out on a journey (death), and clothing and uniforms (nudity). In yet another form of symbolization, which Freud also calls dramatization, unconscious concepts are represented not by words but by images, pictures, sounds, smells, sensations, and actions. Guilt feelings may be represented in a dream by physical pain, while unpleasant odors may represent feelings of sorrow. Although primary thought processes do not reflect logical thinking, they create meaning which can be understood if the code is broken. Once decoded, primary processes seem completely logical, at least if one accepts the basic psychoanalytic axioms regarding human nature.

Primary thought processes and the inherent principles of substitution are elucidated in an example from Freud's oft-quoted self analysis (Freud, 1901). In a conversation about art and frescoes with a fellow traveler on a train journey to Herzegovina, Freud had meant to name the artist Signorelli, but instead he came out with the names Boticelli and Boltraffio. Surprised at this slip, he tried to reconstruct the conversation which had preceded the discussion on art, and remembered that the two had discussed Turkish people who lived in the districts of Bosnia and Herzegovina. These Turks had great faith in doctors, and when told that no more could be done for a dying relative, they replied: 'Herr [Sir], what can I say; I know that if you could save him, you would.' This reminded Freud of a Turkish patient of his who once said to him: 'Herr, when it [sexual life] is over, there is no point in living.' And this memory, in turn, brought to mind yet another which Freud wished to conceal. It was of a patient, from a town called Trafoi, who suffered from a serious sexual dysfunction which Freud was unable to cure, and who committed suicide.

Freud's forgetting the name Signorelli was not an accident, but was unconsciously determined. The name was associated with an anxiety-provoking event, with sexual urges and aggression. Figure 2.1 depicts the processes which were involved in this case of forgetting, or more accurately, in remembering wrong names in place of right ones.

Figure 2.1 illustrates the process of repression representing associative substitutions based on displacement and condensation. The process starts with a repressed anxiety-arousing memory of the patient from Trafoi who committed suicide. This memory was repressed by the force of the anxiety linked to sexual drives and death. As presented in Figure 2.1, the name Signorelli is indirectly associated with the suicide of a patient. The link is made by means of an associative connection (condensation) to the German word Herr which in Italian is Signor. Herr is also part of the word

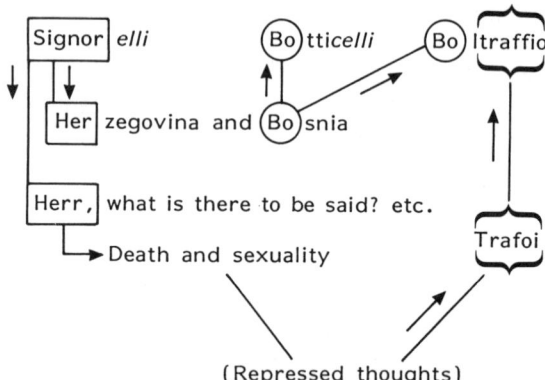

Figure 2.1   The chain of associations that led to the retrieval of the forgotten name of Signorelli. Reproduced by permission from Freud, S. (1901). The psychopathology of ordinary life. Translated by A. Tyson. In *The Standard Edition of the Complete Psychological Works of Sigmund Freud, Vol. 6*, J. Strachey (ed.). London: Hogarth Press, 1960.

Herzegovina (displacement), the region from which the Turks came, who also used the term Herr. Bosnia, too, is an area populated by Turks, and thus related associatively to Herzegovina. Bo, the first syllable of the region's name (displacement) is connected by association to the artists Boticelli and Boltraffio (condensation), whose names are associated with the city from which the patient who committed suicide (Trafoi) came, which is, in turn, related to the sex and death drives implicit in the memory of the suicide that Freud wished to conceal.

The process of repression seems here circular and paradoxical. On the one hand, it creates a substitute that occupies consciousness and prevents the original anxiety provoking memory entry, while on the other hand, the same memory and anxiety still appear in the substitute, albeit in disguise. Thus, repression consists of opposing processes which do not, however, weaken each other, and it simultaneously reflects the inability to remember and the inability to forget. This example and the figure again demonstrate how repression is a substitute-creating process, rather than a simple amnesic barrier. The creation of the substitute without any awareness that it has occurred is at the heart of repression.

Up to now we have examined the process of substitution in repression of the ideational aspects of instincts; however, the same principle is also reflected in the transformation of the instinctual energy activity through the operation of defense mechanisms.

The list of defense mechanisms generally includes the following: internalization, projection, identification, regression, denial, reaction formation, displacement, turning against the self, isolation, undoing, rationalization, intellectualization, sublimation, and, of course, repression. Most of these defense mechanisms operate unconsciously, according to the substitution principle, just like the repression of ideas. As ideational elements replace one another, so the original drive energies are redirected. This can be seen by taking a closer look at some of the defense mechanisms and how they change the original nature of instinctual energy.

The defense mechanism of projection serves almost everyone to some extent; it can, however, take on extreme forms in serious pathology. According to the classic definition, a person projects a part of his or her own personality (usually a drive) onto someone else, perceives it as belonging to the other person, and reacts to that person accordingly. According to Freud, this is a typical defense mechanism of paranoid individuals. Freud assumes that at the root of paranoia is a homosexual sex drive which arouses intolerable anxiety. In order to fend off that anxiety, the paranoiac attributes the homosexual tendency to someone else, and then fights it. In fact, he is dealing with a sex urge, via a substitution. Instead of contending with his own drive, he reacts to another person. The struggle against the other person is fueled by the same instinctual sexual energy from which the paranoiac is fleeing. The drive takes on a new expression, and a substitute for the original is created.

Reaction formation is also typified by the substitution of one form of energy for another. Exaggerated politeness may be an expression of aggressive and destructive drives. The disguise is necessary in order to alleviate superego anxiety. According to Freud, the energy that sustains the reaction formation (i.e., in our example the politeness) is the same as the energy that promotes the original reaction (in this case, aggression); however, its direction is reversed.

In a third defense mechanism, turning against the self, drive energy originally aimed at another is turned against the self. It is usually the aggressive drive which is at the root of this phenomenon. When one's anger or aggression might threaten another, one may turn it inwards, to avoid losing the other person. Self-inflicted suffering replaces the anxiety-arousing threat of loss, and the drive energy that had powered the original aggression against the other now powers aggression against oneself.

These examples show how drive energy functions in defense mechanisms by means of substitution and change, just like drive-related ideas. Furthermore, it can be shown that the substitutions involving energy are also made by means of the two mechanisms of displacement (as in projection) and condensation (as in reaction formation where love and hate are condensed). However the substitution is effected, what is clearly demonstrated is the malleable nature of energy. Energy is reorganized and restructured without the individual being aware of the rules governing that organization.

Freud claims that human nature is based on the flexibility and mutability of the instincts. This flexibility appears in development, pathology, personality change, defense mechanisms, and repression; in fact, it is involved in nearly all human activities. Freud expresses this idea very clearly in his article on 'Instincts and their vicissitudes' (Freud, 1915b), in which he argues that instincts can undergo alteration and be totally transformed. According to his description, instincts are organized along a continuum and can manifest themselves at either of the poles. The three basic continua or axes are:

(a) *Subject/Object*. The drive may be directed at oneself or at the outside world, and may therefore derive satisfaction in either sphere. Sexual satisfaction can be attained by sexual intercourse or masturbation. Aggression can be released by the destruction of others or by self-destruction.
(b) *Pleasure/Pain*. Love (pleasure) may turn into anxiety or aggression (absence of pleasure). Sexual pleasure may sometimes be achieved by self-punishment and masochism.
(c) *Active/Passive*. The drive to kill may be transformed into the drive to be killed; similarly, sadistic tendencies may become masochistic ones, and the drive to rape may become a drive to be raped, according to Freud. Again, these opposing drive expressions are nourished by the same energy source.

Freud describes in detail the transformations of the drive in a person with masochistic tendencies. In Freud's language, masochism is a sadistic tendency turned in on the self. The masochist enjoys experiencing pain just as the sadist enjoys causing it. The switch from sadism to masochism involves numerous changes. Sadism is aggression aimed at the object (another person). The change to masochism involves, first, renouncing that object and substituting the self, and then turning one's aggression against the self. It also entails the substitution of pain for pleasure, and the derivation of sexual pleasure from pain. And, lastly, as the masochist searches for someone who will play the part of the aggressor, it entails a transformation of the drive from active to passive.

Freud's view is that humans are driven by instincts that are given to transformation, thus substitution as the basic principle of behavior and development is established. Repression is no more than a specific manifestation of this substitution; it is the implementation of substitution according to the principles of primary thought processes and reorganization of energy. If repression is no more than a process of creating substitute expressions according to principles of which the individual is unaware, the process of removing repression must be one of discovering the code and exposing the substitution. This is the work of psychoanalysis: decoding with the aid of free association.

FREE ASSOCIATION AND SUBSTITUTION

The technique of free association enables us to see through the disguises which mask unconscious content in the conscious. In this technique, the patient is asked to associate freely to any word or idea that comes to mind: the association may start from a slip of the tongue, or part of a dream, or a fragment of uncompleted memory. The patient is asked to allow the associations to flow freely, uninhibited and uncontrolled. In this manner, with the aid of the therapist's guidance through the associations, the patient reaches the goal: the unconscious meaning of his or her behavior.

What is the connection between free association and the unconscious? What ensures that a chain of associations leads to the discovery of the unconscious material? The answers to these questions are contained in Freud's overall view of psychological determinism.

According to Freud, every behavior, no matter how trivial, is the result of a preceding cause. There is no randomness in behavior. Every behavior occurs because of unconscious forces or reasons.

Psychoanalysis is predicated on the axioms that the unconscious determines the chain of associations which ends in the conscious, and that in reconstructing this chain, the patient and therapist retrace not a random development, but the steps leading back to the unconscious.

Erdelyi (1985) suggests a more flexible approach. In his view, the links between associations are not rigid and unidirectional; rather, many different associative paths lead to the meaning hidden in a given construction. He illustrates his point with the metaphor of a crossword puzzle, in which no single word is the reason for another being there. Rather, all the words are contained in the same structure. As more and more parts of the structure are revealed, the whole becomes clearer. Erdelyi is thus closer to viewing behavior and its components as a Gestalt rather than a strict cause and effect relationship.

In his book *The Psychopathology of Everyday Life* (Freud, 1901), Freud reconstructs the chain of associations that led to the unmasking of a repressed unconscious idea. Freud spoke with a young man who, in order to prove a point, tried to recite by heart a poem by Virgil, but forgot one word (*aliquis*). Freud suggested that he free associate to that word, until the reason for his forgetting that specific word at that particular juncture emerged.

.The chain of association was as shown in Figure 2.2.

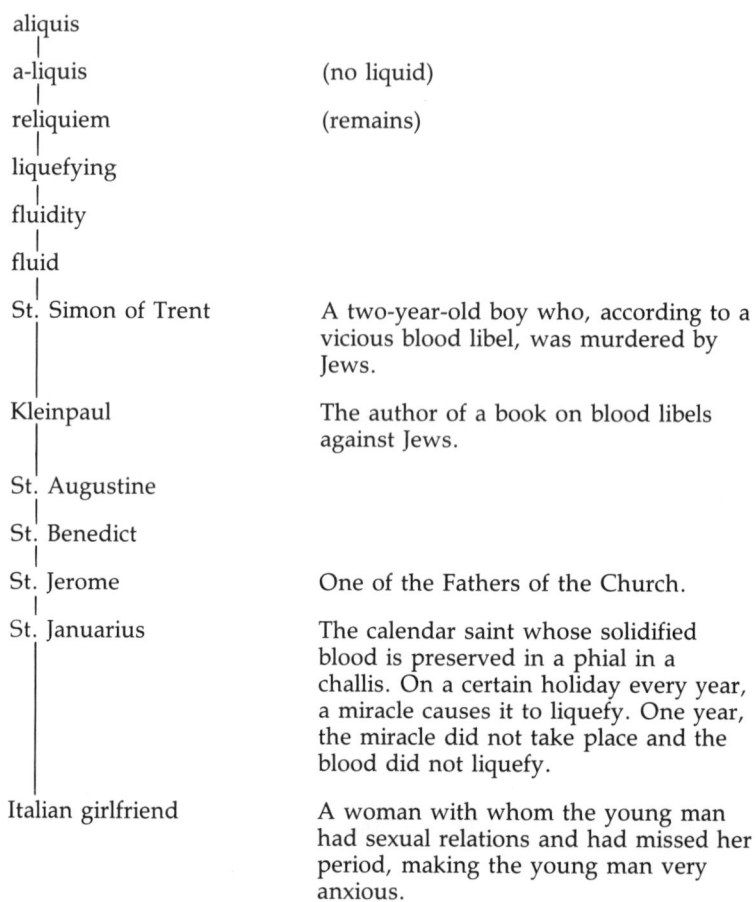

aliquis	
a-liquis	(no liquid)
reliquiem	(remains)
liquefying	
fluidity	
fluid	
St. Simon of Trent	A two-year-old boy who, according to a vicious blood libel, was murdered by Jews.
Kleinpaul	The author of a book on blood libels against Jews.
St. Augustine	
St. Benedict	
St. Jerome	One of the Fathers of the Church.
St. Januarius	The calendar saint whose solidified blood is preserved in a phial in a challis. On a certain holiday every year, a miracle causes it to liquefy. One year, the miracle did not take place and the blood did not liquefy.
Italian girlfriend	A woman with whom the young man had sexual relations and had missed her period, making the young man very anxious.

Figure 2.2 Free association

Freud quickly solved the riddle: the forgotten word was related to the word 'liquid,' which then led to a number of Christian saints, among them a little child; these, in turn, led to the saint whose solidified blood miraculously turned to liquid on a certain festival each year, and from there to the miracle not occurring one year, which in turn led to the young man's anxiety-provoking recollection that his girlfriend had missed a period. Closer examination of this chain shows that its associative links were forged primarily by means of condensation and displacement.

In summary, substitution is at the core of unconscious processes as a whole. Substitution gives new forms to unconscious ideas, emotions, and instincts. The processes of repression and other unconscious activities are based on substitution and the disguise it entails. Furthermore, individuals are unaware of the fact that they create substitutes and, of course, of the manner in which they do so. Substitution is responsible for the fact that individuals do not know themselves as they truly are.

This view entails regarding the unconscious as a form of information processing, rather than as a location, or as a storage space, or as simply forgetting. It is a continuous process of change, substitution, and disguise. Repression cannot be compared accurately to a blocking procedure, like a lid on a pot of boiling water. The various manifestations of substitution are inherent in human nature — not only in the unconscious, but also in normal development and behavior.

REPRESSION, ANXIETY AND PSYCHOPATHOLOGY

We have up to now dealt only incidentally with the motive for repression and its results. Prior to 1917, Freud viewed anxiety as a psychological manifestation of a purely physiological system. Lack of instinctual satisfaction was believed to lead to a build-up of physiological energy and its psychological manifestation is anxiety. Even the expression of anxiety was believed to be modeled after a physiological prototype: the infant experienced difficulty in breathing right after birth. Yet Freud posited that the physical tension may take on psychological manifestations such as anxiety, guilt, fear, shame, etc. Excessive tension may also be manifested in a variety of pathological symptoms. These symptoms, just like repression itself, serve as substitutions as well as safety valves for excessive energy. The key idea here is that repression and inhibition lie at the heart of psychopathology. Every pathological symptom reduces the amount of anxiety; therefore, any attempt to get rid of symptoms and pathology may lead to an increase in the patient's tension and anxiety. However, most symptoms do not provide an efficient defense against anxiety, and thus become an additional source of suffering to the patient.

The assumption that repression causes anxiety is not entirely logical, since if there is no anxiety prior to repression, repression is unnecessary. It was not, however, this logical objection which led to the change in Freud's theory, but rather his observation of clinical phenomena. According to his revised view (Freud, 1926), repression is preceded by and caused by anxiety.

His new view is reflected in his re-evaluation of the case of Hans, the son of one of his patients, who acquired a horse phobia after seeing a horse fall and bite someone. The boy's fear grew, to the point where he was afraid to leave the house.

At first Freud believed that Hans's fear of horses was nothing more than a substitute for aggression towards the father, deriving from an unresolved

Oedipus complex. As Freud understood it originally, the child's wish to get rid of his father so as to gain access to his mother was repressed; in the process his aggression was replaced by fear, and the figure of the father by the horse. On re-examination, however, Freud asked himself what the child actually feared. Was he truly afraid of the horse (an external danger), or was the feared object really his father (repression via change of object)? Was the fear really a disguise for aggression towards the father (repression via change of emotion)? If the instinctual drive at the heart of the phobia was, in fact, aggression toward the father, would it not have been sufficient to redirect it toward the horse? Why the additional change from aggression to fear?

In order better to understand the dynamics of the case, a number of facts must be noted: first, there were clear signs of Hans's sexual attraction to his mother. He had dreams in which intercourse and sex play were symbolized, and he often played with his genitals when his mother bathed him. His mother warned him that his penis would drop off if he continued to play with it (a clear castration threat). In addition, Hans and his father played at horses. The father would gallop with his son on his back and pretend to bite him.

From this point, Freud formulated a new paradigm: The boy, Oedipally attracted to his mother, felt the father's potential aggression and began to fear it. The mother's warnings and the father's feigned biting served as warnings of this extreme punishment. The fear of the father's aggression alone aroused anxiety, and as a defense against the anxiety, the child displaced his fear onto horses, connected to the father by virtue of the games he and Hans played together. Although Freud never dealt with the question of why Hans should be afraid of his father's potential aggression and not his mother's, when it was she who threatened castration, he emphasized, as proof of his explanation, that as relations between the boy and his father improved (under Freud's guidance), Hans's fear of horses decreased.

In this new theoretical formulation, Freud does not see Hans's anxiety as stemming from an excess of energy without an outlet (unsatisfied longing for the mother), but as a realistic response to the father's perceived threats (castration threats) pertaining to the son's attraction to his mother. This type of anxiety is not an instinctual entity deriving from the id, but a realistic ego anxiety. Freud calls it signal anxiety, since it serves as a warning which calls the mechanisms of defense and repression into action. In Freud's reformulated theory, realistic anxiety leads to repression, and not vice versa.

Freud now recognizes two distinct forms of anxiety: one stemming from the id (physical), and the other rooted in psychological reality, which acts as a warning signal. In his final treatment of the issue, Freud finds a much more complex connection between anxiety and repression: anxiety causes repression, which fosters further anxiety, which, in turn, creates symptoms and pathology.

From the clinical point of view, the process of repression begins when the individual experiences a conflict between unconscious drives, on the one hand, and social conventions, norms, or personal values and inhibitions, on the other. Such conflicts may provoke anxiety from one of any number of sources: e.g., punishment threatened by society, represented by the parents, should the drive be expressed; superego anxiety (guilt and shame); fear of abandonment. These anxieties are often referred to as fear of castration. Anxiety serves as a cue for the activation of defense mechanisms. Thus, repression blocks the satisfaction of drives by altering the drive expression. The blocked and distorted drive expression allows only partial satisfaction, and thus drive energy accumulates and is experienced as anxiety and manifested in symptoms and pathology.

The conflict which catalyzes this chain of events parallels the struggle between conscious and unconscious forces for the control of behavior. The chain of tensions, symptoms, and eruptive anxiety is exhausting, a fact that exacerbates the ensuing pathology. Moreover, the pathology entails a chronic lack of drive satisfaction together with ever-increasing drive demands. The latter constitutes pressure exerted by the unconscious, and causes the sensation of a volcano about to erupt. Even after revising his anxiety theory, Freud still held to both versions, i.e., repression causes anxiety, and vice versa.

REPRESSION AND THERAPY

According to psychoanalysis, the individual suffering from pathology is facing an unconscious dilemma. On the one hand, repression is caused by anxiety, and in order to recognize the source of the anxiety, the repression must be removed; however, any attempt to remove the repression may lead to renewed anxiety. On the other hand, it is impossible to begin the therapeutic process without eliminating repression, to enable the individual to recognize his or her true nature, i.e., unconscious wishes. Here we come face to face with one of the paradoxes of psychoanalytic therapy, which causes the patient to resist the therapeutic process. The psychoanalytic approach must therefore be slow, careful and deliberate. Repression must be pried loose gradually; with each revelation of the unconscious, the resulting anxiety must be dealt with before the next stage is undertaken. Psychoanalysis thus requires a prolonged course of therapy.

Psychoanalytic therapy relies mainly on the process of free association to decode and discover the unconscious: this helps to reveal the substitutions of wishes, drives, and memories formed by the unconscious processes. Interpretation of the associations serves as a formula for the decoding process, by means of which the patient learns about him- or herself.

This is not the place to answer the obvious question of just how interpreting and knowing their true nature, or discovering their unconscious needs, helps patients rid themselves of anxiety, and lessens the severity of their symptoms. The fact is that while psychoanalytic theory maintains that this knowledge itself has the power to bring about dramatic change in a patient, the therapeutic process is actually much more complex than the theoretical formulation. Therapists, including psychoanalysts, make use of a variety of strategies that go beyond mere interpretations aimed to discover the unconscious. These include strengthening the patient's ego by empathic support, by discovering alternative ways of satisfying needs, by helping patients cope with anxiety directly and by helping them modify their values and attitudes. All these processes alleviate anxiety and ameliorate the pathology, as indeed does the exposure of the unconscious by breaking the code of substitution.

THE EMPIRICAL BASIS OF THE PSYCHOANALYTIC APPROACH

For many years, evidence of the validity of the psychoanalytic view of the unconscious has rested on clinical analyses. But such evidence involves a good number of subjective, clinical impressions and intuitions, not rigorous scientific criteria. In recent years, however, preliminary objective support has been provided.

Support for the Freudian view of the unconscious involves his tenet that repression aims to eliminate anxiety by inhibiting traumatic and other early anxiety-provoking memories. It is generally accepted that erecting an amnesic barrier is one of the main processes in repression, and there have been several empirical attempts to validate this hypothesis.

One of these attempts is based on the view that the tendency to use repression to deal with anxiety and stress is a personality trait, with some people being more inclined to use it than others. In other words, some people are more anxious and more defensive, and more inclined to use repression than others. It is expected that such individuals will show strong amnesic tendencies, and will recall fewer memories from their past. On the basis of these assumptions, Weinberger, Schwartz, and Davidson (1979) classified persons into four groups according to the combinations of level of anxiety and degree of defensiveness (repression) that they exhibit:

(a) Low anxious individuals, who are low in anxiety and low in defensiveness.
(b) Repressors, who are low in anxiety and high in defensiveness.
(c) High anxious individuals who are high in anxiety and low in defensiveness (non-repressors).
(d) High anxious defensive individuals (unsuccessful repressors).

Using a modified version of this classification, Davis and Schwartz (1987) tested the tendency towards amnesia. Their basic hypothesis was that repressors would be less able to remember experiences associated with negative emotions than would non-repressors. Dividing their subjects into three groups, repressors, low anxious (non-repressors), and high anxious, the authors asked them to recall six types of personal childhood experiences — general, happy, sad, involving anger, fear, and wonder — as well as their age at their earliest memory of each. The results revealed that repressors recalled fewer negative emotional experiences than both groups of non-repressors. Moreover, the earliest negative memories recalled by the repressors were from a later age than those of non-repressors. This pattern indeed suggests that repressors have more limited access to negative emotions than non-repressors.

However, a number of methodological problems somewhat undermine the attempted validation of the Freudian theory of the unconscious in this study. First of all, the results of the study showed that the repressors recalled not only fewer negative experiences than the non-repressors, but also fewer pleasurable ones. If, as in Freudian theory, repression is a means of dealing with unpleasant memories, this study does not show the effect of emotion on recollection and creation of repression, but merely that repressors have a tendency to forget any past event more quickly. Another methodological problem is that the study did not include a group of unsuccessful repressors, high in both defensiveness and anxiety. This leaves open the possibility that the results could simply reflect high levels of defensiveness, rather than successful repression marked by low anxiety and high defensiveness. Finally, in asking subjects to report their recollections, the study had no means of verifying that the subjects were reporting exactly what they remembered. Thus, it may be that the repressors recalled as many experiences as the non-repressors, but for some reason simply chose to report fewer.

To overcome these problems, Davis (1987) conducted a series of three studies, using a modified version of the design of the Davis and Schwartz (1987) study. In these studies, Davis added an additional group of high anxiety, high defensive individuals (unsuccessful repressors). In the first study, the four groups of subjects were asked to recall personal experiences which they themselves had undergone, and events that happened to other people, whether positive or negative. Davis found that the repressors reported fewer experiences, both negative and positive, which involved themselves, and more that involved others.

In the second study, the four groups of subjects were asked to report specific memories of happiness, sadness, anger, and fear. The accessibility of memories was measured both by the number of recollections and by the latency of recall — the time it took each subject to remember an event. (This latency is another indication of repression.) The findings indicated that while all four groups reported similar numbers of neutral and sad memories, the repressors reported the fewest fearful and angry memories, and had the highest latency for memories of this type.

Davis's third study was similar to the second, but the respondents were also asked to recall experiences relating to guilt and self-consciousness. It was found that repressors had the longest latency for memories involving fear and self-consciousness, and that in total they had fewer memories of these. It was also found that the high anxiety group had a longer latency for anger than did the other groups, while the highly defensive subjects had a longer latency for guilt.

In a recent study, Myers and Brewin (1994) have replicated some of the earlier studies with repressors and non-repressors, but they introduced an additional measure of a more objective account of the subjects' actual early experience. They found that repressors indeed free recalled fewer negative childhood memories than did non-repressors and the age of the first negative memory for repressors was older. Repressors also took longer to retrieve negative childhood memories, but not positive memories. Further it was found that repressors' accounts of their childhood were more likely to be characterized by parental antipathy and indifference, as they were less likely to report an emotionally or physically close relationship with their father. This study can be taken as valid evidence for some important theoretical hypotheses of the psychoanalytic approach. A clear link is revealed between childhood anxiety-provoking trauma or lack of need satisfaction, anxiety, and the tendency to repress the unpleasant memories.

Another body of research provides empirical support for the psychoanalytic notion that repression is a defense against unpleasant memories, but the emotions themselves cannot be inhibited and they constantly seek expression. The reduction in subjective distress obtained by the use of repression is accompanied by heightened physiological arousal and behavioral manifestations. Weinberger, Schwartz and Davidson (1979) and Gudgonsson (1981) have investigated the physiological and behavioral responses of repressors and non-repressors when exposed to sexual, aggressive, and other distressing contents. They found that while the repressors reported lower levels of subjective distress than non-repressors, it was indicated that the repressors showed more distress on physiological and behavioral measures.

Highly significant empirical support for psychoanalytic theory is provided by extensive research carried out by Silverman and his colleagues into the relationship between the dynamic activity of unconscious instincts and psychopathology. The basic tenet that they tried to prove was that psychopathology is the outcome of a struggle against unconscious sexual or aggressive longings, using inefficient defense mechanisms. They employed a rather ingenious technique of activating unconscious processes without their subjects' awareness (the subliminal psychodynamic activation, SPA). The idea was that if pathology is, in fact, the outcome of unsuccessful repression of anxiety-provoking wishes, then appropriate stimulation or pacification could either exacerbate or ameliorate the symptoms. The subliminal psychodynamic activation method consisted of projecting onto a screen a sentence or picture relevant to an unconscious wish. The stimulus is shown for a period of four milliseconds, a speed at which 90 percent of the population is unable to grasp any meaning at all, and the remaining 10 percent grasps some meaning by guessing or by partially identifying the letters. Following this type of exposure, the behavioral, physiological, cognitive, and emotional effects are then examined.

Some investigations were carried out on a group of schizophrenics who exhibited thought disturbances. According to psychoanalytic theory, these disturbances derive from oral-aggressive conflicts. The experiments were based on, and set out to prove, the idea that the arousal of oral-aggressive instincts would cause an increase in the severity of the thought disturbances. In one such study, Lomanzino (1969) exposed groups of schizophrenics to one of three verbal stimuli and a parallel pictorial stimulus. The verbal stimuli were either (1) oral-aggressive: ('Cannibals eat human beings'), or (2) non-oral-aggressive: ('The murderer stabs his victims'), or (3) a control sentence having no reference to aggression. As predicted, oral-aggressive stimuli, whether verbal or pictorial, increased the severity of the thought disturbances, while the non-oral-aggressive and control stimuli had no effect on symptom severity.

Fascinating results were also obtained in the study of depression, which, according to psychoanalytic theory, is the result of turning aggression inwards, instead of directing it towards a loved one. In one investigation, Rutstein and Goldberg (1973) studied three groups of women. One group consisted of women who had been hospitalized with depression, a second group consisted of female students who had been classified as passive personalities, and the third group consisted of women who had lost a parent during childhood. The investigators stirred up inner aggression by using a subliminal sentence, 'Destroy mother.' In response, all showed an increase in the severity of depression (inward aggression). No such reaction was found to the control sentence. These findings support Freud's claim that depression is a disguised form of aggression towards a loved person.

One of the assumptions implicit in the above studies is that specific types of psychopathology are related to specific types of unconscious wishes and conflicts. According to Silverman, this association derives from the psychoanalytic notion that certain instinctual conflicts are typical to chronological periods.

Silverman also showed that symptom severity can be decreased by exposure to subliminal stimuli promising fulfillment of repressed wishes. These hypotheses were derived from the assumption that some pathologies are rooted in conflict, or in a deficiency in the mother—infant relationship and inadequate nurturing. The hypothesis was that if depressives or schizophrenics could obtain some kind of unconscious, fantasized gratification of their unsatisfied needs for mothering, their symptoms would be alleviated.

Silverman composed sentences with deep emotional meaning symbolizing the yearning for symbiosis of mother and infant: 'Mommy and I are one,' 'Mommy feeds me,' 'Mommy is always with me,' and 'I can't hurt Mommy.' Exposure to these sentences lessened the severity of the patients' thought disturbances, while sentences expressing ideas threatening this unity, such as 'Destroy Mommy' and 'I am losing Mommy,' intensified the pathology (see, for example, Silverman, 1976).

Research using subliminal stimulation was extended to include non-pathological subjects. In one study (Silverman et al., 1978), subliminal stimulation provoked expression of latent Oedipus conflicts, believed to be universal, in a normal student population. Four groups of male students were exposed to one of the following subliminal stimuli: 'It is OK to beat Daddy,' or 'It is not OK to beat Daddy,' or the control stimulus, 'People are walking in the street.' Following exposure to these stimuli, the subjects were required to throw darts at a target, a symbolic act of Oedipal aggression toward their fathers. As hypothesized, the stimulus 'It is OK to beat Daddy' resulted in higher scores than the other stimuli.

Ariam and Siller (1982) demonstrated the ability of the subliminal stimulus 'Mommy and I are one' to enhance adjustive behavior. These researchers showed that exposing Israeli high school students to this sentence at a subliminal level over several weeks improved their math grades. This study shows that subliminal stimulation of the unconscious can improve normal functioning, demonstrating the powerful impact of unconscious wishes on security and well-being.

Later researchers employed Silverman's technique in their own studies, which have also provided a multitude of findings supporting the validity of psychoanalytic theory. Thus, for example, Leiter (1982) and Fribourg (1981) independently reached the conclusion that different types of schizophrenics differ in their responses to the sentence 'Mommy and I are one.' Differentiated schizophrenics, those whose identities are separate from those of their mothers, were affected positively by the symbiotic sentence 'Mommy and I are one,' while undifferentiated schizophrenics, who confuse their identities with their mother's, did not react to the sentence, supposedly owing to the threat it represented for them.

Similarly, Jackson (1983) found that men reacted to the symbiotic sentence more positively than women, while schizophrenic women preferred the symbiotic sentence when it applied to the father: 'Daddy and I are one.' Carroll (1979) found that subliminal exposure to the sentence 'It's OK to beat Daddy' has greater impact on subjects with efficient defenses than on those with weak defenses.

Recently, Orbach, Shopen-Kofman, and Mikulincer (1994) have again demonstrated that not all individuals can enjoy the fruitful effects of stimulating unconscious fantasies. If the wish for the mother is unconsciously conflictual, it will not have the same positive effects as when the wish is not conflictual. In that study it was revealed that only females with a cohesive self-identity enjoyed a reduction in anxiety following the subliminal stimulation of 'Mommy and I are one.' Females with a low cohesive self-identity, indicating a threatening conflict with regard to the unity with the mother, showed no reduction in anxiety.

Subliminal stimulation has also been found to serve as an effective adjunct to psychotherapy. Bryant-Tuckett and Silverman (1984) found that therapy accompanied by subliminal stimulation was more effective than therapy without subliminal stimulation. Furthermore, it was found that the more frequent the exposure to a stimulus, the more effective the therapy as a whole (Packer, 1984; Palmatier and Bornstein, 1980). Another researcher, Geisler (1986), made sophisticated use of subliminal stimulation in psychotherapy, when she discovered that intensification of the unconscious conflict prior to exposure to the symbiotic sentence enhanced its effectiveness. Bornstein and Rodin (1983) found that only the symbiotic sentence 'Mother and I are one' decreased the severity of the pathological symptoms, and that no semantically similar substitute ('Mother nurses me,' etc.) was effective. Similarly, Silverman, Lachmann, and Milich (1982) found that the word 'Mommy' in the symbiotic sentence is effective only if this was the appellation the subject used for his or her mother in childhood. Other versions, such as Mamma, were also effective only if they were the ones used by the subjects as children.

Several recent studies have focused on the unconscious process itself, not only on the outcome of the subliminal activation. These studies demonstrated that unconscious processes are different in their operation from conscious processes. For example, it was demonstrated that subliminal messages such as 'no one loves me' can produce electrodermal responses in the subjects, whereas supraliminal exposure to the same message does not (Masling et al., 1991). A similar study was reported by Kotze and Moller (1990). Finally, the process of repression and the mechanisms involved have also become a recent aim of the empirical study. Bonanno et al. (1991) have provided a view of the psychological mechanisms that operate when repression takes place, providing initial empirical evidence for Freud's concept of withdrawal of attention (cathexis) as a preliminary step of repression. These investigators have shown that when repressors are provided with auditory stimulation of an unpleasant nature, they avoid it by diverting their attention from the unpleasant stimulation and by employing task-related and task-irrelevant interfering thoughts.

The studies of Silverman and his followers are marred somewhat by the inability of numerous other researchers to replicate these findings (Porterfield and Golding, 1985; Haspel and Harris, 1982; Condon and Allen, 1980). Silverman has been accused of using inappropriate statistical methods, and, since most of the studies in which positive results were obtained were carried out by Silverman himself, by his students, or by close colleagues, of allowing his expectations to influence his results. Silverman, naturally, rebutted these criticisms (1982) and claimed that failures to replicate his results were caused by their poor methodology.

This controversy notwithstanding, Silverman and his colleagues have made an important contribution to the support of psychoanalytic theory. Their studies of subliminal stimulation furnish evidence of the existence of unconscious processes that are organized in a dynamic fashion and that can affect behavior. While it is not clear from the studies that these unconscious elements are in fact 'repressed' memories and constructs, some of them do seem to resemble wishes and instinctual tendencies. These studies also suggest that the unconscious is, in part, a defensive structure, protecting against anxiety; that unconscious activity is different from its conscious counterpart; and that supraliminal stimulation does not affect behavior in the same manner as subliminal stimulation. The studies also show a specific link between certain conflicts and pathologies, in complete accord with psychoanalytic theory; on the other hand, there are universal conflicts and wishes, such as the desire for symbiosis with the mother, which is almost a defining quality of humankind, affecting all people in almost all areas of functioning.

However, some of the findings contradict the psychoanalytic view: the exclusive effect of the specific formulation of the symbiotic sentence 'Mommy and I are one,' these words and no others, contradicts the view of the unconscious as functioning by means of associative symbols and substitutes. It is not logical that only one specific verbal formulation affects an entity as complex, dynamic, and alert as the unconscious. Furthermore, the findings show that people with weaker defenses are not positively affected by the sentence 'Mommy and I are one' (Geisler, 1986). According to these findings, it would appear that those with weaker defenses are more resistant to unconscious influences, which is in direct opposition to psychoanalytic theory.

In this chapter the process of substitution has been presented as the central characteristic of repression and of unconscious activity and its impact on behavior according to the psychoanalytic theory. The substitution process stands behind the transformation of ideational content and energy, as evident in primary thought processes, free association, defense mechanisms, dreams, symptomatic behavior. The principles by which the substitutions are formed are defined by the primary processes. As has been demonstrated, substitution is considered as one of the basic principles of all mental life. While the unconscious is responsible for the formation of substitution that can take on pathological forms, the main therapeutic technique of classical psychoanalysis is the reversal of the transformation through interpretation.

Viewing psychoanalysis from this perspective implies that the unconscious is not a space for hidden content and energies; rather it is a special form of information and energy processing operating according to definite rules.

CHAPTER 3

The Humanist Approach: The Inhibition Model

Our discussion of the humanist approach will include some aspects of the existentialist and phenomenological schools of thought, which contain similar ideas regarding the unconscious. All of these theories emphasize the conscious mind and its central role in the understanding of mankind, to varying degrees negating the existence of the unconscious. Some humanists absolutely reject the concept of the unconscious, claiming that consciousness and subjectivity are the essence of human experience. In their view, human experience should be regarded as a unified whole that cannot be compartmentalized or reduced into parts or structures. This approach does not seem to allow for the concept of the unconscious, which is based on splits in the operation of the mind. In spite of these claims, the humanists' conceptions of unfulfilled potentials within the individual or unrealized potential experiences seems to indicate their acknowledgment that there is an unconscious.

In the humanist perspective, the unconscious may be described metaphorically as the 'dwelling-place' of positive, unrealized potentials within the person. Individuals do not utilize these potentials because they are constrained and inhibited by external factors. As they fail to fulfill their potential, their personality becomes impoverished and their solutions to life's problems become less satisfactory, arousing feelings of emptiness and anxiety. The inhibition of the self's potentials is the essence of repression and the unconscious in the humanist view.

HUMAN NATURE AS CONCEIVED BY THE HUMANISTS

Humanism does not regard behavior as causally determined, but rather views humans as seeking with free will to create and provide meaning in their lives. By creating meaning, they are freed from coercion by life circumstances and overcome limitations. It is the conscious self which governs experience and behavior and strives for meaning in life. The 'self,' the experiential focus of inner representation, is the central concept in humanists' theories of personality (Allport, 1955).

Humans are the only protagonist in their own lives. No unconscious images determine their life choices. They are rational beings, whose conscious goals are determined by mental attitudes not reducible to unconscious instincts or need. The self tends to transcend satisfying basic needs, solving problems and conflicts, and avoiding anxiety. The essence of the self is the striving for self-expression, internal versatility and innovation, for deeper understanding of the world and of itself, and the aspiration for the transcendental and the spiritual.

The phenomenologists and the existentialists (see Rychlak, 1973) view 'intentionality' as the heart of consciousness. Intentionality is the focusing of consciousness on a particular aspect of being. Humans can focus their intentionality toward themselves, their future, their actions, another individual, or any other aspect of their reality. Intentionality creates a comprehensive, integrated perspective and way of life. This is superbly reflected in a negative way in Dan Shavit's book, *A Poet Who Intends to Commit Suicide* (1989). The title character is impotent, unproductive and unauthentic, living an abysmally empty life. Although the poet has no actual intention of committing suicide, his way of life conveys an intentionality toward death. Intentionality is conscious; a man's intentions may be defined and described, and they are freely chosen.

In the eyes of most humanists, humans have a vast reservoir of unfulfilled potential. Beyond their individual talents and abilities, within each person's potential is a positive tendency to behave responsibly, choose wisely, and strive for freedom and self-expression.

Rogers (1961) considers humans to be moral, fundamentally good beings. They have a natural or 'organismic' wisdom that protects and directs them to realize their authentic self. This authentic self naturally aspires to love and be loved, to live in harmony with its environment and to promote the well-being of others. Love is humans' principal motivating force. Without it, their vast potential degenerates and their internal resources are wasted. Acceptance, trust, security, and honesty in their environment strengthen this inherent tendency to direct themselves wisely. Children who grow up in conditions of freedom and trust develop their innate freedom to choose the best path for themselves within the mainstream of their social environment through their organismic wisdom.

The existentialist position (see Yalom, 1980) is radical on the issue of freedom. Not only are humans free or potentially free to shape their world and their life, they rather *ought* to choose to be free in spite of objective forces over which they have no control. The meaning of choosing freedom, according to the existentialists, is taking a firm stance *vis-à-vis* one's life, committing oneself to unwavering adherence to values which transcend material needs.

Natan Sharansky's experience, described in his book, *I Shall Not Fear Evil* (1989), demonstrated the existentialists' meaning of true inner freedom. By maintaining his integrity against the might of the Soviet establishment while he was imprisoned, Sharansky nobly exemplified deep and authentic spiritual liberty.

The delightful Chassidic tale of the Ba'al Shem Tov, founder of the Chassidic movement, illustrates taking an active, firm stance towards life by finding meaning in the most basic behaviors:

> The Ba'al Shem Tov asked the powers-that-be who would be his neighbor in the next world. In answer, he was sent to the home of the only Jew, a large, heavy-set, ignorant youth, in a remote village. He found some pretext to visit him for several days, expecting that he would discover some spiritual virtues — some hidden splendor or glory, learning or even prayer — in this lout. To his dismay, all the lad did was eat! Each day, he got up in the morning, ate his fill, went to work, returning in the evening to devour another gluttonous meal and go to sleep. The Ba'al Shem Tov wondered, 'What right does this youth have to be next to me in heaven?' Thinking to himself that some people reveal their righteousness only on the Sabbath, he persuaded the youth to accommodate him also on the holy day. But even on the Sabbath, the youth did not change his habits — his break from work left him free to indulge his eating from morning to night. 'Perhaps he inherited the right from his forefathers?' The Ba'al Shem Tov examined this idea by asking what his father had done. 'My father was a rag merchant. He was a small, thin man, who spent each day travelling around the villages selling rags. One day the Cossacks caught him. Handing him a cross, they commanded him, "Kiss it, Jew, or we will bury you here." My father refused to kiss the cross. The Cossacks killed him, throwing his body on a bonfire. My father's small, thin body was consumed so quickly and thoroughly that no trace of his existence remained in the ashes. It was then that I decided to eat and eat so I would be big and broad. When the Cossacks catch and burn me, the fire will be seen from all the ends of the earth.' (Folk story)

Through gluttony, this naive Jewish youth achieved meaning in his life. Filling his selfish physical wants became a path to achieving transcendental meaning. Paradoxically, he lived a fully free and responsible life by committing himself to a way of life and choosing a stance towards forces beyond his control.

Freedom and self-actualization make a heavy burden. When individuals live in a loving and accepting atmosphere, it is easier for them to choose freedom, responsibility and selfrealization. Conditions which arouse anxiety and rejection cause individuals to retreat to a defensive stance, to become passive towards life and society, and to adopt needs or wants that are opposed to their nature. This tendency to escape from freedom into states of passivity, dependency, authority and Nirvana (Fromm, 1941) may eventuate in insanity. When the self is not realized, autonomy is relinquished and responsibility avoided, the person becomes prone to feelings of anxiety, dissatisfaction and emptiness.

A number of conclusions may be drawn from the humanist position regarding the unconscious. First, the unconscious is more passive in its influence than is usually portrayed and has no real power to block or influence the individual's way of life. Secondly, unlike the Freudian substitutional model, the humanist model has no concept of dual control, conscious and unconscious. Third, the unconscious is merely abdication of conscious control and abandonment of the self to passivity. It is essentially a condition of absence, omission and lack of self-fulfillment. All human behaviors are a result of rational forces or a response to irrational external forces.

By his explicit manifestation of humanist philosophy in his psychological theory, Carl Rogers's phenomenological approach (Rogers, 1961) provides an outstanding example of humanism. Rogers's most important principles, providing the guidelines for his theory of personality and his psychotherapeutic approach, are the phenomenological perspective and the understanding of the individual through the subjective world. In every individual, there are positive forces striving to be expressed. The incentive for authentic self-expression, which is the reflection of the most fundamental inner truth, is the acceptance of the individual as he or she is. The guiding principle of socialization and therapy is, therefore, provision of a secure and accepting environment which fosters authentic autonomy in the individual. The primary goal of therapy is freedom to express and fulfill the self. Therapy is a corrective experience and an imitation of life itself rather than a remedial technique.

Everyone is endowed with organismic sensors which, with a kind of 'wisdom,' guide them intuitively to the most satisfying and suitable self-expression. Cultural factors, social pressures, education or a hostile environment may, however, interfere with the individual's attention to these sensors. When this occurs, the person's overt self-expression becomes incompatible with the inner self and a sense of alienation ensues.

The so-called basic personality structure of personality is the 'self.' In essence the self is equivalent to subjective conscious experience. This is comprised of the 'phenomenological self' and the 'real self.' The concept of the 'phenomenological self' expresses the subjective perception of the self's actualized potential and the individual's conscious beliefs about him- or herself that have been internalized through socialization. The 'real self' is a composite of one's capabilities, talents, aspirations, diverse needs and values, which reflect the person's true nature.

The phenomenological self and the real self are thus two parts of the same personality structure. The more the phenomenological self and the real self are congruent, the more self-realization, satisfaction and authenticity exist. A large discrepancy between the real self and the phenomenological self creates alienation, failure to actualize the self and a lack of true satisfaction. The unexploited real potential is the unconscious, meaning the unused potentials. Awareness or consciousness is, therefore, this ongoing process of genuine self-expression. In other words, consciousness is the realization of the true potential.

Despite humans' natural tendency toward self-expression and self-realization, and in spite of their organismic wisdom, real self-expression can be distorted or inhibited by education, culture, and society.

Humans have a natural tendency to preserve internal consistency and congruence, which they may maintain by adopting the phenomenological self at the price of denying the real self. A student whose self-image is that of a failure will tend to reject contradictory internal or external information, and will most likely negate a new teacher's positive appraisal.

The discrepancy between the real self and the phenomenological self is also preserved by massive denial. Individuals may regard themselves as content, even happy, and convince themselves that they are adhering to their authentic goals, while actually playing a role which denies them true satisfaction. The following example illustrates this: a student came for consultation shortly before finishing his engineering studies, complaining of an incomprehensible feeling of distress. He should have been feeling satisfied and happy, as he was about to achieve his long-desired goal of becoming an engineer. Yet, he felt sad and dissatisfied. When the student learned to 'listen to himself,' to follow his natural directing senses, he dared to express that in fact he had never really wanted to be an engineer. It had been his father's wish, not his.

Rogerian therapy is based on encouraging self-expression, acceptance, and, above all, listening attentively to the patient's subjective experience. These therapeutic principles create a change in individuals' inner environment, allowing them to establish contact with their authentic self and its unfulfilled potentials.

Roger's approach can be regarded as the basic paradigm for all the humanist theories, despite their differences. We will utilize examples of different humanist theories to provide a more detailed analysis and definition of their principles. The following ideas will be discussed: repression as a process of inhibiting self-expression; environmental influence and life conditions as obstacles to self-expression and self-actualization; and the unconscious as a metaphor for positive potentials.

REPRESSION AS INHIBITION

Inherent in the humanist approach is the definition of repression as the inhibition of the expression of humans' natural organismic potential. The humanists regard inhibition as the more appropriate term, rather than referring to the Freudian concept of repression, because it pertains to inhibiting the development of potentials rather than to repression of instinctual energies.

Ernest Becker (1973) successfully synthesized psychological, philosophical, anthropological, and sociological views into a comprehensive view of human behavior. In his interpretation of Freud, he contended that it is not the Oedipus complex with its accompanying guilt that is responsible for the success of the socialization process. In his view, the universal mechanism of socialization is inhibition. Inhibition may become so pervasive that it becomes the dominant characteristic of life. The price of the relative freedom from anxiety attained through inhibition is limitation of individuals' full experience of their humanity.

Theoretically speaking, Becker asserted, the potential for self-expression is infinite. The compromising ego mediates between natural inner wealth and the demands of reality at the expense of limiting the self's potentials. This compromise involves limitation of the internal world and self-denial in order to cope better with the demands of the external world. Through socialization the child learns to say, 'Daddy, you don't need to punish me any more, I will do it myself [with the help of my conscience].' In Becker's interpretation, the child says, 'Now I am a social creature, because I am not myself any more, because essentially, I belong to you.'

The process of socialization is the consequence of internal conflict, which results in individuals' giving up their internal direction in favor of external direction. Internalized societal taboos form the conscience, which serves as society's tool for controlling the individual through guilt. This is the process creating internal inhibition.

Self-restriction by the conscience and by self-accusation creates the illusion that anxiety is under control. But these diminish spontaneity and devitalize internal life, depriving the individual of inner pleasures. Becker's formula for neurosis is amazingly simple: the child's avoidance of conflict with the external world creates internal conflict between spontaneity and inhibition.

Erich Fromm (Fromm et al., 1968) expressed similar ideas. Children communicate their inner desires to a world in which power speaks. In this world, weak and inferior children are confronted by the power of their, for them, dictatorial parents. Children learn very early to understand the influence of power and its meaning. Their striving for freedom, independence and personal expression submits to a very real, tremendous and threatening power.

Psychoanalysis demonstrated that a mechanism exists which produces guilt and inhibition. The existentialist psychologists contributed the concept of existential guilt, which is born when authentic self-expression is blocked and the individual cannot actualize his or her abilities. Existential guilt is the self-accusation aroused by the failure to realize the self, the waste of the self and lost opportunities.

The essence of human motivation, the humanists maintain, is not in the fulfillment of biological drives and in tension reduction. Human beings are motivated by self actualization, curiosity, innovation, competence, and creative self-renewal (Singer, 1970; Berlyne, 1960; Murphy, 1958; Harlow and Meyer, 1950; Fromm, 1955; Decharms, 1968).

The opposite of creative renewal is the inhibition of spontaneity, rigid adherence to the familiar and action motivated by anxiety. Inhibition and rigidity are two aspects of the same process. Living according to a rigid, continually repeated principle induces self-depletion. Compulsive repetition interferes with creativity, self-awareness and knowledge of the world; it is the source of maladaptation, unhappiness and pathology. In this sense, the unconscious is a way of life based on the individual's blindness to him- or herself and sterile repetition of a limited repertoire.

David Shapiro (1965, 1981) states that the feeling of subjective freedom is composed of two elements: self-direction (will) and the relationship to external authority (obligation). The feeling of freedom develops from infancy through adolescence via individuals' mutual relations with their parental authority figures. The socialization process is fraught with hurdles which are liable to undermine the sense of freedom; for example, the internalization of an authority figure without identifying with his or her goals creates feelings of coercion and estrangement. Internalization of authority to the extent of relinquishing will and self-direction results in perpetually seeking an authority, an overriding principle, or a role model to dictate one's way of life.

Shapiro further clarifies self-direction. According to his view, every human action is based on conscious planning, on the ability to foresee future consequences, to imagine hypothetical situations and to regulate the self. Even the most powerful impulse is only a temptation to act. The action itself is a result of voluntary initiation, which follows processes of appraisal, weighing, and planning. All of the factors involved, whether internal needs, drives and instincts, or external factors, such as authority, create an enriched awareness of the possibilities for choice of action. Action is not the result of an impulse, but rather a reasoned choice based on awareness of the various possibilities that exist.

Behavior that appears to be impulsive is always the result of considered choice. It is true that the sequence of actions that appears impulsive occurs quickly, but awareness and control exist. Shapiro goes further, claiming that there are cognitive styles of behavior that disguise and hinder the experience of personal free will. The hysterical character, for instance, intentionally blurs experiences, feelings, and goals. The impulsive individual formulates every experience in terms of action, thereby limiting awareness and responsibility in an active fashion. The rigid individual tends to be overly aware and indecisive, eventually coming to a standstill, whereas the paranoiac invests great efforts in regarding all behavior as stemming from external forces.

Shapiro delineates and characterizes different forms of behavioral rigidity. One characteristic, which is at the root of all the inhibitions, is the surrender of the feeling of freedom and self-direction. The 'compulsive character' demonstrates most vividly rigid individuals' sense of losing control of internal forces. They experience their own behavior as independent of their will or as an uncontrollable impulse. Compulsive and irrational rituals are the extreme expressions of such behavior.

Another facet of rigidity is demonstrated in the character who always feels he or she must fulfill obligations. This is the experience of 'should.' The feeling of necessity becomes a way of life, so that people who were taught that they must always fulfill obligations never enjoy the experience of living freely. This is the type of person whose self-direction is solely concerned with duties they should perform. Their reading material is chosen on the basis of educational value, not personal enjoyment; they choose to see the movie which is given the best reviews; and they go to a festival because they may be able to complete a business deal at the same time. They determine all of their behavior on the basis of convention, principle or obligation, not on the basis of pleasure or free will. Paradoxically, such individuals will often try to force themselves to be spontaneous or to want something they should want, without allowing themselves to be in contact with their true spontaneous feelings.

Over-planning and overly goal-directed behavior are additional expressions of rigidity. This kind of rigid individual expends considerable effort attempting to control their life and their impulses, while clinging to the perception that their actions are due to free will; their effort to maintain their freedom and spontaneity by refraining from acting on impulses, hiding weakness and being influenced by others, becomes a preoccupation, which is contrary to the real desire. This life pattern, according to Shapiro, is the result of internalizing parental authority without internalizing its goals. In fact, it is an unsuccessful rebellion against that authority.

Inhibition and rigidity are basic to almost all pathology, but they are most apparent in the paranoid individual. Individuals who suffer from this disturbance have serious difficulty with external authority. They tend to regard all that happens to them as resulting from external sources. These individuals grew up with admired authority figures whose expectations they could not attain. This resulted in a feeling of inner defectiveness. Because of this sense of inner deficiency, they became suspicious, vulnerable, sensitive to criticism, and always alert for an attack, especially by authority figures. Such feelings are so difficult to bear that sooner or later, they will place the blame for their imperfection on another person. What was originally an internal threat became externalized, further impairing their feeling of lack of will and freedom.

In varying forms, inhibition and rigidity are related to other mental states. Feffer (1970) found these to be characteristic of schizophrenic thinking in an experiment he performed using the TAT test. This test examines personality characteristics through stories that subjects composed on the basis of a picture presented by the tester. Feffer presented his schizophrenic subjects with pictures containing several characters. He requested that they compose a story and tell it from the perspective of each of the characters. It would be expected that the subject would tell the same story with changes in the version appropriate to the perspective of each character. It became apparent that schizophrenics are unable to make such changes. When they tell the story from the perspective of a particular character, they cannot take the roles of the rest of the characters into account. They compose one story and repeat it for each of the characters. Feffer concludes that the schizophrenic perceives life in a rigid, uni-dimensional fashion.

Rigid self-perception and inability to change one's way of life form one of the central dynamics of self-destructive behavior, according to Shneidman (1982). He views the suicidal person as suffering from a kind of 'tunnel vision,' which precludes perceiving a variety of alternatives. When the idea of committing suicide enters their consciousness, rigid individuals view this as their only possible alternative. (See also Orbach and Bar-Joseph, 1990.)

Inner freedom, spontaneity and self-direction are lost when individuals become rigid and inhibited. They lose the vision to perceive their potential inner riches and possibilities for freedom. As their perception and repertoire of action become more limited, their inner potential becomes progressively impoverished. This experiential poverty is actually a state of mind of unconsciousness.

Consciousness is the opposite of impoverishment; it is an ongoing process of renewal and creativity, of openness to a variety of alternatives and innovations, and a flexible attitude toward the world and toward the self. The concepts of conscious, unconscious and inhibition are not merely a reflection of self-knowledge or the lack of it; they relate to broadly conceived attitudes toward the self and toward life.

Now that the humanist definitions of the conscious and unconscious have been clarified, the etiology of the inhibited, unactualized, unconscious self will be discussed and conditions fostering regression will be described.

LIFE CONDITIONS FOSTERING INHIBITION

According to the humanist approach, the environment plays a central role in shaping personal development and tendencies. Laing (1969) defines a number of life conditions which create existential anxiety and defensive withdrawal. These are social and family conditions which are threatening to self-expression and actualization. The common aspect to all of these is the blocking of authentic self-expression. Laing outlines three threatening life situations:

1. *Engulfment.* This is a family environment in which the parents, who see their children as a natural extension of themselves, 'engulf' the children with demands for conformity. They demand that family members abdicate their individuality, maintaining uniformity and participation in family life while limiting extra-familial relationships. The family prohibits expressions of authentic feelings against its members. These demands rob individuals of their identity and their freedom to feel and relate authentically to themselves and others. Under these life conditions, individuals will prefer to withdraw from the social world into isolation.

2. *Impingement and implosion.* In this condition, family relationships are characterized by intrusion into the child's world. The parents continually demand to know all of the child's innermost, even most intimate experiences. As there are no boundaries between individual members of the family, privacy or individuality is not allowed. The logical reaction to this violation of individual boundaries is to withdraw and disguise the self, presenting a false face to the external world.

3. *Petrification and depersonalization.* In this environment, individuals are treated as objects devoid of emotions, thoughts, or even a life of their own. They are 'activated' like inanimate objects. Ignoring the unique qualities inherent in humanity, in Laing's view, causes 'inner death' and alienation from the self. The child has little choice but to present an inanimate facade to the external world and to preserve his or her inner life secretly.

Another danger to the authentic identity is the 'double bind,' described by the Palo Alto group (Bateson et al., 1956). The 'double bind' is a pattern of family communication, usually between parents and children, which consists of contradictory commands. One is the negative command: 'Do not ..., or I will punish you.' The other command is a contradictory command: 'If you do not do [the same act as forbidden in the first command], I will punish you.' A mother visiting her hospitalized son provides a classic example of such a double bind. When her son put his hand on her shoulder, expressing his feeling of closeness, she shuddered and gently moved his hand. Her son understood the message and removed his hand, whereupon she turned to him and asked, 'What happened? Don't you love me any more?'

There is no escape from the dilemma created by the double bind, as the response to either of the contradictory messages results in punishment. Often the double bind is denied or its identification prohibited, with comments such as the following: 'How dare you say such a thing?'; 'You don't really mean that?'; 'You're just imagining that.' Attempts to expose the double bind may precipitate a more drastic punishment. Because of his dependency, the young child is incapable of escaping this devastating situation.

The double bind is not only a communication problem. It represents a deep conflict within the person giving the message in relation to the receiver of the message. This may be the mother who is ambivalent about her children or who is hostile and anxious about being a mother, or a father who relives his hostile feelings toward his own parents. The double bind is not only confusing; it exposes its recipient to the experience of deep rejection. Denial of reality itself, as well as denial of the genuine subjective experience and genuine emotions, seem to be the only alternative for coping. One can survive a relationship within a double bind only by developing a false self or a false perception of reality.

Watzlawick, Weakland and Fisch (1979) regard massive denial as an additional environmental source of inner inhibition. In some families, the parents utilize denial as their principal method of coping with problems, telling the child, 'If you ignore the problem, it will go away,' or 'That's not really a problem.' When the socialization process is founded entirely on denial, the child learns to deny his or her inner world.

In summary, socialization which consists of massive restriction of individuality, internal contradictions, and massive denial impedes the development of reality perception and of the authentic self, as well as authentic self-expression. Consequently, the true self retreats from the center of awareness into the unconscious, where it is hidden, but safer; thus, an inner split is formed.

THE SPLIT BETWEEN THE REAL SELF AND THE FALSE SELF

Individuals who live in a hostile environment defend themselves by the most effective means possible. A physical attack produces a physical defense, whereas an attack on someone's psychological being engenders an array of defenses which protect the individual's emotional equilibrium. When the real self is under attack, the most effective defense is the substitution of a false self in its place. As with all defenses, this becomes a pervasive method of relating to the environment.

A clinical example will demonstrate this. A woman about 40 years old, emotionally restrained and withdrawn, requested treatment. In a monotonous voice, she complained of an empty life, inability to enjoy herself, absence of internal excitement, lack of direction, inability to enjoy her work despite the obvious skills she had in her field, lack of motivation, and a feeling of boredom. All her life, she had tried in vain to enjoy herself and to feel excitement. She felt angry at her husband for adding further to her boredom and failing to arouse or excite her. Excitement and sexual satisfaction were aroused only by the occasional intense, short-lived romances she tempestuously undertook. At the end of such an affair, she would experience a deep depression with suicidal impulses.

The woman's appearance and behavior reflected her inner world and her life experience. She spoke in a repressed, monotonous fashion, avoiding direct eye contact, and displaying difficulty in initiating a subject for the session. She also placed the responsibility for her boredom in the therapeutic meetings on the therapist.

Eventually, she revealed the story of her mother's cold and humiliating relationship with her. Her mother often mocked her, especially when she expressed enjoyment, affection, closeness, or intimacy. This humiliating relationship explains, at least in part, the withdrawal, restraint, and inhibition in this woman's closest relationships, and the feelings of emptiness and longing that prompted her to seek sensations outside of these close relationships. The momentary chance embraces with strangers served to release some of the authentic self's energy while protecting her from the pain she had learned to expect in close relationships.

Laing's (1970) concepts of the 'embodied self' and 'unembodied self' can contribute to a better understanding of this woman's experience. The 'embodied self' is the authentic self, in which body and mind are experienced and function as an integrated, harmonious entity. The 'unembodied self' develops in a situation of constant threats to the self. It is as though the individual's mind becomes split off from his or her body, and the real self is split off from the unauthentic self. The 'unembodied self' is the real self, which has been detached, in a sense, from the body and from immediate experience. The false self, which is based on convention, norms, imitation, and conformity to the expectations of others, replaces the real self. When they have developed such defenses, individuals may actually experience themselves as detached from their body. The body is depersonalized as an estranged, inanimate object.

In the following anecdote, Laing demonstrates the efficiency of this defensive splitting of the self. When a young man was attacked in a narrow alley at night, he fought off the two attackers with no hesitation. Later he related that he did not feel their blows, because he felt that he was not in his body — it was as if someone else were there. As a one-time defense, the split is effective. When it becomes pervasive, it interferes with the development of authenticity and the formation of real and satisfying relationships, and reality testing. The individual becomes robot-like, automatic and passive. Experientially, he feels counterfeit.

In another example, Laing (1969) described a patient who told him that he loved mathematics in school and hated literature. When he had to write a composition on Shakespeare's *Twelfth Night*, he overcame his youthful distaste for the play and wrote a composition praising it. The composition won a prize, despite his insistence that not one word was authentic. Only later did he reveal that he had loved both the play and writing the composition, but had not acknowledged this even to himself. His real affinity for Shakespeare was completely hidden in order to defend his authentic self from criticism. He would be far less hurt by criticism of his false self.

A defensive split of the self into a hidden authentic one and a false one impoverishes the personality. When the real self does not enjoy a vivid, genuine experience of the world and itself, it loses its potential for vitality, creativity, and satisfaction. The individual's inner potential atrophies, leaving him or her empty and mentally impotent.

THE UNCONSCIOUS: 'STOREHOUSE' OF POSITIVE FORCES

From the humanist perspective, repression is a way of life characterized by inhibition, impoverishment and rigidity, and the unconscious is a storehouse of unactualized potentials. When, as a result of life circumstances, individuals' natural potentials are not actualized, these remain unconscious — thus, in essence, the unconscious is the reservoir of unfulfilled potentials. To live in self-denial of one's authentic potentials means to live unconsciously.

The Gestalt approach is one which considers the unconscious as a reservoir of authentic and positive human assets. In the terms of this approach, the authentic self is the 'background,' while the actual self is the 'figure' in the inner Gestalt.

Work on a patient's dream performed by Fritz Perls, one of the founders of Gestalt therapy, can illustrate this approach. Perls considers the dream to be an expression of the unconscious, as does Freud, but his interpretation of the unconscious and utilization of the dream is quite different. As he writes,

> Freud once called the dream the 'Via Regia,' the royal road to the unconscious. And I believe it is really the royal road to integration. I never know what the 'unconscious' is, but we know that the dream is definitely the most spontaneous production we have. It comes about without our intention, will, deliberation. The dream is the most spontaneous expression of the existence of the human being ... all the different parts of the dream are fragments of our personalities. Since our aim is to make every one of us a wholesome person, which means a unified person, without conflicts, what we have to do is put the different fragments of the dream together. We have to repossess these projected, fragmented parts of our personality, and repossess the hidden potential that appears in the dream.
>
> Perls, 1969, p. 71

Perls presents his analysis of a dream, performed with the patient, Linda (Perls, 1978, pp. 85–7):

LINDA: I dreamed that I was contemplating ... a lake ... drying up, and there is a small island in the middle of the lake, and a circle of ... porpoises — they're like porpoises except that they can stand up, so they're like porpoises that are like people, and they're in a circle, sort of like a religious ceremony, and it's very sad — I feel very sad. Because they can breathe, they are sort of dancing around the circle, but the water, their element, is drying up. So it's like a dying — like observing the death of a tribe of people or a flock of animals. And they are mostly females, but a few of them have a small male organ; so there are a few males there, but they won't live long enough to reproduce, and their element is drying up. And there is one that is sitting there near me and I'm talking to this porpoise and he has prickles on his tummy, sort of like a porcupine, and they don't seem to be a part of him. And I think that there's one good point about the water drying up, I think — well, at least at the bottom, when all the water dries up, there will probably be some sort of treasure there, because at the bottom of the lake there should be things that have fallen in, like coins or something, but I look carefully and all that I can find is an old license plate ... That's the dream.

FRITZ: Will you please play the license plate?

LINDA: I am an old license plate, thrown in the bottom of a lake. I have no use because I'm of no value — although I'm not rusted — I'm outdated, so I can't be used as a license plate ... and I'm just thrown on the rubbish heap. That's what I did with a license plate; I threw it on a rubbish heap.

FRITZ: Well, how do you feel about this?

LINDA: (*quietly*) I don't like it. I don't like being a useless license plate.

FRITZ: Could you talk about this? The dream went on for so long before you came upon the license plate, I'm sure this must be of great importance.

LINDA: (*sighs*) Useless. Outdated ... the use of a license plate is to allow — give a car permission to be driven ... and I can't give any more permission to do anything because I'm outdated ... In California, they just paste a little — you buy a sticker — and stick it on the car, on the old license plate. (*Faint attempt at humor*) So maybe someone could put me on their car and stick this sticker on me, I don't know ...

FRITZ: Okay, now play the lake.

LINDA: I'm a lake ... I'm drying up, and disappearing, being soaked up by the earth ... (*with a touch of surprise*) dying ... But when I am soaked up by the earth, I become part of the earth — so maybe I irrigate the surrounding area, so ... even in the lake, at its bottom, flowers can grow (*sighs*) ... New life can grow ... from me (*cries*) ...

FRITZ: You get the existential message?

LINDA: Yes, (*sadly, but with conviction*) I can paint — I can create — I can create beauty. I can no longer reproduce, I'm like the porpoise ... but I ... I'm ... I ... keep wanting to say I'm food ... I ... As water becomes ... I water the earth and give life — growing things, the water — they need both the earth and water, and the ... and the air and sun, but as the water from the lake, I can play a part in something, and producing — feeding.

FRITZ: You see the contrast: On the surface, you find something, some artifact — the license plate, the artificial you — but when you go deeper, you find the apparent death of the lake is actually fertility ...

LINDA: And I don't need a license plate, or a permit, a license in order to ...

FRITZ: (*gently*) Nature doesn't need a license plate to grow. You don't have to be useless, if you are organically creative, which means if you are involved.

LINDA: And I don't need permission to be creative ...

These selections speak for themselves. They illustrate the immense difference between Gestalt therapy and Freud's analytic—investigative approach. The concept 'Gestalt' refers to perception of total entities, rather than parts. In its Freudian explication, the dream is a form of hallucination created by instinctual drives and expressing instinctual fragments. The dream, in the Gestalt perception, expresses the self as a whole entity; it is considered as creative self-expression rather than a hallucination. In seeking the basic truth of each patient in part through dreams, Freud discovered infantile sexuality and the Oedipus complex. The search by

Gestalt theorists yielded concepts of creativity, vitality, authenticity, and inner strength. In this approach the dream releases inner creative energies, generates a sense of wholeness and renewal, and indicates new, often daring directions for problem solving. In Linda's dream, her initial self-perception is that she is useless, withered, dependent, helpless, old-fashioned, and needing support. When allowed expression, her inhibited self reveals itself to be nurturing, creative and life-giving. This revelation of the unconscious is achieved through self-direction. Within an accepting atmosphere, individuals may express their previously hidden reactions to current issues in their lives and learn to be alert to all of their feelings, thus revealing and discovering their positive potentials.

Gestalt therapists encourage their patients to become acquainted with every detail that becomes available through dreams, fantasies, stories, or reports of daily life, on the assumption that these details reveal the many and varied facets of the self. By focusing on each of these aspects, individuals become acquainted with various unfamiliar internal parts of themselves, which they are then able to assimilate afresh into a more integrated and complete self. Internal worlds are revealed in a new light, the positive, productive, but forgotten side is revealed, and new learning takes place.

The most outstanding proponent of the school of thought which regards the unconscious as a reservoir of positive energies and processes is Milton Erickson (see Haley, 1973; Erickson, Rossi and Rossi, 1976). Although Erickson did not formulate an original theory of the unconscious, it is possible to infer his premises from his work methods and from others' theoretical summaries of his work (Haley, 1973; Yager, 1987).

One of Erickson's basic premises, demonstrated in his hypnotherapy, is that the unconscious is intelligent, wise, and omniscient. It is like a superior self, knowing how to control and direct the individual, understanding the self and the world, self-protective and striving for internal harmony. For Erickson, it is important to help patients become aware that their unconscious is wiser than they are. It stores an abundance of knowledge, and knows how to guide the individual in a way that the conscious mind cannot. Erickson encouraged his patients to permit their unconscious to assume responsibility for much of their functioning (Erickson, Rossi and Rossi, 1976).

Erickson's suggestions to his hypnotized patients convey his theory of the unconscious. The ability of the unconscious to distinguish and choose between good and evil and act wisely is reflected in the following instruction:

it is important for a person to know their unconscious is smarter than they are. There is a greater wealth of stored material in the unconscious. We know

the unconscious can do things, and it's important to assure your patient that
it can. They have to be willing to let their unconscious do things and not
depend so much on their conscious mind. This is a great aid to their
functioning.   Erickson, Rossi and Rossi, 1976, p. 9

The idea that the unconscious contains endless abilities and potentials is
expressed as follows: 'you can go into a trance to find out a whole lot of
things that you can do. And they are so many more than you dreamed of'
(Erickson, Rossi and Rossi, 1976, p. 43); 'you can enjoy using your abilities
. . . A process that you don't know you have but abilities that are in your
unconscious mind' (ibid., p. 173). The individual's unconscious accumulates a wealth of information, not repressed memories, which cannot be
retained in awareness but exists for him or her to employ: 'In the course of
living from infancy on, you acquired knowledge, but you could not keep
all that knowledge in the foreground of your mind' (ibid., p. 198); and
'You don't have to remember. The important thing is to have certain
experiences recorded in your mind. Some day their presence will be of
service to you. It is necessary for you to be aware that you know they are
there. The important thing always is to do the right thing at the right time'
(ibid., p. 260); 'In the development of the human being learning in the
unconscious became available in any time of need. When you need to feel
comfort, you can feel comfort. When you have a need for relaxation, you
can have it' (ibid., p. 155).

Even forgetting and repression are talents, vital abilities of the
unconscious. 'Your unconscious learned a lot yesterday. It also learned
that we could learn a lot without intruding upon the personality' (ibid., p.
207).

Instead of regarding the different states of consciousness as oppositional,
Erickson views them as complementary and harmonious:

Now there are some different ways in which the mind can function in which
the unconscious can join with the conscious, many different ways in which
the unconscious can avoid the conscious mind without the conscious mind
knowing that it has just received a gift.   ibid., p. 43

Erickson implicitly portrays the unconscious as a form of unique communication within the self and with reality. More emphatically, Erickson
suggests that the essence of the unconscious is this unique process of
communication with the self or with others. The unconscious language is a
metaphoric, childlike language of early intrapersonal and interpersonal
relationships. As described in his work, Erickson's 'contacts' with the
unconscious are developed through primary and friendly communication.
While hypnotized, the patient enters a primary, childlike state. This is not
an emotional or intellectual regression or a primitive state; instead, it is a

childlike condition in which the patient's self-expression becomes imaginative, spontaneous, playful and symbolic. Erickson allies himself with the unconscious by creating a friendly, yet authoritative relationship with the patient.

The unique communication of the unconscious consists of metaphors, symbols and imagery; playfulness and entertainment, flexibility, and diversity in the use and meaning of language; and meta-communication. This communication exploits the patient's innocence and faith in it to enhance his or her well-being. Erickson's exceptional method stimulates these processes, inducing the patient to enter the primary, conflict-free, and childlike position necessary for communication with the unconscious.

The following quotes illustrate his use of authority in a playful fashion to induce the child-like state: 'I am now going to awaken you and I want you to be very surprised ... you won't be able to bend your legs ... and you won't, will you? (*Pause*) You will see them but you won't be able to feel them after I awaken you. Agreed?' (Erickson, Rossi and Rossi, 1976, p. 174); 'What happens after that is going to surprise you ... You are pretty well aware of all the things you can do, but the most surprising experience ...' (ibid., p. 143); 'Or would you like to have it as a surprise? Now or later?' (ibid., p.142).

Erickson sometimes prepares patients for the childlike state by talking with them about their childhood, their children, or about children in general:

> The unconscious is much more childlike in that it is direct and it is free. Children have asked me why I walk that funny way when their parents had not even noticed that I limped. ... The children saw something they wanted an understanding of. ... The patient thinks like a child and reaches for an understanding. ibid., p. 255

He can subdue the patient's mature thought and enhance an inner dialogue based on sensuality, intuition and openness.

> You give them the opportunity to open their eyes ... use their nose to smell and ears to hear, their fingers to feel ... One can learn by reading, by seeing, by feeling, ... by experiencing, and the best way of learning, to use folk language, is by getting the feel of it ... You get the feel of a poem, the feeling of a picture, the feeling of a statue ... We do not just feel with the fingers, but with the heart, the mind. You feel with the learnings of the past. You feel with the hopes for the future. You feel the present. ibid., pp. 251–3

Even in the most serious of situations, Erickson encourages the patient's childlike, playful acting out (see Haley, 1973). He tells the story of a young woman who appeared for treatment, opening with the remark that this would be her last attempt. If therapy was not effective this time, she would commit suicide. Erickson instructed her to withdraw all of her savings to buy new clothes, and to dress in her new clothes and apply fashionable cosmetics for work. She told Erickson that at work she frequently met a young man at the water fountain who apparently liked her. Erickson told her to fill her mouth with water the next time they met and spray it into the young man's face through the (troubling) hole between her teeth, run a step in his direction, and then run away from him. As anticipated, the story ended happily: the young man ran and caught her ... and the ensuing romance ended in marriage.

Sometimes Erickson enlists unconscious forces to 'trick' the conscious. A woman who had been unable to have sexual relations even after marriage came for therapy. Erickson understood that her rebellious unconscious was responsible for the problem, and that her anxiety stemmed from conflict about submission. Allying himself with the rebelliousness, he persuaded her to have sexual relations on any day she chose, except for one specific day. As expected, she burst into his office the morning after the 'forbidden' night, declaring that she had enjoyed sexual relations the night before!

Erickson also enlists the innocence and childlike nature of the patient in problem solving. He achieves a childlike response through axioms and laconic questions evoking the answer 'yes.' When he asks a critical question, the patient inadvertently answers affirmatively. To handle ambivalence, his requests are phrased ambiguously to avoid arousing defensiveness. Instead of openly requesting compliance from a patient, he asks, 'When would you like to do it, now or two minutes from now?'

Dialogue with the unconscious is obtained through symbols, metaphors, images, analogies and informal, colloquial expressions. Erickson creates a meta-language which reaches several levels simultaneously. A single message can be impregnated with multiple meaning, meaning both semantic and metaphoric. Such messages can elicit responsiveness on several levels simultaneously.

When a couple seek sex therapy, Erickson tends to choose an indirect, metaphoric approach. He might help them change a particular aspect of their life which is analogous to sexuality, thus influencing their sexual relations as well. With one couple, he might discuss the importance of dining together, and accommodating their different preferences. She likes an appetizer before meals, while he pounces on the meat and potatoes immediately; the woman prefers a quiet, enjoyable meal, while he just wants to finish the dinner. Erickson might conclude the session with the suggestion that they go out to dinner together (Haley, 1973).

For Erickson, the unconscious is a lifelong metaphor. Haley (1973) demonstrates this with an example. For many years, an institutionalized mental patient claimed to be Jesus. Nothing convinced him otherwise. One day, Erickson approached him, saying that he understood the patient was an expert carpenter. In this manner, Erickson succeeded in engaging him in the first productive work he had performed in many years. 'Being Jesus' was a metaphor; communication with the metaphor effected the desired change. In Erickson's view, the metaphor does not conceal contents, but rather serves as a means of experiencing life. Instead of interpreting the metaphor, he utilizes it therapeutically.

These examples clarify Erickson's view of the unconscious as a multi-dimensional, unique communication system. The metaphoric language *is* the unconscious; not only a reflection or expression of the unconscious. The unique characteristic of this communication is its primary, childlike, playful, and non-defensive nature. Being in an unconscious state means communicating genuinely and freely with oneself and others in metaphors, meta-language, imagery and many-tiered meanings.

THE UNCONSCIOUS: PATHOLOGY AND TREATMENT

The relationship between the unconscious, anxiety, and pathology according to the humanist inhibition model may now be summarized. Anxiety results from inhibiting inner potentials and self-expression. This is a consequence of life conditions which block the natural development of the child or the natural tendencies of the adult. These inhibiting hostile environmental influences may take the form of contempt, prohibitions, confusing messages, inflated demands, and falsified realities. In order to protect itself from psychic injury, the authentic self withdraws from a genuine interaction with the environment. This withdrawal leads to an inner detachment and inhibition of true self-expression.

Inhibition culminates in developmental and emotional arrest. The result is a progressive deterioration, impoverishment and deficiencies in coping. A false self is erected instead, adopting the expectations and goals of others but failing to realize authentic potentials.

Inhibition in all its forms causes anxiety, alienation, and pathology. Inhibitions limit the individual's ability to adapt and to innovate. Fear of responding in new, creative and authentic ways results in rigid, habitual maladaptive responses which fail to satisfy vital needs. A vicious circle is formed. External inhibitions cause inner inhibitions and impoverishment, which engender anxiety. This, in turn, further exacerbates inhibition.

The humanist definition of the relationship between the unconscious and pathology is the opposite of the psychoanalytic definition. Whereas in psychoanalytic theory, anxiety induces repression, in the humanists' view, inhibition creates anxiety.

This formulation dictates a different therapeutic approach. The humanist view that human nature is essentially positive determines the therapeutic goal, which is to remove inhibition and summon up the potential that has been blocked and therefore remained unconscious. This does not require caution in uncovering the unconscious, as the delicate balance between anxiety and repression postulated by the Freudians does not exist. Full, authentic self-expression can come about without fear of intensifying anxiety. On the contrary, the faster inhibition is removed and self-expression enhanced, the faster anxiety will diminish. The humanists' central therapeutic principle is the active, persuasive encouragement of full self-expression. The means to achieve this are varied, but all strive to reach the most comprehensive possible realization and expression of the subjective potentials.

Since the external environment — family, culture, society — maintains the threat that inhibits authentic self-expression, environmental change is an additional therapeutic strategy for creating internal changes. It is surmised that removal of the external threats and limitations will enable the authentic self to grow almost autonomously, while acceptance and encouragement of the individual will considerably increase the pace of growth. This is the principle which underlies Carl Rogers's and others' concept of the 'corrective emotional experience.' The process of development is positively re-lived, figuratively speaking, by the patient in conditions of trust, respect and acceptance.

Environmental change also underlies Laing's concept of the therapeutic community, an innovation he introduced within treatment institutions on the basis of his existentialist theories. According to his description, within this positive environment his patients were capable of partial or completely normal functioning during most of the day, only later retreating to the community's protection and to their 'illness.' These conditions enabled suffering individuals to undergo a process of self-healing by self expression through their illness, leading to healthier reorganization than that which existed before the illness. The change of environment itself is the key to the therapeutic developments which ensue.

As a humanist, Fromm (see Fromm et al., 1968) also believes that environmental change brings about internal change. In his view, little Hans, whose irrational fear of horses was explained by Freud as resulting from the Oedipus complex, was not cured by the psychoanalytic interpretation that he loved his mother and felt hostile towards his father. The cure lay in his father's newly protective accepting toward him.

The humanist approach sees humans as conscious and rational creatures and as essentially positive. The wholeness and completeness of the subjective experiences should not be fragmented. This position seems to reject an assumption of unconscious. Yet a careful examination of the humanist approach shows that it implicitly contains a conceptualization of the unconscious in the form of inhibition of organismic potentials. Certain life conditions, such as double binds, massive denials, rejection, excessive demands, depersonalization and others, prevent self-realization. As a result of this, inhibition of genuine self-expression occurs. The unconscious stores precisely the strong, positive, and creative energies of the individual.

This model deviates significantly from almost all other existing theories of the unconscious. While most other theories view the unconscious as serving to defend against anxiety, the humanist approach maintains that it represents the most positive and creative aspects of the human being. The therapeutic goal is to release the unconscious, enabling it to attain self-expression and full actualization. This goal is obtained by encouraging self-expression and becoming familiar with the self, unconditional acceptance, and changing the environment to engender freedom and authenticity.

CHAPTER 4

Dissociation: The Unconscious as Lack of Control and Inner Split

THE ESSENCE OF DISSOCIATION

A contemporary of Freud, the French psychologist Pierre Janet (1859–1947), constructed a theory of the unconscious that is as comprehensive and explanatory as psychoanalytic theory. For various reasons the Freudian approach took priority and played a central role in the development of psychological theory, while Janet's dissociative model gained little recognition. Hilgard restores Janet's theory to its rightful prominence in psychology, establishing it as a basis for research on the unconscious and further developing the theory into its present form as the neo-dissociative model of the unconscious.

Dissociation is a state in which a personality structure functions independently of the executive control system ('ego' or the 'self'). Loss of control and splits within the personality are the two basic processes which characterize dissociation. When these processes occur, the ego is unable to monitor or control the dissociated behavior. The individual in this state becomes incapable of inhibiting behavior voluntarily, as the dissociated behavior becomes automatic and independent of the central control.

Janet (see Van der Kolk and Van der Hart, 1989) utilizes the hysterical person, whose emotional difficulties represent dissociative behavior, to exemplify pathological loss of control. He maintains that the hysterical person lacks the willpower that is necessary for mental synthesis or integration. Instead, part of the personality becomes a system of relatively independent automatic actions. The central control systems surrender to secondary controls, such as drives and instincts.

Compulsive symptoms, such as rituals, troublesome obsessive thoughts and irrational fears, are additional pathological forms of losing control. Compulsive behavior operates autonomously rather than 'obeying' the central control of the personality. The second aspect of dissociation is the splitting off of a part of the personality, meaning that there is no connection between some aspects of personality and the central control. This is evidenced by lack of awareness of the split-off entity. In other words, one part of the personality is unaware that another part exists. Splitting is also demonstrated, according to Janet, in the phenomenon of forgetting traumatic events which become encapsulated, forming a separate entity within the personality.

In a case example, Janet (1889) reports that a young girl sought therapy for hysterical blindness. This symptom resulted from the unpleasant experience of being forced to sleep in the same bed with a child who had impetigo. The incident was recalled only in hypnosis. The dissociation expressed itself in the split between the event and becoming blind. The memory did not disappear, but was split off and became an autonomous part of her personality. Retrieval of the forgotten event under hypnosis demonstrates that a split off, encapsulated part of the personality 'survives' and affects the person's behavior.

According to Janet, dissociation is generally related to a traumatic event that triggers a strong emotional reaction. The unusual nature of the event, the unbearable emotions it arouses, and the lack of appropriate schemata for its assimilation impede its integration into the personality. When this occurs, a new personality nucleus, the subconscious, is formed as an independent personality sub-system. The event and all related feelings and thoughts become part of this new nucleus. The undercover operations of the autonomous sub-system are often expressed in frightening perceptual distortions, disturbing ideation, and psychosomatic symptoms.

The above phenomena are results of the dissociation of the traumatic event which ensues from failure to process cognitively the frightening event. The event is experienced through auditory, visual, and physiological sensations rather than through verbal symbols which facilitate reconstruction. These events are therefore recalled on behavioral, emotional, and physiological levels, as in flashbacks, but not in words. This results in a paradoxical situation: the individual is unable to assimilate the trauma, yet cannot really forget it. As a result, the traumatic experience appears in the form of symptoms and disturbances in the individual's adaptability.

Not all dissociation is pathological. In Hilgard's modern (1986) formulation of dissociation, loss of control and splitting off of a part of the personality are not caused by a traumatic event. These two principal characteristics are found in normal functioning. From this perspective, the personality is comprised of many sub-systems, all of which are monitored and controlled by several control centers. This is reflected in the many different roles that an individual plays. A person may be a teacher, friend, spouse, parent, club member, amateur violinist, etc. Each role represents a different, somewhat independent 'personality cluster,' yet the roles are interrelated and coordinated by the central control. They 'communicate among themselves,' and the dominant role 'remembering' that the others exist in the background. A certain degree of dissociation is an essential part of normal behavior.

Another adaptive aspect of dissociation is that it facilitates conscious attention on several external and internal foci simultaneously. More than one level of awareness or more than one course of action may be maintained. Hilgard shows that commonplace conversations between people often exemplify this. While listening to someone, individuals may plan their answer; then they may adjust their answer to the expressions that they observe in the other's face as they are responding. At the same time, they may also think to themselves that the conversation has gone on far too long and try to devise a way to end it.

In conformance with Hilgard's theory, Ludwig (1983) maintains that dissociation is the mechanism which transforms complex activities into automatic ones. It facilitates such activities as the 'automatic' driving which makes the ride smooth and pleasant. This type of dissociative functioning saves considerable mental effort and enhances efficient functioning. Dissociation aids in solving difficult conflicts and coping with traumatic experiences by creating an amnesic barrier, which is at times the most appropriate coping strategy. Dissociation becomes problematic when the sub-system of the personality is completely split off and removed from the personality's central core, so that it functions in an almost completely autonomous manner.

To a certain extent, Hilgard's approach rests on Deikman's (1971) differentiation between passive and active consciousness. Passive consciousness relates to the passive perception of stimuli by the sensory system, many of which may be perceived unintentionally and almost indiscriminately. The active aspect of consciousness is voluntary and intentional, while the passive perceptions occur in a dissociated fashion.

Comparing the psychoanalytic and dissociative models, Hilgard clarifies the distinction between dissociation and repression. The topographical psychoanalytic model of repression postulates a depth psychology created by a block of repression between 'upper' and 'lower' parts of personality. Repression functions vertically. In contrast, the dissociative model posits a split not between 'upper' and 'lower' parts of the personality, but between different parts of the personality on the same level, without assuming a depth psychology. Thus, the different personality parts may or may not coexist in consciousness. The barrier between these parts need not be a defensive one, while the block created by repression is defensive. The distinction between the two models is described in Figure 4.1.

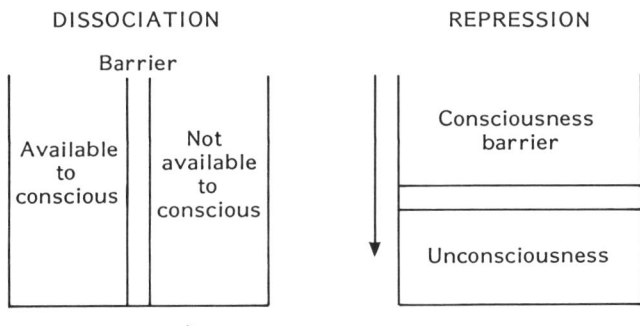

Figure 4.1 Psychoanalytic and dissociation models of the unconscious and repression (based on Hilgard, 1986). The diagram on the right is the vertical model, which emphasizes the barrier formed by repression between different levels of depth. On the left, the horizontal model illustrates the split between parts of the personality, which occurs on the same plane rather than between different layers of depth. The arrows represent the dissociative/repressive direction.

Even Breuer (Breuer and Freud, 1893) maintains that dissociation is not necessarily a pathological defensive process, but also may exist as a normal tendency within the personality. He wrote that Anna, who suffered from a series of hysterical and dissociative symptoms, had a tendency to dissociate throughout her life, unrelated to her later illness. Her frequent, non-pathological tendency to daydream, in a kind of hypnotic state, reflected a dissociative tendency. When she was under emotional stress, her normal dissociation intensified and became pathological. Freud originally agreed with Breuer's opinion, but soon his psychoanalytic theory developed in a different direction.

This idea that dissociation is a part of the normal behavioral repertoire, but becomes pathological under certain conditions, is central to the dissociative model.

FACES OF DISSOCIATION

Dissociation is quantitative and dissociative phenomena exist on a continuum. At one extreme, dissociative phenomena consist of a small degree of dissociation. This is true of daydreams, imagination, selective perception and divided attention, dreams and hypnotic states. At the other end of the continuum are those with extremely dissociative features, such as fugue states, multiple personalities, amnesia, and hallucinations. In the middle fall the hysterical reactions, various forms of compulsion, somnambulism, estrangement, depersonalization and hypnosis.

One of the most interesting and dramatic aspects of Hilgard's work is his discovery that there are different levels of awareness within the dissociative state. His concept of the 'hidden observer' contradicts Freud's sharp distinction between consciousness and unconsciousness. The following paragraphs will describe some dissociative phenomena (following Hilgard, 1986) in order to illustrate different aspects of dissociation.

Multiple Personality

Multiple personality is a fascinating psychological phenomenon. The character of Dr. Jekyll, whose personality is transformed into Mr. Hyde, is a famous literary example of this phenomenon, while the movie *The Three Faces of Eve* is based on the true story of a woman who suffered from multiple personality. There are differing forms of multiple personality, but in all of them two or more personality constellations exist simultaneously or alternately. Sometimes one omniscient personality knows of the existence of its alternates, while the latter are completely unaware of any additional personality. In other phenomena, the different personalities know of each other's existence and deeds.

Generally, three principal criteria are used to characterize multiple personality:

1. Two or more personality structures exist, each of which is dominant at a given time.
2. The dominant personality determines behavior while it is in control.
3. Each of the personalities has a complicated, well-organized identity, with its own specific behavior patterns.

Martha, a 36-year-old married woman, suffered from multiple personality. Her case was described by Frankel (1976), to whom she was referred for therapy of her hysterical conversion reactions, which consisted of difficulties in walking and uncontrollable vocalizations. When she began treatment, she appeared in a wheelchair with a scarf around her neck to prevent her, as she said, from making the unwanted sounds. Martha was eventually persuaded to 'free' the alternative personality, Harriet. Harriet, the healthy personality, willingly demonstrated that she could walk freely. In the therapy session, Harriet claimed that she was Martha's childhood friend who died when Martha was five years old. The historical basis for this story could not be confirmed. Harriet was convinced that Martha's suffering and illness were her response to pressure from her husband. While Harriet was continually aware of Martha, Martha became aware of Harriet only occasionally. Harriet retreated into Martha's personality before the session ended, and when Martha reappeared, she was totally unaware of Harriet's having 'attended the session.' Interestingly, the latent, subordinate personality in this case was healthy, organized and independent.

Kluft (1984) enumerates four essential characteristics and processes in multiple personality, as follows:

1. A biological tendency to dissociate must exist.
2. Multiple personality is usually produced in reaction to a trauma. It is interesting to note that Putnam et al. (1986) found that more than 90 percent of the patient population suffering from multiple personality had endured a trauma, such as sexual exploitation, violent physical abuse, or witnessing brutal deaths. The researchers also found that there was a significant correlation between the number of traumas suffered by the individual and the number of personalities he or she developed.
3. In order to adapt to the trauma and cope with its effect on his or her life, the individual splits off the traumatic experience from the rest of the personality.
4. The dissociative defense becomes fixated and develops into an additional personality with an organized structure. This fixation occurs, in Kluft's opinion, when no therapeutic intervention or nurturing emotional experience is provided to correct the split that ensues from the intolerable trauma.

In the multiple personality, a traumatic event or a conflict that cannot be resolved has prevented sufficient integration of the different parts of the 'self.' As the central control system of the personality loses control, sub-systems or sub-personalities consolidate and act independently. The split is expressed in the amnesiac block that is formed between the personalities in many cases.

Dreams, Imagination and Hallucinations

Dreams, imagination, and hallucinations are all based on dissociative illusions and detachment from reality to some degree. The extent of voluntary control over each of these three processes differs.

The study of imagination, which is a dissociated but voluntarily controlled state, may be utilized to some extent in order to understand dissociative states in general. Hilgard (1986) refers to the association between imagination and right brain hemisphere function. Verbal abilities and analytic tasks, such as mathematics, are under the control of the left hemisphere, whereas the right brain hemisphere is responsible for global functions, such as imagination, spatial perception, and perception of music. Hilgard cites studies which demonstrate that recitation of the words of a song without the music activates the left hemisphere, while humming the tune activates the right hemisphere. Both hemispheres are activated by singing the words.

The dominance of a particular hemisphere creates a tendency to prefer activities controlled by that hemisphere. Since one or the other hemisphere is dominant in a large proportion of the population, researchers have been able to demonstrate that those people with dominant right hemisphere have a greater natural tendency for dissociative activities, such as imagination and hypnosis, than those whose left hemisphere is dominant.

From these facts, it can be inferred that dissociative activities such as imagination are activated by the right hemisphere. Since dreams and hallucinations are similar to imagination, it can also be inferred that they can be regulated to a certain extent. In an attempt to find a connection between these dissociative phenomena and hypnosis, Hilgard found right hemisphere dominance in people who tended to respond to hypnosis. However, these inferences are highly speculative and further research is required to validate them.

Dissociation in Hypnosis

Hypnosis is a classic example of dissociation, and it can shed light on the subject of dissociative phenomena. Hypnosis, which occurs within the context of a special relationship between two people, is a condition in which the authority of the hypnotist directs the subject's behavior by suggestion. Two factors influence the subject's ability to enter the hypnotic trance: suggestibility and hypnotability. Suggestibility is the tendency to be influenced by and obey instructions. Hypnotability is the ability to enter a hypnotic trance.

To enter a hypnotic trance, the subject has to be responsive to a series of suggestions which are monotonous, repetitive, and incremental. Suggestions are given in a monotonous voice which repeats simple, clear words. The communication may begin with a suggestion: 'You are sitting in your chair, feeling more and more calm.' The suggestion is repeated, 'Relaxed ... relaxed ... comfortable ... and restful ...,' and again, 'relaxed ... relaxed.' At some stage, the suggestion becomes more intense: 'You are sinking into a deep, deep, deep sleep.' After a few minutes, the suggestion becomes more complex: 'When I do thus, you will feel you can't lift your hand ...'

The first suggestions are usually ideomotoric, which means that they convert the image of a motor action into the action itself. A suggestion may be given to intertwine one's fingers and imagine that a magnet is making them inseparable. In another image, one hand is lighter than air, while the other is heavier than a stone. The subject should respond according to the image, raising one hand and dropping the other involuntarily. Such a suggestion affects the particular limb so that it becomes dissociated from the body following the directions of the hypnotist.

This seemingly autonomous behavior is dissociative, in that the subject does not direct or control its execution. The events that occur under hypnosis are usually forgotten when the subject returns to consciousness, even without a specific suggestion to this effect. Other spontaneous reactions in the hypnotic trance are relaxed facial muscles, fluttering eyelids, separated lips, dry mouth, shivering, slow and deep breathing, catlophas, hypolgesia or analgesia.

While in a hypnotic trance, the subject may perform a series of complicated physical and mental activities at the hypnotist's instruction. A few hypnotic phenomena which contribute to understanding Hilgard's neo-dissociative theory will be the focus of the following discussion.

Age regression

Regression to a younger age can be accomplished under hypnosis in several ways. One method is behavioral 'primitivization,' which refers to evoking the general atmosphere of a certain age. In another age-regression technique, the subject may be helped to re-live or re-experience a specific event or a particular age. In yet another age-regression phenomenon, the subject may 'observe' an early life event as if in front of him.

A dramatic case of age regression illustrating the power of hypnosis was reported by Hilgard. The subject was a Japanese American student. As a young child, he was taken to a displacement camp after the Japanese attack on Pearl Harbor. The student did not know Japanese, and remembered speaking English all his life. During age regression to the age of seven, he spoke English, but used several Japanese words. When the age regression was continued to the age of three, suddenly his speech erupted into fluent Japanese. Upon returning to the age of seven, he reverted to English. This session was taped and played back to him, but he did not understand his own words. With encouragement from the hypnotist, he attempted to remember the hypnotic experience of his 'Japanese episode.'

> It was like my lips all of a sudden would move into these funny shapes. And then I would want to say something and wouldn't know what I was really saying. The words just came out and I wasn't sure whether they were real or not. The strangest thing is that my muscles without my volition would just take over. It was really like my mind wasn't involved in it.
> Hilgard, 1986, p. 47

It became apparent that this young man made himself 'forget' the Japanese language because of the negative connotations it had during his childhood. This episode illustrates both the split and the loss of control that occurred while he was speaking. Through the hypnotic episode, the student's lack of control of one part of his personality was demonstrated. The lips of a three-year-old child took control and emitted syllables the young man did not understand.

Amnesia and Hypermnesia in Hypnotic States

Forgetting and clearly remembering experiences that occurred in the distant past are striking hypnotic phenomena which are actually mirror images of each other. The difference between normal forgetting and hypnotic amnesia was demonstrated in several studies performed by Kihlstrom and Evans (1976). In this research, it was found that learned material that had been forgotten in the normal way was recalled in the chronological order of the learning sequence. However, when subjects received instruction to forget and, despite this, the forgotten material was retrieved under post-hypnotic suggestion, they retrieved the material in random order. When a new hypnotic suggestion eliminated the hypnotic amnesia, the process of remembering became chronological again. It follows, then, that hypnotic amnesia does not damage the organization of memory, even when a post-hypnotic instruction has been given to forget the material.

Hilgard studied the way in which the amnesiac block is formed in hypnosis, which is essential for understanding dissociative processes. From an examination of the subjective experience of hypnotic subjects, he identified several processes. The first is the influence of the hypnotist's words. The subject submits to the hypnotist's instructions. One subject described the experience this way:

> I wasn't sure I was going to forget them after he told me to forget. I tried to remember or review them right after, and I couldn't. I would get only the first or the first two words and no farther. Later on I couldn't remember those . . . You know it's there, you can *feel* it's there but it feels like a blank space. You can't get to it.   Hilgard, 1986, p. 77

When the hypnotist instructed him to remember, the subject said: 'It was not like a revelation hit me. I still had to try to remember. This time, I could remember' (ibid., p. 77).

It is the suggestion that is so powerful, rather than the words themselves. The hypnotic subject relinquishes control to the hypnotist. At times, the subject may repeat the instructions, making the external suggestion a self-suggestion under the hypnotist's supervision.

Another device for inducing amnesia is selective inattention to, or purposeful diversion from, the material that the subject is instructed to forget. In order to attain the amnesia, the hypnotic subject must actively cooperate in the process. 'Suddenly it was as though a shade was drawn between the words [that were to be forgotten] and myself,' recalled one subject (ibid., p. 78).

Imagery may also aid in creating amnesia: 'When told to forget, my head fills up with something soft and all the ideas were squashed against the side of my head, against the bones, like styrofoam that can be squashed with a weight. When the weight is removed, the ideas and words bounce back' (ibid., p. 78). Thus, the hypnotized person responds to the hypnotic instructions with various cognitive mechanisms to create the dissociation.

Hypermnesia, the recall of material usually unavailable in the waking state, can be achieved through hypnosis. Hypermnesia is an effective therapeutic device for retrieving past experiences which underlie pathological reactions. Hilgard refers to Janet's treatment of Mary, who suffered from recurring symptoms that consisted of terror, delirium, and vomiting of blood during her menstrual periods. When other treatments had failed, Janet resorted to hypnotic age regression to discover the roots of her fears. Mary regressed to the age of her first menstrual period. He then ascertained that she had been frightened by the menstrual blood she saw, and to stop its flow she had immersed herself in a barrel of cold water. As a result, she became ill and experienced blurring of her senses for a few days. Subsequently, her menstruation stopped for five years, and when it reappeared, she suffered from the symptoms described above. As Janet summarizes:

> I was able to succeed only thanks to a singular means. It was necessary to bring her back into the initial circumstances of the delirium, convince her that the menstruation had lasted for three days and was not interrupted through any regrettable incident. Now, once this was done, the following menstruation came at the due point, lasted for three days, without any pain or delirium. Hilgard, 1986, p. 44

Several stages in Janet's treatment of Mary can be identified: achieving a more distinct memory by the process of hypnosis; significantly revising the character of the traumatic event in her memory by suggestion; and, in the third stage, recreating amnesia of the event through hypnotic suggestion.

Hypnosis can work wonders when interrogating eye witnesses to serious crimes, by enabling the investigator to help the witness remember the forgotten events that the latter observed. Kroger and Douce (1979) describe several thrilling cases in which FBI agents succeeded in capturing criminals with the aid of witnesses and victims who remembered information under hypnosis. Among others, the authors describe the kidnapping of two girls, aged 7 and 15, by a member of the Symbionese Liberation Front, a militant underground group in the United States during the 1970s. He took the two girls to Mexico. When they arrived at a motel, he raped the older girl. He released the girls after several days, but threatened that if they told anyone what they had undergone, they would be killed.

The girls found it difficult to remember the events clearly. The older one remembered the motel, but investigators could not find any concrete evidence there to assist them in identifying the kidnapper. Under hypnosis, she recalled important details about the car, such as rust spots in various places, its color, the brand name of the paper towels that were in the car, and the kind of cookies that were on the back seat. She also remembered that the window squeaked when opened. While hypnotized, the girl remembered an exchange between the kidnapper and a mechanic at a garage on a hill, in which the mechanic said the kidnapper needed freon. She also remembered that the kidnapper paid by a red, blue and white credit card. FBI agents found the garage, the mechanic, and a copy of the credit card receipt. When the suspect was arrested at his home, an examination of the car confirmed all of the details the girl had remembered under hypnosis (Kroger and Douce, 1979).

This is only one of many cases that demonstrate the power of hypnosis in reconstructing events that have been forgotten. In spite of this, Chapnik-Smith (1983) casts doubt on the reliability of hypnotic reconstruction of facts. She maintains that hypnotic memories are not reliable unless additional verification is provided by other means.

In an exhaustive article, Chapnik-Smith maintains that the hypnotist influences the memories through suggestions containing subtle hints. In a series of laboratory experiments, she demonstrated that reconstruction of learned material under hypnotic suggestion was not more accurate than remembering under conscious direction. After extensively reviewing the literature, she advances the proposition that several factors may at least partially explain the apparent efficacy of hypnosis in improving memory. Hypnotic subjects are undoubtedly more suggestible, and may 'create' facts because of their strong wish to produce results. (See Buckhout et al., 1981; Zelig and Beidleman, 1981; and Hastie, Landsman and Loftus, 1978.)

One of the factors which may enhance memory with or without hypnosis is encouragement to guess details or events even when unsure of their existence. Signal detection theory postulates that such encouragement in uncertain situations increases the individual's willingness to risk more guesses, thereby increasing the chance of guessing correctly as well.

Smith (1979) reports a very interesting finding. Memory improves in direct correlation to the greater number of details provided about the context and the situation in which the events to be remembered occurred. This was demonstrated when subjects learned two lists of words in two different rooms. When examined, those who were tested in the room where they had studied remembered more words than those who sat in a different room for the test. When subjects were encouraged to remember the context in which they learned, they remembered more extensively than those who did not receive this encouragement, although the actual context was different. Moreover, two hypnotic techniques, repetition of the attempts to remember and utilization of imagery and imagination, increase the accuracy of memory.

Hilgard (1986) provides interesting information about memory functioning while under anesthesia. He reports that, under hypnosis, some patients were able to remember what occurred during their operations, including conversations between the doctors. This finding verifies that events are observed and remembered, at least by some people, even in extreme dissociative states.

It seems that amnesia and hypermnesia are phenomena which occur in hypnosis, although the contributing factors and processes are not yet completely understood. Suggestion clearly influences their formation. It was demonstrated that amnesia and hypermnesia open and close the doors between the different parts of the personality and between various mental functions and states. The techniques used for this purpose both under hypnosis as well as in the waking state can be useful in creating and lifting dissociation.

Automatic Writing and Dichotic Listening

The phenomena of automatic writing and divided attention also shed light on dissociative processes. In automatic writing, a conscious activity (reading) and an unconscious one (writing) are performed simultaneously. Usually, while the subject is hypnotized, he is given a post-hypnotic suggestion to perform two different or opposing functions. The hypnotist requests that he answer questions aloud affirmatively or negatively, while simultaneously writing the opposite answer. Hilgard claims that this phenomenon demonstrates the existence of a split between the motoric, executive function on one hand and the regulating function on the other hand. The subjects report experiencing such a split: 'I found myself in a contradiction. How can I be thinking and verbalizing something and doing precisely the opposite with my hand? ... I felt I had set up a conflict' (Hilgard, 1986, p. 144).

In a complicated research project, Stevenson (1976) examined automatic writing. He examined subjects' ability to read the names of colors and write a series of numbers simultaneously. He divided his subjects into several groups. One group performed the automatic writing under the influence of post-hypnotic suggestion. The second group simulated being hypnotized, rather than undergoing hypnosis, and received the same suggestions as the first group (see Orni, 1972). Stevenson also examined the performance of automatic writing while the subject was under hypnosis (unconscious functioning) and without hypnosis (conscious functioning). Finally, he introduced different degrees of difficulty into the performance of the automatic writing, such as writing numbers serially as opposed to writing a series of arithmetical additions.

Interestingly, Stevenson found that automatic writing done consciously was performed better than that performed in an unconscious, hypnotic state. This difference in the groups' achievements increased with the difficulty of the arithmetical problem. Unconscious writing of the numbers created greater interference with reading the names of colors than did the conscious writing task. The results of comparing the simulators to the hypnotized subjects were even more surprising: the simulators generally performed better. In other words, there was less interference with reading the names of colors from the conscious performance of arithmetical tasks than from the same activity when performed unconsciously.

Stevenson's study demonstrated that two processes interfered with performing two of the tasks under hypnosis. The first interference was the maintenance of one task in the unconscious, because this requires substantial mental effort. The second disturbance resulted from competition between the two tasks. The fact that the simulators functioned better than the hypnotized subjects demonstrates, paradoxically, that a hypnotic trance is a truly unique state of consciousness. Often, the comparison between functioning under hypnosis and by simulation is used to measure whether or not hypnosis is actually occurring. These studies clearly demonstrate that the belief that hypnosis always improves mental and physical functioning is simply incorrect.

Dichotic listening is a perceptual task defined by the ability to perform competing tasks on two different levels (subliminal and superliminal) of consciousness, or even on the same level. In dichotic listening, two competing pieces of auditory information are provided simultaneously to an individual; one becomes the focus of attention, while the other is purposefully rejected or provided subliminally. Despite this, the rejected or subliminal information is not lost; it can be retrieved. The information is apparently processed in parallel fashion. One set of data is consciously perceived, while the other perception occurs unconsciously. It appears, therefore, that inattention to one of the auditory stimuli may function as a dissociative block, and that parallel processing may occur simultaneously on both conscious and unconscious levels.

The findings on automatic writing and dichotic listening can contribute to understanding some aspects of dissociative processes and their related mechanisms. First, graduated exercises or appropriate instructions, not only hypnosis, can also create dissociative states in which two competing activities can be performed simultaneously. Most importantly, regulation of attention between different functions may be the principal mechanism for forming dissociation between these functions.

THE HYPNOTIC EXPERIENCE AND THE 'HIDDEN OBSERVER'

The mystery of the hypnotic phenomenon may be clarified by understanding the subjective experience of the hypnotized subject. Hilgard investigated this by interviewing hypnotized subjects about their experiences and found four distinct characteristics of the hypnotic experience:

1. *Heightened suggestibility.* In the hypnotic state, most of the subjects felt that they were more than normally submissive to the power of the hypnotist's suggestions.
2. *Intensification of imagery and imagination.* These usually spontaneous responses to hypnosis facilitated compliance with the hypnotist's instructions.
3. *Decreased planning ability.* Owing to a sense of passivity and reduced motivation, the hypnotized subject relinquishes the initiative to the hypnotist.
4. *Decreased judgment and reality testing.* The hypnotized subject does not discriminate between true and false information, and accepts hypnotic suggestions that distort body image and real time, as well as other strange concepts.

To his surprise, Hilgard discovered an additional layer of awareness within the hypnotic state, with different characteristics. In an experiment on inducing temporary deafness by hypnotic suggestion, Hilgard discovered an unexpected phenomenon, which he called the 'hidden observer.' When Hilgard demonstrated induced deafness by hypnosis in a blind student in class, one of the students asked whether or not the subject perceived the voices 'on some level.' Examining this immediately, Hilgard asked the hypnotized student to raise his index finger if he was aware of noises. To everyone's surprise, the subject raised his finger, and added, 'Please restore my hearing so you can tell me what I did. I felt my finger rise in a way that was not a spontaneous twitch ... and I want to know what you did' (ibid., p. 186).

Hilgard restored the student's hearing with another hypnotic suggestion and asked him to describe his experience. The student told the class that he became deaf when the lecturer counted to three; then he became bored and began thinking about a statistics problem. Suddenly, he felt his finger rising involuntarily. He asked what happened, but Hilgard continued the experiment before explaining to him. He hypnotized the student again, then said:

> When I place my hand on your arm like this (*he demonstrated*) I can be in touch
> with that part of you that listened to me before and made your finger rise —
> that part that could hear and knew what was going on when you were
> hypnotically deaf. When I question that part, it will be able to answer me and
> tell me what it knows about what happened. But this hypnotized part of you,
> to whom I am now talking, will not know what you are saying — or even that
> you are talking — until, out of hypnosis, I shall say, 'Now you can remember
> everything.' All right, now I am placing my hand on your arm.
>
> ibid., p. 187

The subject accurately reported the events which had occurred from the moment he was hypnotized. He recalled the question leading up to the experiment, the experiment itself, and all the other questions he had answered. When he was awakened from the hypnotic state, he did not remember the events which had occurred, and asked the class to describe what had been happening.

Following this discovery and its replication in additional experiments, Hilgard concluded that there is more than one state of awareness within the hypnotic state. Beyond the familiar hypnotic state, there is a state which Hilgard named the 'hidden observer.' This state of superordinate awareness is only a metaphor for the cognitive process which occurs during hypnosis.

Hilgard continued to investigate the phenomenon of the 'hidden observer' in a number of experiments on pain reduction. In a combination of pain reduction and automatic writing, he measured the pain reported verbally while the subject's hand was held in iced water on a scale of 0 through 10, with 10 representing great pain and the desire to remove his hand from the water. Under hypnosis, the subject was asked to keep his hand in the water while verbally reporting the level of pain. He was given a hypnotic suggestion that he would not feel the pain. Simultaneously, he was asked to write his sensations with his other hand, which presumably expressed the perceptions of the 'hidden observer.' The results confirmed the existence of two states of awareness within the hypnotic state: the subjective experience of the hypnotic state; and the 'hidden observer' experience. The 'hidden observer' reported experiencing a higher level of pain than the subject reported verbally while under the hypnotic suggestion that he would not feel pain.

Evidently, the 'hidden observer' represents a superordinate hypnotic process in which awareness of reality is heightened at least to a degree similar to that of the waking state. Although hidden, this process is discerned and assimilated unconsciously, but it influences overt behavior.

Furthermore, Hilgard thinks that the 'hidden observer' phenomenon supports the horizontal dissociative model (see above), rather than the vertical psychoanalytic model. The 'hidden observer' is 'omniscient,' characterized by clarity, accuracy, organization, maturity, and protecting the hypnotized individual, contrary to the unconscious as described in the psychoanalytic model.

Hilgard regards the hidden observer as an additional dissociation within the dissociative state of hypnosis, as described by one of the subjects:

> The hidden observer seemed like my real self when I'm out of hypnosis, only more objective. When I'm in hypnosis, I'm imagining, letting myself pretend, but somewhere the hidden observer knows what's really going on. I think this is part of the same process as the tendency in hypnosis to stand back and say: Look what's happening to you. You're slowly going under hypnosis. Hilgard, 1986, p. 209

Hilgard thus concludes that there are three levels of awareness: consciousness, hypnotic consciousness, and the 'hidden observer.' Yet, an important question might arise. Why is it not possible to maintain the usual categorization of awareness vs hypnotic states, and why is the 'hidden observer' different from the normal state of awareness which the hypnotist calls upon to participate in the hypnotic process? In another critique of Hilgard's discovery, Spanos and Hewitt (1980; see also Bowers, 1989) maintain that the 'hidden observer' is not an expression of the dissociation of different mental aspects, but of the hypnotized subject's response to a hypnotic suggestion that engages its functioning.

These researchers provide empirical evidence for their claims. Two groups of subjects who were highly responsive to hypnosis participated in a study of pain tolerance. Half of the group received instructions which induced expectations that the 'hidden observer' would increase their tolerance for pain, while the others were told that the 'hidden observer' would reduce their pain. The results in each case accorded with the subjects' expectations. This casts doubt on the 'hidden observer' as an authentic entity which observes events occurring while the subject is hypnotized, implying that it may be a process that was hypnotically induced by suggestion just like other phenomena created by hypnotic suggestion.

This penetrating criticism does not succeed in negating the value of Hilgard's dissociative model, which is based on dissociation between different control centers that regulate behavior. Whether the 'hidden observer' is a separate entity which manifests itself in a particular situation or simply an expression of compliance to suggestion, the split in functioning in the hypnotic state has been clearly demonstrated. From the moment of its creation, the 'hidden observer' functions as a behavioral motivator outside awareness even in the hypnotic state.

HILGARD'S NEO-DISSOCIATION THEORY

On the basis of a thorough examination of the various dissociative phenomena, Hilgard (1986) formulated a theoretical model of dissociation. He suggests that complex behavior is initiated and directed by two major systems, the executive system and the monitoring system. The executive system refers to such entities as the ego, although Hilgard refrains from utilizing this term. The executive initiates behavior, plans goals and means of achieving them, makes decisions, resolves conflicts, activates a specific mental function while inhibiting others, and so on.

The monitoring system, which functions alongside the executive system, is responsible for such mental activities as observation, screening, attention focus, judgment, and appraisal. These activities supply the individual with information about internal and external events. The monitoring system is dynamic; it regulates the flow of attention selectively to appraise, evaluate, and determine the factors which are relevant to attaining goals or realizing plans. The concepts of superego, self-image, and reality testing are congruent with this description of the functions of the monitoring system. The two systems, executive and monitoring, are coordinated and provide reciprocal feedback.

In addition to the central system, secondary sub-systems and more specific tertiary systems exist. There is a hierarchy of systems which govern behavior, beginning with the central system, and continuing with subordinate systems and then various minor sub-systems. These minor sub-systems relate to habits, attitudes, interests, specific skills, and others. While the functioning of the central system is complicated and requires coordination between the various high mental processes, such as perception, thought, and emotions, a minor sub-system is a specific habit or mechanism that is independent of the central controls and responds to a specific stimulus in a specific field.

A very important principle that Hilgard incorporates into his dissociative theory is the relative autonomy of the different sub-systems. Despite the hierarchical relationship and the links between the lower and higher systems, the different systems can operate independently. The control of the central system over the secondary and lower systems is not absolute; they can be split off from central controls. The executive and monitoring systems may also be mutually split off or function in isolation from one another.

The autonomic functioning of certain sub-systems is demonstrated in such everyday activities as driving a car or typing. In certain reactions, the split between thought and emotion also generates autonomic functioning. Compulsive behavioral symptoms and phobias result from such splitting. Although suffering individuals know that their behavior or fears are irrational, their emotional reactions have been removed from their central system's control.

Dissociation also occurs between the executive and the monitoring systems, which are normally coordinated in their operations. The obsessive-compulsive person's monitoring system may 'inform' the executive system that compulsive behavior is inappropriate, but to no avail. Similarly, the monitoring system may predict that an emotional outburst will have undesirable results, but the executive system may dissociate and act inappropriately despite this information. In other cases, the monitoring system may dominate and dissociate itself from the executive system. When a young man's excessive fear of being rejected impedes his inviting the girl of his dreams for a date, this is the result of the monitoring system's interference.

In fact, Hilgard views personality as being composed of many 'self' systems, although he does not utilize this concept. The scope of the functions of the different personality structures or selves differs; some function openly, others in concealed fashion. The relationships between most of these structures are coordinated hierarchical relationships, although some of the structures function completely independently. Hilgard believes that all behavior, whether adaptive or maladaptive, involves dissociative processes. Hypnosis provides a clearly discernible example of dissociation because control is transferred to an external power, but, as Hilgard suggested in his book, dissociations occur in all behaviors.

At this point, the various factors involved in generating dissociation may be summarized:

1. *A constitutional tendency to dissociate.* It is assumed that there are inherent individual differences in the inclination toward dissociative behavior. The exact mechanisms and processes responsible for this tendency cannot be explained yet, but a number of authors believe that this tendency is constitutional. Janet believes that dissociation is rooted in a biological weakness.

2. *Personality structure.* Hilgard's approach suggests that dissociation is also a function of the degree of tightness or inner integration within the sub-systems and functions of the personality. The higher the inner integration, the lower the probability for dissociation.

3. *Trauma.* Janet presumes that trauma automatically produces a dissociative reaction.

4. *Repetitions and automation.* Through monotonous repetition, any particular action becomes automatic and unconscious, unavailable for critical examination by the central systems, such as the monitoring system. Many repetitions of behavior, whether motoric or ideational, strengthen the autonomy of the sub-systems involved in the specific type of behavior and detach it from central control.
5. *Split attention and selective inattention.* Attention processes are voluntary and within conscious control. Focusing attention and concentration on one activity or object causes background factors to withdraw into the pre-conscious. Similarly, selective inattention may cause dissociation, inducing the unattended part to settle into the unconscious.
6. *Hypnosis and suggestion.* The transfer of control to another person creates dissociation by relinquishing willful control over behavior.
7. *Imagination.* Imagination and imagery are additional voluntary mental devices for creating inner splits in mental functioning, distancing from reality, and limiting executive and monitoring controls.
8. *Forgetting.* Intentional or unintentional amnesia may assist in creating the dissociative block.

It seems to me that the two most important and basic mental mechanisms involved in creating dissociation are imagination and actively shifting the focus of attention. The ability to utilize imagery and ideomotoric responses can help in forming the altered state of mind and ideational reality found in many dissociative behaviors, such as hallucination, conversion, yoga, etc. The power of imagery can influence sensations and perception to the extent of altering internal experiences and external reality.

The ability actively to employ and deploy focusing of attention and to control inattention seems to be the process responsible for creating splits and inner blocks which compartmentalize the personality structure. Focusing attention or inattention is involved in memory and forgetting, avoidance of unpleasant experiences, automatic behavior, blurring of thought, etc., all of which are involved in dissociation. Imagination and attention or inattention create a distancing from reality or from the focused self. Both of these functions culminate in the experience of absorption (Spiegel, 1989), which is 'a disposition for having episodes of single and total attention that fully engages one's representational (i.e. perceptual, enactive, imaginative and ideational) resources' (Tellegen and Atkinson, 1974). Absorption, then, seems to be one of the major processes which occur in the dissociative state and it can take on both involuntary and voluntary forms.

One of the states accompanying absorption is the loss of generalized reality orientation (Shor, 1970). In waking life, Shor claims, the context of generalized reality provides a frame of reference in the background. Within this context, we interpret all ongoing conscious experiences. This orientation to generalized reality can, Shor maintains, fade into the distant background of the mind under certain conditions, such as hypnosis (or the dissociative states). These ongoing experiences are isolated from their usual context. When that happens, the distinction between imagination and reality disappears.

Relating these formulations to the therapy of dissociative states, it can be said that therapeutic manipulation of attention and imagery can be instrumental in lifting pathological dissociative blocks.

DISSOCIATION AND PATHOLOGY

Looking at pathology from the perspective of the dissociative approach, the following sequence of processes is noteworthy. Usually, pathology begins with a trauma which causes such an overwhelming shock to the individual that the traumatic event cannot be assimilated. Almost automatically, the response to trauma is an immediate rise in sensory and perceptual thresholds and diversion of attention from the traumatic event. The dissociative response develops from the drastic change in these thresholds and the diversion of attention. The traumatic event and the reactions to it are then encapsulated as an autonomous and disconnected personality sub-system or a schema.

In essence, the dissociative response reflects the two major characteristics common to all forms of dissociation, loss of central monitoring and control functions, and splitting. Loss of control is expressed in symptoms such as flashbacks, visual images, recurring thoughts, incomprehensible and uncontrolled emotional outbursts, multiple personalities, and similar phenomena. The split assumes the form of loss of the memory of the trauma, experiences of numbness and bluntness, distancing from reality, and estrangement.

Horowitz (1981) formulates this in a similar, but more detailed manner. He identifies two major elements in the response to trauma. The first can be denoted over-alertness, which includes agitation, hyperactivity, aggressive outbursts, anxiety, nightmares, intrusive recurring flashbacks of the trauma, and the tendency to relive the traumatic experiences compulsively, without emotional control or regulation. The second aspect of the response to trauma is distancing, which includes introversion, with numbing of the senses, withdrawal, isolation, forgetting and feelings of self-alienation. According to this formulation, there is a two-phase post-traumatic reaction. The first is intense panic and over-alertness. The second phase alternates between emotional outbursts (loss of control) and withdrawal accompanied by numbness (split).

According to Janet, dissociation is the direct consequence of the trauma itself (see Van der Kolk and Ducey, 1989). Indeed, some studies demonstrate that most people who suffer from the dissociative response of multiple personality experienced a trauma in childhood (Putnam et al., 1986). This trauma cannot be absorbed into individuals' cognitive schemata about themselves and their world because of its strange or frightening nature; thus, it is maintained outside the existing schemata. Verbal recreation of the trauma enables the individual to 'redigest' it and incorporate it into existing schemas. Verbalization of the trauma facilitates a process which makes the memory more tolerable for the individual. Unless it is verbalized and formalized, the trauma retains its shapeless, unprocessed, and primary form, creating a split in the subjective experience of continuity. Although remaining forgotten, the trauma activates different autonomous responses.

Horowitz et al. (1980) hypothesize that the response to trauma represents repeated attempts to integrate the trauma into long-term memory, but because appropriate schemas for its absorption are unavailable, the trauma is absorbed only on the level of the working memory. Full absorption of the trauma does occur, but slowly. Until this process is completed and an appropriate schema is formed, the unassimilated trauma thrusts itself into consciousness. Strong affective responses of anxiety or depression are also generated by the inability to assimilate the trauma. These affects were dominant at the moment of the trauma, and their appearance reflects an effort to achieve catharsis.

Spiegel, Hunt and Donershine (1988) describe a different intermediary mechanism that connects the trauma and the dissociative response. They maintain that people who tend to utilize imagery apparently tend to escape from traumatic situations through dissociation. This hypothesis is reinforced by their findings that individuals who undergo a dissociative post-traumatic response are also highly susceptible to hypnosis and tend to use imagery as a form of escape. Thus, in their view, dissociation does not reflect difficulties in absorbing an unusually frightening event into an appropriate schema; rather, it represents a form of escape by using the most available mechanism for dealing with a difficult situation. Dissociation is thus the immediate defense utilized to cope with pain and anxiety stemming from the trauma itself.

Self-hypnosis is another, similar process which is regarded as connecting between trauma and the dissociative response. Putnam et al. (1986) maintain, in accord with Janet, that the basis of escape through dissociation is the human tendency to perform self-hypnosis during or following a traumatic event.

The studies of Noyes and his colleagues (1976, 1977) shed additional light on the relationship between trauma and dissociation. They compared the dissociative responses of accident victims and hospitalized psychotic patients. In this comparison, three principal characteristics of the dissociative reactions were found:

1. Depersonalization, which included responses such as distancing from reality and from one's body, distortions in body perception, isolation of emotion, etc.
2. Blurring of cognitive and sensory functions, such as perception, thought, memory, etc.
3. Mental alertness, expressed in vigilance, perceptual clarity, heightened sensitivity, rapidity of thought, feelings of control, etc.

Despite some similarities in the dissociative responses of the two groups, especially with regard to establishing distance from the traumatic event, many of the responses were different. Accident victims reacted with general mental alertness, focused attention, clarity of thought, sharpening of perceptual functioning, and emotional distancing, while the psychotic patients responded with blurring and numbing of the senses, diffused attention, and intense emotions.

The most important conclusions reached in this study are that there is no single dissociative response, and that dissociative responses may be adaptive or maladaptive. The adaptive dissociative response prevents anxiety and enhances self-control, and is usually characteristic of the reaction to a single traumatic event, whereas the maladaptive dissociative responses of psychotic patients result from continuous conditions which provoke anxiety and depression.

It would be reasonable to hypothesize that reacting in a dissociative manner is adaptive when coping with an acute, momentary trauma, facilitating escape from dangerous situations, but without losing control, and then slow reintegration and enhanced functioning. Continuous emotional traumas, which pose a mental as well as physical threat, apparently cause a continuous and disintegrating form of dissociation. Traumas in which individuals undergo experiences that upset their internal stability to the point of loss of control are essentially different from those momentary traumas which endanger someone's physical existence.

Dissociative reactions are related to a broad range of psychopathology. Van der Kolk (1987) established that trauma and dissociation play a role in the formation of borderline character disorders, hysteria, panic, and anxiety reactions. Horowitz et al. (1980) believe that dissociation has an important role in psychosomatic reactions, depression and anxiety. Pitman et al. (1986) reveal a connection between dissociation and depressive reactions, suicidal tendencies and schizophrenia. Pierre Janet himself regarded the compulsive reaction as the prototype of dissociative reactions. No hypothesis, however, has been presented to explain the involvement of dissociation in such a wide range of pathologies. Apparently, these theorists regard trauma, rather than conflict, as the basis for the formation of pathology.

In contrast to psychoanalytic theory, the dissociation model does not delineate the specific relationship between anxiety and dissociation. From the literature, several assumptions can be reached. First, the traumatic event or internal conflict arouses unbearable anxiety, which is warded off by the dissociative response. A second hypothesis is that anxiety is a response to the symptoms which accompany the dissociative response, such as flashbacks and lack of self-control. Yet a third assumption to be derived from the literature is that anxiety is not an essential element in the development of dissociation.

DISSOCIATION AND TREATMENT

The two basic therapeutic goals for pathology which involves dissociation and dissociative disorder are the restoration of central control of the executive and monitoring personality systems, and elimination of internal splitting in order to achieve internal integration.

In fact, from the standpoint of the dissociation model, the overriding principle of therapy is restoration of flexibility to the control and splitting or integrating functions. Full control includes the ability to create or eliminate splitting, and to enhance or relinquish control as required for maximal coping. Individuals may allow their feelings freedom or limit them, and may choose to disregard or confront unpleasant events. In the same vein, they may choose to dissociate adaptively (day dream, let go, be absorbed) or heighten control and inner integration (be logical, delay gratification, concentrate).

Describing the use of this principle, Horowitz (1981) maintains that the treatment of those who suffer from post-traumatic syndrome should consist of facilitating regulation of the form and intensity of the repeated experience of the trauma. The individual should be helped to remember at moments and to forget at others, to concentrate on the events when necessary and at other times divert attention from them. In his article on symptomatic treatment of compulsive disorders, Janet (see Putnam, 1987) asserts that the doctor should help the patient feel the doctor has full control in treating his or her problem, so that the patient will also feel able to control the problem. Symbolic contents and their meaning should not be treated; rather, the focus of treatment is learning to control the pathological condition. Patients should not be allowed to sink into skepticism. They should be forcefully encouraged to follow their healthy inclinations, despite the fear or uncertainty this arouses. Similarly, patients should be helped to control their attention and motivation.

Paradoxically, one of the most common methods of restoring control is utilizing the dissociative state of hypnosis. In hypnosis, the individual yields self-control to an external agent in order to regain it afterwards. Regaining control is achieved by eliminating the factors that interfere with the individual's self-control. The reacquisition of self-control through hypnosis circumvents the need for unpleasant self-confrontation.

Van der Kolk (1987) recommends another way to regain self-control. This method consists of a long succession of therapy sessions in which a slow, gradual, but steady attempt is made to reawaken the painful trauma. The goal is to recreate the trauma with all of its emotional contents, so as to achieve verbalization of the traumatic experience and emotional catharsis, which are the two most efficient methods for regaining control of the dissociated trauma. This requires a slow process of working through and overcoming resistance and anxieties. The slow retrieval and working through can be accompanied by simulation techniques and directed imagery.

Removal of dissociation and restoration of control may be achieved by 'canceling' the trauma through forgetting or revising the memory, as was demonstrated by Janet in the case of Mary. Janet produced a change in Mary's symptoms by planting a new, different memory of the traumatic event. Spiegel, Hunt and Donershine (1988) report that they succeeded in eliminating the nightmares symptomatic of the post-traumatic syndrome in a similar manner.

However, studies performed by Kihlstrom (1977) raise several questions regarding this therapeutic conception. He demonstrated that original memory contents remain firmly implanted despite their apparent removal under hypnosis. When the hypnotic suggestion is removed, they reappear. In the case of Janet's treatment of Mary, the revised memory which Janet induced to eliminate the trauma could not compete with the real memory. A possible reply to this criticism is that revision of the memory of the traumatic event may not erase the original memory, but it can completely dissociate the frightening trauma so that its effects no longer trouble the individual. Another speculative answer to the criticism is that intensifying the memory of the real trauma during the first stage of hypnosis produced a cathartic effect which provided such relief that the symptoms disappeared.

A number of cognitive and behavioral techniques may also be utilized to enhance flexible central control and integrate splits of personality sub-systems and split-off behaviors. These include positive reinforcement of desired behavior and negative reinforcement of undesired behavior;

training in stopping undesired thoughts and substituting them with desired ones; training to shift attention and inattention, desensitization, relaxation and guided imagery techniques to dissolve undesired dissociation and enhance more desired and controlled forms of adaptive dissociation, as well as loosening central control when needed; practicing paradoxical intentions to enhance control; enticing contextual details of the traumatic situation to facilitate retrieval of forgotten experiences, and the like.

The dissociation model has abandoned depth psychology in favor of a psychology of hierarchical structures with different central power which have dynamic and flexible interrelationships. The unconscious is defined in terms of splits among the structures and loss of control of central structures. Unlike the psychoanalytic model, this theory suggests that dissociation can also be adaptive. Only extreme forms of dissociation are considered pathological, and these usually reflect the involvement of a trauma. Dissociation is based on normal psychological processes, such as attention, imagery, hypnotability, suggestibility, etc. Under extreme conditions, these processes start to function in the service of defense. The main therapeutic goal of this model is to re-establish the volitional flexibility of control over behavior. The recent comeback of the dissociation theory of the unconscious holds great promise of wide implications for the behavioral sciences. However, extensive research is required to establish it as a comprehensive theory of behavior.

CHAPTER 5

The Cognitive Approach to the Unconscious

In this chapter, three different cognitive approaches to conceptualizing the unconscious will be discussed. The first approach views the unconscious from the perspective of information processing. The second views the unconscious from the perspective of hidden cognitive structures. The third approach views the unconscious from the perspective of higher cognitive processes of attention and comprehension.

THE UNCONSCIOUS AS HIDDEN INFORMATION PROCESSES

Cognitive psychology is, by definition, the study of consciousness. Consciousness can be described as a composite of processes of attention, perception, memory, thought, and imagery. These mental activities create some of the products of consciousness: registering of phenomenological experience, retrospection regarding past experiences, formation of categories of knowledge, rules of judgment, comparisons, problem solving, selective attentiveness and, finally, execution of behavior based on the above-mentioned cognitive activities.

The principal functions of cognitive activity can be summarized in two categories:

- *monitoring*, which refers to organization of perceptions, including memories and thoughts, and their representation in consciousness;
- *control of the self*, enabling the individual to initiate and cease behaviors and cognitive activities voluntarily.

Modern approaches to cognitive psychology focus on the study of cognition through information processing: the registration, interpretation, categorization, storage and retrieval of incoming information. Much of this information processing is believed to take place out of consciousness. Yet the products of this unconscious processing influence the content of consciousness as well as behavior. The unconscious processing is an inseparable part of the information processing in general, and as such it assists in monitoring and controlling cognitive processes and behavior.

Kihlstrom (1984) presents two models of information processing with different implications for the unconscious. The first is the multi-store model of memory. This model describes the processing of stimuli from the sensation of a stimulus until the point of storage. In this version of a multiple-stage memory system, there are three levels of information storage, and on each storage level the information undergoes a different form of processing. Each of the three levels reflects a different degree of awareness. The three centers of storage are the sensory register; the short-term memory; and the long-term memory.

Simply described, the process consists of the following three stages. The first station for receipt of stimuli is the sensory register. The stimuli are recorded in a completely unconscious process, but this registration initiates instant contact with higher cognitive brain processes, where components and patterns (voice, light, form, etc.) of the sensory information are unconsciously analyzed and receive their initial meaning. In the next stage, when attention is focused on material, the incoming information becomes part of awareness, and processing (assignment of meaning) becomes conscious. At this point, the information is actually part of the short-term memory. In this stage, the information processing is continued by rehearsing the material many times. The material is then transferred for storage to the long-term memory, where it is not conscious but is available for rapid retrieval into consciousness.

A second version of information processing is the uni-store model of memory. In this there are also three information-processing centers, but only one of them serves as the storage center. The information processing begins, as in the previous version, with the sensory system. In the second stage, the processing is transferred to the memory storage system, where the stored material becomes conscious only if attention is focused on it. Attention brings only relevant material into consciousness, leaving the rest in the unconscious (or the pre-conscious).

According to the second model, most of the information processing occurs unconsciously in this model, by contrast with the multi-stage model. The material is perceived in the sensory system and it is unconsciously analyzed and classified in a preliminary fashion. In the following stage, the processed contents are transferred to the memory and linked with similar material or encoded in the appropriate category. All of this procedure remains unconscious. However, if at this stage attention is enlisted in a 'search' for information relevant to that specific moment, the desired material becomes conscious, because it was relevant to the organism's immediate needs. Until the material becomes conscious due to a shift in attention on it, it functions unconsciously, influencing thought, perception and general behavior. Attention is the filter which chooses contents for transfer to consciousness so that the cognitive functions occupying the individual at the specific moment may be performed.

Kihlstrom (1984) also defines stored memories from the standpoint of their availability for retrieval into consciousness. He differentiates between three types of stored memories:

(a) A memory that cannot be retrieved, but is not considered unconscious because it disappears completely from the information-processing system and it stops influencing behavior.
(b) A memory that can be retrieved from the storage center. Because it can be recalled easily, this material also is not considered unconscious.
(c) Material that is recorded in the phase of sensory registering and processing is the only material that is considered unconscious. It is not easily retrieved, yet it influences behavior.

Differentiating further between forms of conscious and unconscious memories, Kihlstrom (1984) defines and distinguishes between procedural memory, which is unconscious and relates to cognitive skills, and declarative memory, which is conscious. Procedural memory relates to memory of information and knowledge that has become automatic and remains unconscious, such as grammatical knowledge and its use in speech, driving skill, styles of automatic thinking, and the many different motor skills. This memory functions outside the individual's awareness. Declarative memory is a system of facts and contents, such as vocabulary, names, categories of classification, etc., which can be recalled consciously.

One of the processes responsible for transformation of unconsciously stored information into consciousness is its relevance to the 'self.' Events which are related to the self automatically become the focus of attention and are therefore consciously processed. An subjective occurrence is naturally experienced as 'I am doing this' or 'this is happening to me.' Information which is unrelated to the self is processed unconsciously until it becomes relevant to the self or the self's needs. This view is in sharp contrast to the psychoanalytic or dissociation models which posit that some information is diverted from consciousness precisely because it is relevant to the self in a threatening way.

Marcel's (1983) presentation of another form of information processing is relevant to this discussion. In Marcel's opinion, after the stimuli undergo sensory information processing, the processed material is converted into a set of hypotheses about the perceived stimulus. These hypotheses are examined by placing them in categories and pre-existing schemata according to the meaning of the stimuli. The process of creating and evaluating these hypotheses, finding the relevant schema and choosing the preferred hypothesis on the basis of that schema is unconscious.

Pawer and Brewin (1991) provide another approach to the subject of conscious and unconscious information processing. In their opinion, unconscious processing functions simultaneously within different systems, not in successive stages. For example, the word, concept or object 'mother' may be processed in relation to past experiences with the mother, but also in relation to a current situation with a girlfriend. Moreover, the unconscious processing is performed in modular fashion, independent of any other internal system. This process occurs quickly and automatically, without the individual's attention or mental effort. Conscious processing, which is logical, occurs in sequential stages. It is not modular, but dependent on other systems and stages. Because conscious processing demands effort and concentration, it is executed slowly.

Lazarus (1991), who discussed processing of emotional contents in particular, emphasizes another important difference between the conscious and unconscious forms of processing. He maintains that an emotional reaction and the behavior which follows are always a result of the individual's appraisal of the triggering situation (whether the situation is internal or external). When a particular situation is appraised as threatening, pleasing, challenging, etc, it arouses corresponding emotions. The specific emotion is a result of the appraisal rather than the situation itself. Often, however, people experience an emotional state without recognizing that they have appraised a situation or even without being able to identify which reality situation aroused the emotion. Lazarus considers this to be the result of unconscious appraisal.

He maintains that the principal characteristic of unconscious information processing is that it is automatic. Because it is automatic and very rapid, this processing occurs outside of awareness and appears to be executed without the involvement of higher cognitive appraisal systems. Moods which appear without reason or which seem to have no basis in appraisal of reality are created in such a fashion. They are based on processing which is performed so automatically and rapidly that it is imperceptible. According to Lazarus, one of the reasons for the processing being so automatic and rapid is that it is built on archaic unconscious structures or schemas which respond swiftly to certain specific stimuli. In contrast to Freud, who defined them as instincts, the cognitive theorists (Pawer and Brewin, 1991) emphasize that these archaic structures are cognitive systems.

Gilbert (1989) further develops these ideas, defining four primary schemas which process incoming information in automatic-emotional fashion: care eliciting, care giving, competition, and cooperation. These structures represent innate programs devised to process external material according to the permanent emotional characteristics contained in the particular program. Each program may produce a certain emotional state. For instance, according to Gilbert, depression results from a schema concerned with loss of the care giver or from a structure relating to failure and loss of status in a competitive situation. Since all stimuli connected to these subjects may be processed unconsciously and automatically, individuals may find themselves suffering from a depression without knowing the reason for it.

Additional differences between the various forms of conscious and unconscious processing were distinguished by Epstein (1983), who maintains that identical material may undergo two different forms of processing. Conscious processing is rational, while unconscious processing is symbolic and experiential.

Some of the hypotheses about the form of unconscious information processing presented above are reinforced by the parallel distribution processing (PDP) theory formulated by Rumelhart and McClelland (1986). The PDP model postulates the existence of a large number of processing units rather than a single control processing system. Each processing unit is devoted to a specific task. When activated, the unit excites some additional units and inhibits others along a rich network of associative links. Thus, the incoming information is distributed widely across the processing system rather than localized in any particular unit.

The activation of individual processing units can vary continuously. In addition, although each unit is connected to others, it operates independently under different rules and principles. Hence, information processing is performed by the different systems in a parallel manner rather than sequential stages. Parallel processing permits a large number of activated units to influence each other at any particular moment; thus, different aspects of the same information are being processed independently and simultaneously. This means that the greater the number of units, the more elaborate the processing.

Research in two principal areas has provided evidence and examples of unconscious information processing. One of these is subliminal perception and the second is the influence of unconscious memories.

Two researchers, Somekh and Wilding (1973), who were among the first to examine subliminal perception, demonstrated that subliminal processing is more precise and accurate than conscious processing. The researchers showed the words 'sad' and 'happy' on a screen both above and below the threshold of awareness, after which they showed the subjects an expressionless face, asking them to rate the degree of pleasant feeling it aroused. The subjects rated the picture according to the subliminal word they had been shown, sad or happy; however, this was not the reaction when the stimuli were presented above the threshold of awareness. When the experiment was expanded to include deception of the subjects by screening the words 'sap' and 'harry' both subliminally and superliminally, only the subjects who had been overtly exposed to the decoy words responded as though the words were 'sad' and 'happy,' while those who had been presented with the deceptive stimulus subliminally were not deceived into being influenced by these words in appraising the expressionless face.

Research by Forster and Govier (1978) also indicates that subliminal perception may be more accurate than conscious perception. In their experiment, subjects were conditioned by receiving an electric shock simultaneously to exposure to the word 'ships.' Later they were provided with the words 'ships,' 'boats,' and 'shings' subliminally in one ear while in their other ear segments of prose were read. During their exposure to the words, the subjects' GSR (galvanic skin response) was measured. The subjects responded with elevated GSR to the words 'ships' and 'boats,' while the GSR remained the same in response to the decoy word, 'shings.' In contrast, there were more errors, or elevations of the GSR, to the word 'shings' when it was presented above the threshold of awareness than below the threshold. It appears that differentiation and discrimination are more accurate when the stimuli are presented on the subliminal level (see Dixon, 1981).

Studies in dichotic listening have also produced relevant findings. In an experiment performed by MacKay (1973), the subjects received overt information in the form of an ambiguous sentence with two possible meanings, 'They threw stones toward the bank yesterday.' In the other ear, one group of subjects was exposed to the word 'money' subliminally, while the other group heard the word 'river.' The subjects interpreted the sentence in line with the meaning which accorded with the information they had received unconsciously, without having any idea of the reason they chose this particular interpretation. This experiment illustrates a more important process. A vague, undifferentiated stimulus might be perceived by the short-term memory, influence the perception and interpretation of a specific emotional behavior, and then disappear from the mental system. This could create a condition of 'history without memory' (Bowers, 1984). In this condition, the source of a particular interpretation or emotional state cannot be recalled, because it has totally disappeared and therefore cannot be retrieved nor freed from the unconscious state.

It has also been found that unconscious perception is more complex, sophisticated and richer than conscious perception. Marcel (1980) demonstrated that when information, superliminal or subliminal, has multiple meanings, many more meanings are unconsciously derived from the word than consciously. For example, when the word 'palm' is screened above the threshold of awareness, it is interpreted either as a tree or as the palm of the hand, while when it is screened subliminally, both meanings of the word are recognized.

It is apparent, then, that stimuli which are provided above the threshold of awareness circumscribe and inhibit perception and meaning much more than subliminal stimuli, which contribute more flexibility and richness. These findings regarding the sophisticated nature of subliminal perception were duplicated by Groeger (1984, 1988). He presented subjects with certain words (target words) above the threshold of awareness and subliminally. Later, he gave them a pattern of several words (arranged in the form of a puzzle), and asked them to identify the target word within the puzzle pattern. The pattern did not actually include the specific target word, but words that were similar in form or meaning were provided. It was found that the subjects who had been exposed to superliminal stimuli chose words that were similar only in their form, while those who had been exposed to subliminal stimuli chose words that were similar to the original in meaning.

Experiments performed in the area of unintentional unconscious learning further demonstrate the sophistication of unconscious perception and processing. People can unconsciously learn a complicated set of rules and transfer their acquired knowledge to new situations. Reber (1976) presented subjects with simulated rules of grammar used with a string of letters, and then examined whether they could transfer the rules to a new set of letters. Subjects who had learned the logic of the set of letters unintentionally (while unaware of learning) performed the new task better than those who learned the principles of the new grammar consciously. Reber maintains that in this fashion an individual can augment his problem-solving intuition. Intuition is not some mysterious, inexplicable sixth sense, but rather a rational system that has been internalized but is not available for conscious reconstruction.

Knowledge which is unconsciously recorded in memory may influence behavior without the individual being aware of the knowledge itself or the way in which it is influencing behavior. Jacoby, Walshyn and Kelley (1989) performed outstanding experiments illustrating this influence. They demonstrated that, under certain conditions, subjects confuse the phenomenon of 'familiarity' with the phenomenon of 'fame.' Using the technique of dichotic listening, Jacoby, Walshyn and Kelley provided their subjects with names of various people under the condition of dichotic listening (unconscious) and full attention (conscious condition). In the dichotic listening, the subjects were provided subliminally with some names in one ear, while in the other ear they received different information superliminally. Later, they were given the task of appraising the degree of fame of each person named. In spite of the fact that they could not reasonably know the names of these people, the participants in the dichotic listening situation rated them as though they were actually famous, rather than recognizing the experimental presentation as the source of the names' familiarity. In another, even more remarkable study, the same findings were attained while subjects were anesthetized prior to undergoing operations (Jelicic et al., in press).

Several relevant conclusions may be drawn from the information processing models and research with regard to the unconscious:

- Conscious and unconscious information processing are different and distinguishable from each other.
- Unconscious and conscious information processing do function in parallel fashion and affect each other. Unconscious processes can influence cognitive functioning, emotions and behavior.
- Unconscious information processes can be, at times, more sophisticated and more precise than conscious processing and therefore have adaptive value.

UNCONSCIOUS STRUCTURES AND HIGHER COGNITIVE FUNCTIONS

Meichenbaum and Gilmore (1984) constructed a model of unconscious information processing which involves higher cognitive functions, such as thought, that are also unconscious. In their theory, they divide cognitive activities into three principal components: cognitive events, cognitive processes, and cognitive structures. The cognitive event is essentially cognitive activity, such as thought or belief. Cognitive process is a principle by which information is organized, stored and retrieved. For example, unconscious cognitive processes can be expressed in an inclination to regard some stimuli as more important than others or a tendency to consider preliminary material as more significant than information acquired later. The third component, the cognitive structure, is an internal paradigm which adapts information to conform to the paradigm itself. 'Schemas' or 'programs' are examples of cognitive structures.

To summarize briefly, Meichenbaum and Gilmore describe the development of unconscious influences on behavior as follows. External information is perceived by the internal structures. While this is occurring, the information is influenced by the various cognitive processes, becoming cognitive events which constitute the individual's consciousness and influence his or her behavior. Meichenbaum and Gilmore think that these components and processes function mostly unconsciously.

We will now attempt to delineate their theory in its complexity. The cognitive events, such as thoughts, images and planning, normally become conscious in the following four situations:

1. Situations requiring new thoughts and images, such as acquiring new skills (e.g., driving). Until the skills become automatic, awareness and attention are focused on the activity, maintaining it at the forefront of consciousness.
2. Situations which require reasoning and choosing between alternatives, usually those preceding decisions about specific actions.
3. In situations of distress or difficulty, when seeking alternatives to customary ways of thinking and acting that have become ineffective or worthless.
4. When attempting to recall forgotten material.

In these four situations, individuals become aware of the cognitive events which they would not normally perceive in awareness. Thought, imagination and contemplation do not stop functioning when they are not the focus of awareness.

Meichenbaum and Gilmore utilize the concept of 'automatic thoughts' (Beck, 1976) as examples of unconscious thought which influences behavior unintentionally. In Beck's opinion, automatic thinking is the main mechanism involved in depression and its negative emotional state. The result of this ongoing unconscious flow of negative thoughts is a negative position towards the self, pessimism, and feelings of depression and despair. The fact that the depression appears at times without any evident trigger does not mean that a trigger does not exist; the reason lies in unconscious negative thoughts. In this model, the unconscious functioning includes a wide range of cognitive activities, such as self-appraisal, symbolic thought, imagery, expectations, etc.

In order to comprehend the operation of unconscious cognitive activity, one must look at two other components of unconscious activity: the processes and the structures. Unconscious processes shape the information perceived from external sources and change it into mental representations according to several pre-existing principles. The four main principles — that is, cognitive processes — believed to shape perceptions are: principles for storing information; principles for retrieving information; inferential processes; and principles for search and review of information.

These cognitive processes are exemplified in meta-cognition, which Meichenbaum and Gilmore regard as the basic principle activating thoughts, memories, decisions, etc. This term refers to the rules and styles utilized automatically by the individual to organize his or her cognitive world without being aware of this principle or its mode of action. Meta-cognition functions unconsciously, but is accessible for conscious reconstruction. An example of utilizing meta-cognition in trying to recall a forgotten name may be found in recalling memories and associations in relation to the person whose name has been forgotten. A similar use of this basic principle would be remembering an event connected with that person. A third example of using the process of meta-cognition is the request for help from another person who knows the forgotten individual's name. The functions of meta-cognition, as exemplified here, reflect individuals' accessible but usually unconscious knowledge of their cognitive processing.

Inferential processes and interpretations of reality operate according to three principles: availability, representativeness, and confirmation bias. The principle of availability reflects the individual's tendency, when information is vague, to regard the most available information as the most relevant. This process may produce distortions of reality, as the most relevant facts are not necessarily the ones that are most available.

The principle of representativeness reflects the tendency to accept information only if it accords with the pre-existing knowledge in the individual's conscious awareness at the time. By basing decisions on consciously known facts, the individual may omit important new information that would change the evaluation of a situation. The depressed person may be very selective in perceiving reality, relating only to those aspects which agree with prior pessimistic conceptions and ignoring aspects of reality which could contribute to a more optimistic outlook.

According to the principle of confirmation bias, people seek automatic confirmation of their theory or hypothesis about reality, and by acting on this principle unknowingly transform the reality so that it corresponds to their outlook. If, with or without justification, an individual believes another person is competing with her, she may find evidence that 'proves' this, and then behave according to her 'confirmed' hypothesis so competitively that she provokes others to compete with her.

In contrast to the cognitive process, the cognitive structure functions as an internal readiness or tendency to perceive the world in a special, pre-defined way. It acts as a schematic profile which filters or shapes the stimuli, influencing their particular organization according to its structure. In other words, these structures are the pre-defined and stable characteristics of the modes of organizing perceptions. These charac-teristics, which have been established on the basis of previous experience, contribute to understanding and provide meaning to reality.

Schemas serve as good examples of cognitive structures. As Meichenbaum and Gilmore describe the functioning of the schema, it receives and filters information, but also changes in response to this information. The information which is received with the help of this program immediately becomes part of the program itself. Another important aspect of the schema is that it contains a system of unconscious aims. According to some theorists, each individual's schema contains intentionality towards the world which guides his behavior towards achieving specific goals, although he is unaware of his schema, its intentionality and his goals. Other examples of cognitive structures include cognitive styles, strategies of problem solving, etc.

Meichenbaum and Gilmore's contribution is important in that it provides a theoretical basis for understanding the unconscious operation of high cognitive mental activities. In discussing the concepts of cognitive events, processes and structures and their unconscious influence on behavior, their theory advances a step beyond basic unconscious information processing.

THE UNCONSCIOUS AS LACK OF ATTENTION AND COMPREHENSION

The parallel between subjective experience and consciousness is Bowers' (1984) point of departure for the formulation of his cognitive theory of consciousness and the unconscious. Our subjective experience is the most important basis for understanding ourselves and our world. Most of the knowledge comes from introspection or observation of others. It is universally agreed, however, that introspection cannot encompass all internal events. Despite its advantages, introspection is a potentially defective tool for complete and accurate understanding.

An anecdote by Nisbett and Wilson (1977) demonstrates this point. In their research, they asked a random sample of customers in a big shopping center to evaluate which of five pairs of nylon stockings placed in a row they would choose as the best. The study participants examined the nylon stockings, picking them up and feeling them, looking at them from all angles, inspecting them in all possible ways. The customers said they were inspecting the quality of the material, its softness, color, etc. Most of the customers then chose the last pair of nylon stockings as the best. Since all of the nylon stockings were identical, the determining factor seemed to be their position in the row and nothing else. When the researchers informed the customers that their judgments had been based on position alone, they all categorically rejected this discomfiting information. This exemplifies the potentially erroneous nature of introspection, which does not always provide accurate reality testing or comprehension of motivation.

The conclusion that introspection is often faulty led Bowers to base his theory of the unconscious on analysis of the methods people use to characterize and achieve understanding of the world and of themselves. He distinguishes between two types of knowing or not knowing: one is noticing or not noticing, whereas the other is comprehending or not comprehending. Bowers denotes lack of consciously noticing as first order unconsciousness, and denotes lack of comprehension as second order unconsciousness. Bowers defines the unconscious with the aid of these concepts of unnoticed and uncomprehended.

Beginning by analyzing the concept of the unnoticed, Bowers distinguishes between perception and consciousness. The first relates to the information processed, which is the perception; whereas consciousness relates to awareness of the act of perception itself. Attention to a specific phenomenon may transform the process of perceiving, which may be unnoticed, into a noticed experience. It is reasonable to assume, according to Bowers, that perception precedes awareness, since the perceptual process itself occurs before the processed information reaches awareness. It is, therefore, logical that certain knowledge may be perceived (processed) without having been noticed. Bowers' definition of the unconscious as lack of noticing rests on this basis. Any external or internal event which occurs without being noticed is essentially unconscious.

Utilizing this definition, Bowers delineates four forms of unconsciousness which may be characterized as psychological processes which are unnoticed but which influence behavior. These four areas are the known phenomenon of subliminal perception, memory (forgetting), repression, and dissociation. By definition, subliminal perception refers to perceiving stimuli without noticing them because they exist far below the threshold of conscious human perception. Memories may also have a similar influence; in other words, unnoticed material that is recorded in memory may influence behavior.

In Bowers' opinion, dissociation is yet another specific example of internal mental stimuli or events which may influence behavior without having been noticed. Daydreaming is an example of dissociation which may not be noticed. Bowers cites Breuer's description of the famous case of Anna, the young woman who suffered a series of neurotic dissociative symptoms while tending her dying father. Breuer writes that her daydreams contained material that was highly charged with emotion, including sexual fantasies. Although the contents of her fantasies aroused tremendous anxiety and generated a variety of pathological symptoms, Anna was totally unaware of her daydreaming and its influence on her. Again, Bowers emphasizes that the influence of unnoticed events has important implications for the understanding of pathology. As unnoticed external stimuli may be perceived and leave their trace in behavior but not in memory, so may daydreams and imaginings with negative contents produce feelings of sadness or depression. The feelings of sadness or depression might remain long after the unnoticed contents of the daydreams and imagination have disappeared. Because they were not noticed, it will be futile to attempt to reconstruct the memory of the events or causes for the negative feelings. Such attempts may arouse spurious memories of events which have no relationship to the emotional reaction.

Bowers is also convinced that repression may be defined as an expression of an avoidance reaction to a thought that occurred before it reached awareness. He is defining repression as an attentional avoidance (the act of repressing) of attentional avoidance (the unpleasant thought). People are not aware of the fact that they divert attention from unpleasant thoughts, wishes etc. This is a 'cover up' of the 'cover up'.

So far, this discussion has focused on first order unconscious processes, or the unnoticed. Now it will shift to the second order of unconsciousness, lack of comprehension. Individuals may notice a certain phenomenon without paying attention to it, because they do not understand it. They fail to see the causal connections between the different factors involved in the creation of a phenomenon. This lack of comprehension of a phenomenon and its causation is a state of unconsciousness. Whether the processes and events in question are external or internal, they are regarded as occurring unconsciously because they are uncomprehended.

Bowers performed an experiment which illustrated the unconsciousness of uncomprehended internal events. He showed subjects a series of postcard reproductions of portraits and landscapes in pairs, asking them to state which of the two reproductions in each pair they preferred. After clarifying each subject's preference, Bowers reinforced the opposite preference in the ensuing series of trials. In other words, the subject who preferred landscapes received reinforcement each time he chose a portrait, and vice versa. As expected, some of the subjects changed their preferences as a result of the reinforcement. The researcher discussed this with one subject, asking her which type of picture she preferred. When she answered that she preferred a landscape, he asked if she noticed his reactions during the experiment. She said she noticed that he said 'good' each time she chose a landscape. 'Do you think your tendency to pick landscapes was influenced by my reinforcement of them?', asked the experimenter. 'Of course not! I picked the landscapes because I liked them better than the portraits. Besides, you only said "good" after I made my choice, so what you said couldn't possibly have influenced my selection of pictures.'

The subject, who had no knowledge of reinforcement processes in behavior modification, did not recognize the rule that reinforcement applied after a certain reaction increases the tendency to repeat that reaction. In this case, when the reason for the behavior appeared after the behavior's occurrence, the subject did not understand that the reinforcement was influencing her, despite having noticed it. Because she applied her knowledge of the laws of cause and effect inappropriately, she misunderstood the situation. Her incomprehension of the reinforcement process is an example of second order stage of the study the subjects were hypnotized, half receiving post-hypnotic suggestion for a good mood, and the other half for a depressed mood. Then they were asked to recall the events of the week, as recorded in their diaries. As expected, those in a good mood remembered more of the pleasant events, and vice versa. Moreover, when the subjects were asked to regrade the events on the pleasantness — unpleasantness scale, they tended to change their original grading to match their current mood. This study, as do others, illustrates the natural tendency to create inner congruence between different parts of an experience by altering attitudes and evaluations.

Rachman and Lopatka (1990) provide another example of spontaneous matching of emotion and mood with memories. Unlike many other researchers, they examined subjects in natural, as opposed to artificially induced, emotional states. Female subjects were observed in two situations, one during their menstrual periods, and one at another time in the month. In each situation they were asked about the degree of pain they felt and about their moods, and they were also asked to recall personal events from the past. Later the subjects were reminded of the experiences they had recalled in each of the conditions and were asked to grade them according to the degree of pleasantness — unpleasantness which the experiences aroused in them. The experiences which were recalled during menstruation were rated as less pleasant than those rated during the rest of the month. The relationship between the degree of pain felt in both conditions and the extent of pleasantness — unpleasantness of the recalled experiences was not direct, but was mediated by the mood which accompanied the pain. In other words, there was no correlation between unpleasantness and pain, unless the mood accompanying the pain was taken into account.

These studies cast doubt on the validity of one of psychology's basic tenets — that past events are the cause of current mental occurrences. They also undermine the psychoanalytic assumption that the unconscious preserves past events, which thus continue to influence the present. The above studies clearly show that one's current state of mind influences one's view of the past, and not only vice versa.

In this context, the following case is relevant. In treatment sessions a patient would speak at length about his miserable childhood. He was asked to bring family photographs to a session, and lo and behold, he found among them a picture of his family, together, with his 'rejecting' mother hugging him, and he was grinning happily. He was astonished, and could not get over his surprise, and said that perhaps his childhood had not been so terrible, and that maybe he himself had contributed to his severe world outlook and difficult relationship with his mother. Truth is thus flexible, and not always uni-directional.

unconsciousness. All uncomprehended influences on behavior, according to this model, are unconscious. As the causation of phenomena is not comprehensible from observation or introspection (but instead is inferred from them), we may remain unaware of many phenomena which influence our behavior unless we create a system of concepts with solid foundations to explain them.

Bowers proceeds to include the phenomenon of intuition as a form of unconscious thinking influenced by unnoticed and uncomprehended processes. In his view, intuition is intellectual sensitivity to information from the internal and external environment which has not yet been fully processed (noticed or comprehended), but which guides inquiry and observation toward deeper insight. In other words, individuals have not noticed that they already know necessary information. Bowers analyzes a number of important discoveries that were made in states of dreaming or daydreaming. He notes that individuals' intuition impels them to investigate certain ideas before they understand the reasons for the investigation or the meaning of it. Intuition connects between two seemingly unconnected ideas that exist in the same problem context to provide the solution. In all likelihood, individuals had been aware of each of the ideas, but had not discerned any special connection between them until the moment of insight. The intellectual sensitivity directing observation and investigation toward discovery of the connection between different events and facilitating their assembly into a clear structure is called intuition. Bowers maintains that this unconscious intuition guides a large proportion of cognitive activity.

THE UNCONSCIOUS: PATHOLOGY AND TREATMENT

In contrast with dynamic approaches, cognitive approaches are unanimous in their perception that pathology is not an expression of an unconscious defensive system. The presence of unconscious contents or processes may cause pathology because they have a negative influence, but not because they represent a defensive system against anxiety which becomes pathological in itself. The unconscious contents and processes are by-products or part of information processing, and, like all information, they influence behavior.

There are several cognitive theories which find a link between the unconscious and pathology. Beck (1976) presents the concept of unconscious automatic thoughts with negative content about the self and about self-worth. As a result, these individuals focus unwittingly on the negative aspects of their life and personality. When such automatic thoughts are continuous, the person's mood is negatively affected, sometimes to the extent of clinical depression. Depressed individuals do not always know what caused their depression, and may not provide an objectively realistic reason for it. Not only automatic thoughts cause pathology; unconscious systems of goals, assumptions and beliefs about the self and the world may cause maladaptive behaviors. An individual may lead a way of life according to beliefs that everyone is selfish, or all women are aggressive, or that one has to attack before being attacked, or that power is the only important asset in life, and so on. Such unconscious systems of belief may influence individuals' feelings and behavior without their being aware of their existence and influence. Individuals may believe that they live according to one set of cognitive beliefs, but function in reality under the influence of a different, even contradictory, set of unconscious beliefs. Although this conflict has a strong maladaptive effect in many areas of life, individuals have no control over these processes while they are unaware of them.

According to Meichenbaum (1977), the basis of unconscious processing is not a system of distorted beliefs about the self and the world, but rather hidden self statements which are derived from these beliefs. It is the hidden negative self statements which generally lead to ineffective functioning.

Bowers (1984, 1987) described the aforementioned phenomenon of 'history without memory' which may contribute to our understanding of the manner in which problematic information processing may create maladaptive reactions without awakening any conflict. The individual may be influenced by an external event or internal events which do not register even in short-term memory, and then 'decay,' or vanish entirely. However, the impact of such a stimulus may be long lasting. Under such circumstances, there is no possible way to retrieve the information causing the negative reaction, so the maladaptive reaction remains.

Another path leading to maladaptation is individuals' lack of awareness of their own expectations from their environment (Novaco, 1975). Lack of correspondence between an unconscious system of expectations and real events cause not only unexplained disappointment, but also inappropriate reactions toward the environment.

The cognitive-behavioral approach also emphasizes the importance of the unconscious learning processes behind pathology. The individual may be ignorant of the learning processes which engender a powerful, maladaptive emotional reaction, such as irrational fear. These learning processes may occur subliminally or the individual may be inattentive to the learning process.

Many of the therapeutic principles and methods are based on this common principle of cognitive theory, all of which in one way or another recommend raising consciousness about the manner in which information is processed. Developing new patterns of behavior based on new ways of information processing.

These principles and methods may be divided into three major groups:

1. Discovering the unconscious contents.
2. Changing the method of processing information.
3. Circumvention of unconscious contents by directly changing behavior.

The principle of discovering the unconscious contents and the method of processing information is a direct conclusion from Beck's (1976) and Lazarus' (1991) theory that automatic thought and appraisal are the bases for pathology. Beck's approach of exposing hidden beliefs and their effects provides a good example of cognitive therapy. Beck teaches his patients to focus on their feelings, the thoughts that precede these feelings, and the behaviors that ensue from the thoughts and feelings. Events from the past and the manner in which they were interpreted are regarded by Beck as important for discovering the individual's inner world. Through exposing these thoughts, the therapist and the patient both reach conclusions about the patient's hidden system of beliefs which contribute to the situational cognitions and appraisals which lead to negative feelings.

During the next stage, patients learn how they reach conclusions, generalize them, exaggerate their meaning, and that the ensuing feelings are necessary results of their cognitions and beliefs. In a further stage, changing beliefs about the world of the self in general lead to changing specific cognitions and appraisals of the world, and these again engender altered feelings. During treatment, patients learn to perform self-monitoring of their current inner cognitive world and its impact on their emotional state. They also learn to observe the changes in feelings that result from changing their system of beliefs and thoughts. This technique is a prototype for the various cognitive therapeutic techniques.

The cognitive-behavioral approach is based on circumventing usual internal reactions and cognitions to bring about change. These approaches utilize techniques of exposure to threatening situations, systematic desensitization, and flooding of emotions in order to change feelings and behavior directly with minimal involvement of the internal cognitive system.

The cognitive approach views information processing and all related structures and mechanisms as the main process behind the construction of conscious and unconscious life. Unconscious processes are natural givens of mental functioning. Many of the high mental functions simply operate unconsciously. Unconscious functioning can be sophisticated, complex, precise, and utilize abundant material accumulated by unconscious learning. We can learn, perceive, think, and formulate beliefs without being aware that these processes are occurring. Yet, the unconscious processes and their products continually affect behavior.

In addition to a unique formulation of a model to understand the unconscious, the cognitive approach provides clarity to some of the processes delineated by the other models. Processes such as repression, inhibition, dissociation, amnesia, and so on become much more clear when examined from the perspective of the cognitive approach.

CHAPTER 6

The Unconscious as Internal Incongruence

One of the most important principles in understanding life from a biological perspective is that of homeostasis, or equilibrium (Stagner, 1961). This pertains to the regulation of biological processes so that inner functions remain constant despite external changes; for instance, maintaining a consistent body temperature. The organism is adjusting to changes by regulating its biological pathways in response to internal and external stimuli, so that basic functions remain constant in order to preserve its very existence. This principle of equilibrium has been adopted by psychological theories to explain the regulation and dynamics of mental processes.

Mental equilibrium is the basic principle underlying all theories which view development and personality from the aspect of internal balance, congruence, and the striving for consistency and stability. According to these theories, individuals endeavor to preserve their self-image, self-esteem, level of achievement, family security, emotional arousal, their system of beliefs about the world, the way they satisfy their needs, etc. When the status quo is undermined, certain mechanisms, defense mechanisms, are activated to preserve it.

In the approach adopted in this chapter, the state of internal congruence, internal equilibrium, resonates with the concept of consciousness, and inconsistency, incongruence, resonates with the unconscious. The unconscious represents a gap or discord between mental aspects and creates inner tension. Before analyzing the concepts of internal consistency or harmony and the unconscious more thoroughly, it is important to understand the theoretical—philosophical basis of the principle.

EQUILIBRIUM AND STRUCTURE

Mental activity from the viewpoint of homeostasis is clearly illustrated by Piaget's structural approach (Piaget, 1968). This approach looks at mental life through biologically based structures, schemas, and patterns. These direct development and embody the rules of behavior.

Such schemas or structures may be found in perception. Perceptual gestalt is the organization of the external world according to the relationship of the part and the whole, the proximity of the stimuli to each other, their similarity to each other or their diversity, etc. These principles of perception are inherent in an individual's perceptual mechanism and they organize perception. The pattern of language is another structure, creating the meaning and understanding of words according to consistent rules. The mathematical schema is that by which an individual organizes the quantitative aspects of the world. In the same way one may speak of schemata which regulate interpersonal relationships, and so on. Similarly, one may refer to emotive patterns which control the special way in which an individual regulates emotional behavior. One can thus identify an appropriate structure for each area of mental activity.

Piaget calls the constant and recurring pattern a 'schema,' and he defines it by means of three special characteristics: totality, transformation, and self-regulation.

Totality is related to the fact that the structure is organized as a gestalt whose whole is more than the sum of its parts. The schema comprises different components, principles of action, and rules, which do not combine mathematically; each organizational change produces a totally new structure.

Despite its consistency, stability, and cyclical nature, the structure is by no means static; on the contrary, it undergoes transformation — it develops and changes form in the course of growth, accumulating experience and learning. The change is gradual, in accordance with internal and external developments, while preserving consistency and stability. Changes in the structure itself cause changes in the stimuli absorbed. Thus, changes may occur in Weltanschauung (general outlook), in social relationships, and in one's consciousness, in accordance with the existing schema and with changes it undergoes.

Self-regulation refers to the control which the structures exercise over themselves to ensure their stability and preservation. In other words, changes in the schema may not be the result of reaction to external influences, but are mediated by self-regulation systems.

These three processes are meant to achieve internal balance within the structure. Balance is thus a result of changes, dynamic adaptations, and internal adjustments arising from changes in reality, or from anticipation of future changes, from new learning and experiences. In this way there is perpetual development, yet stability is preserved.

Developments, changes, and adaptation can be better understood with the help of the concepts of assimilation and accommodation. In biology, these are two distinct but simultaneous processes. For example, in the process of digestion, food is assimilated into the body. At the same time, accommodation takes place as the digestive system adapts itself to suit the specific food which has been absorbed. Assimilation is the absorption of small soluble food particles, the end product of the process of digesting ingested food; accommodation is the process of adjusting the digestive system to the specific food. Assimilation changes the stimulus to suit the structure; accommodation changes the structure to suit the stimulus.

A similar process occurs in cognitive schemas. The cognitive system changes when it absorbs new stimuli. A two-year-old child knows that everything that flies in the sky is a bird. Every bird the child sees flying undergoes assimilation into the existing structure and strengthens it. When one day the child sees a helicopter — a large, noisy, flying object which does not fit into the bird schema — he cannot assimilate any more and an imbalance is created. The structure must undergo accommodation to the new stimulus in order to be able to contain it; henceforth, flying objects may be birds, planes, kites, etc. The schema has expanded, changed, differentiated more finely, and can thus assimilate new objects. A new balance has been established, which will prevail until a new disharmony or imbalance is caused, which will once again result in new assimilation and accommodation.

In every adaptive behavior, there is a balance between assimilation and accommodation. When the two processes are incongruent, the result is non-adaptive behavior. Psychotic individuals, for instance, who suffer hallucinations, delusions, or other distortions of reality, are exhibiting behavior based only on assimilation. They try to assimilate reality into their structure, without changing the structure in accordance with the dictates of reality. Children's games of fantasy follow the same rule. On the other hand, purely imitative behavior is based on accommodation alone, with the schema and reaction changing constantly according to the stimulus, and no assimilation or change of the object to fit the existing schema.

When the processes of assimilation and accommodation do not take place properly and the structure cannot assimilate new stimuli, the internal balance is disturbed. This is reflected by internal tension and occasionally by reversion to more primitive schemas. The tension serves as a catalyst for change in the schema. When a new balance is struck, the tension disappears. The most important conclusion to be drawn from this is that an unbalanced schema is an obstacle to development, to new understanding, to assimilating new experiences; that is, the organism is at a developmental standstill. On the other hand, achieving internal harmony removes the obstacles and allows for new development and progress.

There are two principal causes of internal imbalance. One is inherent in the nature of the stimulus or event requiring assimilation. A rare object or exceptional event may be so different from the norm that the schema is unable to absorb, categorize, and assimilate it; in fact, there may not exist an appropriate structure for such exceptional events. Sexual abuse of a young child, being such an exceptional and frightening experience, may be an example of such an event. The second cause is a defect in the coordination of the processes of assimilation and accommodation. The child immersed in a fantasy world, or the psychotic person suffering from delusions and false beliefs, employs only the assimilation process without accommodation. Someone totally identifying with an external image undergoes only the process of accommodation.

The two processes (assimilation and accommodation) operate in all areas of behavior, not just in intellectual development. Interpersonal relationships, immigration to a new country, adapting to economic developments, or reaction to a loss, may all be analyzed according to the principles of assimilation and accommodation. Moreover, both processes operate the same way in the emotional as in the cognitive realm. One may refer to emotional reaction patterns as a schema or structure. Reactions to emotionally loaded events are regulated by emotional schemata which function and develop in the same way as cognitive ones.

Piaget's perspective may be extended, with important implications for the internal incongruence model of the unconscious. Every behavior of a structure has both cognitive and emotional elements. Every cognitive change is accompanied by a corresponding emotional change. The process of assimilating a new experience — the birth of a sibling, starting school, moving house, discovering something new about a spouse, a surprising grade in an examination — cannot be fully described without an appropriate emotional change accompanying the cognitive one. The argument presented in this chapter is that the emotional changes which accompany the cognitive are essential for adaptive behavior. In general terms it may be claimed that the perception of a loss is naturally associated with grief, a pleasant surprise with happiness, and failure to achieve a goal with frustration. The restoration of internal harmony cannot take place without an appropriate emotional reaction accompanying the structure's cognitive change. Absence of such accord disturbs the balance and its creation restores the balance.

THEORIES ON CONSISTENCY AND INTERNAL CONGRUENCE

Various theories of personality explain behavior from the perspective of internal congruence, or inner consistency. Although they are not based directly on his premises, Piaget may be regarded as the originator of the theoretical and philosophical foundations of all these theories. What all the internal harmony theories have in common is humans' basic tendency to maintain stability in the face of a changing world, and preserve the accord between their inner world and the environment.

Lecky (1945) was one of the first theorists to lay down the principle of striving for internal consistency as a central factor in understanding behavior in the context of theories of personality. He saw a human as a system of ideas organized around, and regulated by, the self, aiming to preserve inner consistency and congruence. This is achieved by preventing internal contradictions and conflicts between different systems within the personality, and by avoiding friction between the concept of self and the external world.

There are several approaches to the idea of inner consistency. Some emphasize congruence of the inner world, for example, Festinger (1957), whose cognitive dissonance theory stresses the harmony between the individual's beliefs and perceptions. Higgins and his colleagues updated this theory in their own version (see, for example, Higgins, 1987, and Strauman and Higgins, 1987). Others place the emphasis on the congruence of the internal and external worlds. Kelly's personal construct theory (Kelly, 1955) stands out among these. A third group unites the two principles, that of internal congruence, and that of congruence of the internal and external. An example of these is Fiske and Maddi's theory of constant arousal level (Maddi, 1980). Three of the above theories will be outlined here, those of Higgins, Kelly, and Fiske and Maddi, to acquaint the reader with a view of the personality from the perspective of inner consistency.

Higgins: Self-representation

Higgins' (1987) cognitive theory speaks of different foci and angles in the perception of self, and points out the possible discrepancies that may exist between them. He views the self not as a totality, but as comprising different representations and variations. He enumerates three focal points, or domains, of the self:

1. The actual self, which is our representation of the attributes that are believed to characterize ourselves.

2. The ideal self, which is our representation of the attributes believed to be ideal attributes.
3. The 'ought' self (normative self), which is our representation of the attributes which we believe we ought to have.

Higgins calls the ideal and the 'ought' self regulators, or monitors. These are the belief systems which guide behavior, and by which individuals judge and evaluate themselves, and regulate their behavior.

In addition to the above domains or foci of the self, Higgins distinguishes between two different aspects from which the self is viewed: from the individual's own point of view, and what the individual believes that significant others might think.

Combining each of the three domains with the two perspectives gives six different versions of the self:

1. The actual self viewed by self.
2. The actual self viewed by others.
3. The ideal self viewed by self.
4. The ideal self viewed by others.
5. The normative self viewed by self.
6. The normative self viewed by others.

The relationship between the different domains can be one of congruence or incongruence. Congruence means that there is accord between the attributes in the different domains. For example, individuals aspiring to be clever think that they already are. A gap exists between the domains when there is inconsistency between their attributes, e.g., individuals wanting to be clever actually believe that they are not. According to Higgins, a gap between different representations of the self results in negative feelings; the individual tries to eliminate them by closing the gap. People differ in their grading of the importance of different aspects of self and in the type of gap they attempt to close. Some try mainly to close the gap between the actual and the ideal self as viewed by the self, while others attempt to bring the actual and the 'ought' (normative) selves as viewed by others closer together.

Higgins' major contribution is his clarification of the relationships between the different internal discrepancies and the emotions and motivations which they arouse. He claims that the greater the gap between representations of the self, the greater the ensuing emotional reaction. Higgins clearly differentiates between two basic types of emotion: first, those resulting from unachieved objectives, mainly feelings of depression — dissatisfaction, frustration, disappointment, and sadness; second, emotions arising from the realization of unwanted results, which arouse feelings of tension such as fear and threat. As a rule, any discrepancy between the actual self and the ideal self, from whichever viewpoint, will cause feelings of depression; whereas a gap between the actual self and the normative, from any aspect, will trigger feelings of anxiety. Higgins in fact goes beyond this, and makes a finer distinction between the relationships of various discrepancies and different emotions:

1. The gap between the actual self and the ideal self, both viewed from the self, will cause feelings of disappointment, dissatisfaction, and frustration.
2. A discrepancy between the actual self from the standpoint of self and the ideal self from the other's view brings about feelings of shame, embarrassment, and loss of self-esteem.
3. A gap between the actual self seen from the point of view of the self, and the normative 'ought' self seen from the standpoint of others, leads to feelings of tension through fear, threat, and anger.
4. A discrepancy between the self views of actual self and normative self arouses guilt-type emotional tension, self-contempt, and discomfort.

Kelly: The Personal Construct

Kelly (1955) also sees the need for stability and congruence as the major motive in behavior. In contrast to Higgins, Kelly stresses the need to maintain congruence between one's subjective image of the world and external reality. Humans are fundamentally inquisitive, knowledge-seeking, and high-grade problem solvers. Their central interests are understanding the world and its operational rules, predicting events, and hence being able to control them. Acting like scientists, humans look for congruence between their hypotheses about the world and actual events.

The formation of hypotheses about reality starts with questions about the laws of nature, proceeds to the identification of repeated patterns of events, and the formulation of principles according to which these patterns occur. The next stage consists of the attempt to apply these principles to new events and situations, and the resulting revision of the principles to yield improved results. This is a never-ending process.

Kelly called this system of hypotheses the personal construct, defining it as a set of assumptions about a particular aspect of reality in a systematic, simple, clear fashion. There is a concomitant tendency to ignore or distort phenomena that do not fit the construct. Prejudice provides an extreme example of this.

As the construct directs behavior, it assumes the nature of a self-fulfilling prophecy, thereby achieving the objectives of homogeneity, stability, and security. Every individual has his or her own constructs for different areas of life: the self, interpersonal relationships, economics, religion, politics, education, achievements, and personal philosophy.

We will illustrate the function of the construct with the following example. A young couple are trying to calm their two-month-old baby who is crying continuously. Their first hypothesis regarding reality, representing the child-rearing construct, is that babies cry when they are hungry. They test the hypothesis by trying to feed the baby. If this fails to achieve the desired result, i.e., the baby keeps crying, they will turn to the next, competing construct, i.e., the hypothesis that babies cry because they are in pain. This can be tested by attempting to calm the baby down through relieving the assumed pain. If this is also unsuccessful, the parents may reach a third hypothesis, based on repeated observations: every time they pick the baby up, it stops crying, and when they put it down, it starts again. Their conclusion is that the baby is crying because it wants to be cuddled.

The same operational principles are found in more complex constructs. The extent of congruence or incongruence of the construct and external events produces specific emotions typical to the nature of the discrepancy. When individuals feel that the construct is failing to predict events and that it requires a radical change, they experience anxiety. They feel the same when the construct offers unpleasant predictions. Attempts at forcefully imposing or expanding the construct are accompanied by feelings of aggression. Acting in contradiction to one's construct causes guilt feelings.

In trying to impose congruence between the construct and reality, individuals may deny real events or ignore their system of constructs (repression). Alternatively, they may completely abandon their own constructs and adopt those of others (identification), or apply their own system of constructs to others (projection).

In Kelly's view, pathology also results from problems of incongruence between one's constructs and reality. Pathological behavior is generally characterized by repeated inflexible use of constructs which do not match reality — the mentally ill believe that they must change reality and not their system of constructs.

Fiske and Maddi: Levels of Arousal and Activation

Fiske and Maddi (Maddi, 1980) offer a different theory of internal congruence and incongruence. They refer to consistency and balance in the emotional arousal and activation levels. They claim that humans' prime tendency is to preserve the match between their constant level of energy and that of a particular moment. Just as people have a natural need to be active, to create, to be alert and responsive, so, too, do they have a natural need to maintain a constant level of arousal and activation.

When Fiske and Maddi speak of arousal and activation levels, they do not mean the simple expenditure of energy; they refer to mental activity, searching for purpose, meaning, self-renewal, and creativity. The objective is not to stick to the familiar, to habit and routine, but to discover changes, variety, and development, at the same time preserving the balance with the existing level of excitation.

Everyone has a given level of arousal and activity, but this may change for external reasons, such as pressure, or internal reasons, such as tiredness and anxiety. When such a disturbance occurs, various mechanisms are brought into play to re-establish the balance. These can operate by monitoring and adjusting the level of activity. Boredom and disinterest can cause arousal which raises the activity level. Too high expectations, which require over-exertion, and repeated failures, can lower the arousal level. A feeling of routine can lead to a search for novelty, and too high a stress level at work may bring about a slowing of the pace. The same rule applies to different areas of life.

For the arousal level of the stimulus to be maintained, it must be further differentiated. Differentiation introduces novelty, renewed interest, a fresh perspective, and hence new development. This process can be extended until the whole world can be seen in a grain of sand, this representing the highest degree of emotional and cognitive differentiation.

To illustrate: a painting may, at first glance, create a certain impression; it loses its effect, however, unless the viewer discovers new aspects which create excitement, fresh thought, and new associations. In order to maintain the excitement level, the differentiation has constantly to be extended. After a time the painting looks totally different from the way it appeared at first, but the level of arousal has been preserved. In the absence of differentiation, the painting loses its ability to stimulate, and interest in it is dissipated. The process of differentiation allows development to take place, and new tools to be acquired which may be put to use in new areas.

Continual and increasing differentiation and exposure to novelty produce a level of arousal which cannot be maintained for long. In this situation, a monitoring mechanism is brought into play which reduces the arousal level. This integration process is the opposite of differentiation. One's arousal level may be reduced by finding factors common to different stimuli, by putting different stimuli into broader categories, by identifying familiar patterns, i.e., by smoothing over differences.

Fiske and Maddi thus show that the differentiation and integration processes are responsible for maintaining the balance between development and stability, between change and consistency. The interaction between these two mechanisms results in changes in personality, although the activation level remains constant.

Despite the highly abstract nature of Fiske and Maddi's formulation, the relevance of their theory of constant activity and arousal levels to real-life situations is apparent. The principles underlying the monitoring functions of differentiation and integration apply to all aspects of life.

THE UNCONSCIOUS: INNER INCONSISTENCY AND INCONGRUENCE

Having presented the broad theoretical basis of homeostasis, and several theories in psychology based on it, we now describe the unconscious from the viewpoint of inconsistency and lack of internal congruence. This approach derives from the assumption common to Piaget's and other theories of congruence, that humans strive toward internal congruence, which is essential for normal functioning and development. The absence of congruence is associated with tension and pathology. Internal congruence is disturbed by threats from the external or internal world inconsistent with one's beliefs, feelings, self-perception, or one's subjective view of the world. A lack of congruence or consistency prompts immediate attempts to return to a state of congruence and restore the balance.

One method of doing this is to distort perception and to dissociate inconsistent elements from each other. This creates an artificial, forced balance or congruence based on denial. This false consistency is defensive, limiting the individual's awareness and self-expression. This condition describes the unconscious. Its opposite, inner congruence, is based on creating new states of congruence through development, assimilating all the incongruent elements and forming new relationships between them, expressing a deeper awareness and a richer consciousness.

The basic relationship regarding internal incongruence and the unconscious finds support in Piaget (1951), who views the unconscious as reflecting a condition in which internal experience and perception of reality are inconsistent. Piaget maintains that this situation arises as a result of assimilation occurring without accommodation.

Our view of the concept of congruence, unlike those presented hitherto, refers to harmony or balance on an experiential level. Every experience consists of different elements. We focus on three major ones: perception (or memory) of reality, interpretation of perception (appraisal, meaning), and emotional response. These components of experience are not related to each other hierarchically in a chain of causations, but occur simultaneously. When one of the components is distorted, dissociated, or denied, the experience is incomplete, leading to incongruence and tension. In contrast, the different elements of a harmonious experience are associated with each other, creating a rich interrelated system of experiential elements. This theory does not oppose other internal congruence theories or even other theories of the unconscious, but for the most part complements them.

We do not intend to offer here a complete theory of personality, but confine ourselves to the unconscious from the viewpoint of internal consistency.

Experience: Its Components and Their Interrelationships

The use of the term experience instead of schema or construct reflects the attempt to de-emphasize the role of cognition as the dominant feature in the determination of inner consistency. The term experience and its determinants as a major organizing principle have been used by a number of theoreticians. Janet (1911) speaks of feelings, emotions, thoughts, activities, and memories as components of experience. Myers (1892) gives prominence to just three factors, emotions, cognition, and memories.

The definition of experience in the present context relates to three aspects: first, the perception of reality, including memories. We confine the term perception, somewhat artificially, to mean perception of facts before they have been internally processed and fully interpreted. This aspect of experience also includes memories of past facts and events. The second is cognition, referring to the constant flow of thoughts, appraisals of, and the subjective meaning attributed to present and past facts. The third is emotion, referring to the affect accompanying the mental activity of perception and cognition.

Each of the components of the internal experience makes an important contribution to the individual's adaptation. Human existence itself, which is based on satisfaction of physiological and psychological needs, requires the efficient, coordinated, and congruent functioning of each element and its associated processes.

Perception also has an adaptive value. Knowledge of the immediate and the distant environment, contact with reality, and distinguishing between the real world and the imaginative world — all these are of supreme importance for the individual's existence. Perception of the past is also a part of our conceptualization of the present. Neither self-awareness nor meaning can be considered without taking memory into account. It is an integral part of self-identity (Markus and Wurf, 1987). According to Janet (see Van der Kolk and Van der Hart, 1984), concordant activity of the memory is vital for healthy adaptive functioning. Consciousness comprises organized memories relevant to the specific situations. Janet thus views the ability to forge an appropriate link between different memories as an inherent condition of mental health.

Appraisal and attribution of meaning express the human need to organize conceptually and bring order to life, according to Greenberg, Rice, and Elliot (1993). Cognition may be regarded as playing an additional role. The meaning provided by the creation of internal schemas that depict and define the essence of the self and the world and the rules by which they function serves as a guideline for personal existence and survival.

Emotions have a major contribution to adaptation. Greenberg, Rice, and Elliot (1993) regard emotion as an internal cue signalling individuals to organize and orient themselves biologically and psychologically to satisfy a particular need. The desire to satisfy a need or eliminate a frustration reflects an emotional-motivational disposition, based on preceding physiological arousal, for meeting the need. This physiological arousal also purveys a special character or color to the entire experience and gives the experience its unique, emotional quality of fear, joy, excitement, longing, etc. The role of emotion in adaptation can be defined as a signal to the individual about his or her state in relation to the satisfaction of a specific need. The particular emotion signals the existence of the need (for example, yearning, fear) and the measure of the satisfaction (frustration, fulfillment). Therefore, emotion anchored in biological disposition plays an important role in survival, in that it furnishes individuals with the internal orientation towards the fulfillment of their needs. For this reason, attention to inner emotional signals is extremely important.

Congruence between the three components and their related processes is no less important for adaptation than the existence of each component. The adaptational value of each of the elements in the experience is reduced when need satisfaction signals function without the benefit of fairly accurate reality perception, or these are unaccompanied by meaningful interpretations or classifications which approximate the way the world operates and the optimal methods of functioning in it. Moreover, lack of internal congruence between the three components — perception, meaning, and emotion — results in confusion, internal contradictions, and thus in uncoordinated functioning. It is hypothesized that this congruence developed because it is functional for the human organism's very existence. Although congruence is a naturally enhanced tendency, it does not always develop automatically; past experience, education, and values may enhance or impede and distort internal congruence.

One of the first to offer an interactional model of the relationships between perception, memory, meaning, and emotion was Minsky (1980). He suggested that consciousness is based on memories that are bound in a web of emotional association and the meaning attached to them. However, the nature of this relationship can be understood only after the issue of the primacy of emotion vs. cognition has been studied.

This old controversy (Arnold, 1960) has been revived recently (Ortony and Turner, 1990) and reflects a strong polarization of unsettled theories. On one hand, there are those (Lazarus, 1982, for example) who claim that emotion is always a by-product of the type of appraisal of the situation, and that emotions are shaped by environmental factors. Thus, emotions do not have an independent status, and the neurological and physiological systems which elicit emotions are subordinate to cognitive functioning. Lazarus (1991) claims further that appraisals can be made in an automatic unconscious level that always precedes the emotion. For example, anger is always a result of an appraisal, made consciously or unconsciously, about a situation or a person making a threat of a demeaning offense. On the other hand, there are those (see Zajonc, 1980) who claim that emotions and cognitions, although interrelated, represent two different mental and neurological systems that can operate independently and that emotional reactions do not always require a prior appraisal of the situation. Zajonc showed that certain emotional responses to particular stimuli are likely to be instantaneous without cognitive intermediation. A familiar stimulus, for example, may immediately arouse feelings of affection before any cognition regarding the stimulus has been formed.

In between this extreme polarization there is also an intermediate position which tries to compromise between the two extreme theoretical approaches (e.g., Plutchik, 1968, 1989; Johnson-Laird and Oatley, 1989, 1992; Stein and Trabasso, 1992) which see emotional behavior as an end result of an interaction between some biologically given, basic emotional tendencies and patterns on one hand and higher cognitive processes on the other hand. However, in this discussion I will focus mostly on the relative independence of emotion and cognition approach, as this approach serves as a theoretical basis for the congruence model of consciousness and unconsciousness.

The case for the independence of emotion from cognition begins with two arguments. One is that the two functions are based on two separate brain systems, and the other is that there are basic emotions which are biologically constituted.

Zajonc (1980) hypothesizes that emotion and cognition represent distinct systems, the former being based primarily on the energetic arousal system, and cognition on the informative system. Appraisal and meaning can take place in different stages of emotional processing and, conversely, an emotion may be aroused at different stages of information processing, e.g., during registering, coding, categorization, recall, etc. In Zajonc's view, emotions are present at every stage of cognitive processing. When someone tries to remember, reconstruct, or identify a particular structure or content, the emotional-energetic system is the first one encountered. A person usually chooses a particular job because it interests him, and having made the choice, will then find a justification for it.

Thus, emotion can be the dominant aspect of, and the basis for, enhancing experience (Langner, 1967). In fact, emotions appear automatically and involuntarily. Since emotion represents the energetic element of behavior, it is necessarily less controlled by cognitive processes. In addition, from a developmental point of view, Zajonc claims that the primacy of emotion and its independence of cognition can be easily demonstrated. A baby is capable of smiling, of feeling pleasure and pain, before it acquires cognitive skills. Izard (1984, 1991) expresses similar ideas.

Isen (1987) also illustrates the independence of emotion from cognition. She shows that emotions have a great effect on behavior in general, and on higher cognitive functioning in particular. Inducing a good mood in people, for example, influences their generosity towards others and towards themselves, their willingness to act cooperatively, their ability to take risks, their intuitive thinking, and it improves their memory, their effectiveness at problem solving, mental flexibility, and efficiency of categorizing material, and their differentiation and integration skills.

Recently, evidence from the field of neurology verifies that the two aspects are relatively independent of each other, and demonstrates their possible interrelationships and combinations. Weinberger (1990), relying on LeDoux (in press), maintains that the brain center which is responsible for emotions (the limbic system) is relatively independent of the cortical centers, such as the left hemisphere, which are responsible for processing verbal information. Moreover, Gazzaniga (1985) maintains that an independent sub-system of the brain has been identified which is responsible for creating interpretations and meaning. This sub-system is independent and operates separately from the other sub-systems, but also forms combinations with other sub-systems to process experiences.

The second argument for independence of the emotional functions rests on the notion that there are several innate, basic emotions (Izard, 1984, 1991; Ekman, 1992; Panksepp, 1989, 1992) and that emotional development follows a biological blueprint (Piaget, 1986). A basic emotion (usually fear, anger, happiness, and sadness) is defined mostly on the basis of the following characteristics:

1. It is a universal emotion that is distinguished cross-culturally.
2. It has a distinct and unique physiological pattern activity that can be identified, thus forming the assumption that it is a separate brain entity.
3. It has a unique facial, expressive component. That is, each basic emotion has a similar facial expressive pattern that can be identified cross-culturally.

The relationships between emotion and cognition as two independent functions have been defined in several ways. Markus and Nuris (1986) claim that the relationship between emotion and cognition is based on a cyclical and reciprocal influence. The interaction between the self representation and emotions towards the self may be described thus: when the self representation is negative, it creates a negative emotion, and this emotion will itself have a negative effect on the self-concept.

Heise (1977) stresses that emotions which accompany cognition serve as the guiding principles in the interpretation of reality. Humans' prime objective is the preservation of the validity of some basic emotional guidelines or structure and the interpretations which arise from them. Thus, for example, a maternal image has positive emotional associations, and the purpose of behavior is to preserve these positive emotions which, in turn, confirm the positive maternal concept. If these emotions cannot be preserved, a new concept of a maternal image must be constructed to correspond better to reality. The approach of Markus and Nurius, and that of Heise, indicate the tendency to maintain the delicate internal balance between change and stability through a constant interaction between emotion and cognition.

A most comprehensive theoretical model of the interaction between cognition and emotion is that of Greenberg and Safran (1984, 1987, 1989), who base their arguments on the theoretical and empirical work of Leventhal (1979). They also view emotions from a biological, adaptive perspective as motivational dispositions to act; emotions are translated into tendencies to immediate action. In humans, these tendencies are mediated by higher-level information processing which elaborates the action tendencies into conscious emotional experience and intentions. In Greenberg and Safran's view, emotions are primary structures aimed at motivating adaptive behavior.

The structure for certain primary core emotions is wired into the human organism. The neurological substrate for emotional experience is wired in, and it includes a code for specific configurations of expressive motor behaviors that correspond to specific primary emotions, including at least the six emotions with identifiable facial expressions — fear, anger, sadness, surprise, disgust, and joy. The basic neurological template for emotional experience becomes elaborated in the human being into subtle blends of emotional experience, such as love, pride, envy, and humility, that are characteristic of human functioning.

Safran and Greenberg (1987), following Leventhal (1979), actually speak of three parallel information-processing levels: the expressive motor level, the schematic level, and the conceptual level. The expressive motor mechanism is largely an innate or wired-in system whose initial function does not depend on past learning. Sensorimotor activity appears to function in a manner like perceptual activity. In the same way that particular properties of the environment elicit specific visual perceptions, particular stimuli such as approaching objects (looming), high-pitched vocalizations, configurations that are face-like, and pain and contact/comfort experiences elicit specific expressive-motor reactions in neonates, without prior learning.

The second major system of processing is the schematic emotional memory mechanism which functions at an automatic level. It is a representation of particular post experiences, and is concrete and episodic in nature. Thus, it functions as a repository of automatic reactions for effectively significant situations. It also sets up expectations regarding what will occur in the emotional realm and directs attention to specific features of the perceptual field. In addition, it influences the encoding of the situation and activates or amplifies perceptual-motor inputs to give it a place in focal awareness. It also functions to integrate information generated at the perceptual-motor level. This schema represents prior emotional experiences and is elicited by many of the same stimuli that activate expressive-motor processing. In fact, this schema, once developed, is likely to be the major source of continuing spontaneous expressive-motor outputs. Expressive-motor responses, as well as being generated in direct response to a situation, can also be generated by this schema.

The third system in the hierarchy of processors involved in the construction of emotional experience is the abstract conceptual system which is responsible for conscious, sequential, volitional processing. It is a higher-level system containing abstractions from more concrete experience. This higher-level processing can act upon lower-level processing and is of great significance in the analysis of concrete experience, i.e., in drawing causal attributions, volitionally directing attention to specific experiences in memory, anticipating the future, etc. It is a highly flexible system used for reasoning and symbolic and verbal activity. It is a repository of memories and operations about feelings, their situational antecedents and their consequences. It does not, however, contain feeling memories themselves.

This system is responsible for our conscious attitudes and for evaluations of concrete emotional experiences. In addition to generating attitudes, the system is used in the control of emotional experience. It does so indirectly by controlling expressive behavior and by retrieving concrete images, rather than by directly eliciting emotional schemas. Emotion is usually regarded as non-volitional, because it cannot be directly elicited by this system. However, with practice in expressing and imaging, one is able voluntarily to feel anger, sadness, happiness, etc. Skilled actors demonstrate that individuals can learn to produce some degree of volitionally controlled states of feeling.

The human organism is seen as responding to the environment in an immediate, reflexive fashion. The type of immediate appraisals which humans make of the environment relate to biological and psychological survival. People engage in immediate perceptual-motor appraisals of environmental events which are not dependent on a prior stage of conceptual appraisal. These events are, however, subject to an ongoing conceptual appraisal as they take place, which becomes increasingly sophisticated as the organism develops. As this parallel appraisal process takes place, the individual accumulates memory stores consisting of images of eliciting environmental events, evoked expressive motor responses, associated autonomic arousal, and conceptual appraisals. Emotional experience thus becomes coded in memory structures of networks.

When an individual either attends to information or internally generates information which matches one of the components of the network, the probability increases that other associated components will become activated. As Long (1983) maintained, an emotion prototype is activated and processed automatically when an individual attends to information which matches sufficient coded propositions in the prototype. Once the right propositions or combinations thereof are matched in a stimulus array, the entire emotion prototype is automatically activated and processed. The individual thus consciously experiences an emotion, resulting from the pre-attentive integration of autonomic/expressive-motor, schematic, and conceptual components of the network. The experience of emotion thus indicates that a cognitive-affective network has been activated and is currently operating.

Problems can arise from the automatic cueing, at a pre-attentive level, of schematic emotional memories without their being fully processed consciously. This automatic processing can lead to inexplicable problematic feelings. Problems can also arise from discrepancies between levels of processing, particularly when the conceptual level contains injunctions against material in schematic memory or against certain expressive motor responses. Finally, schematic memories can be repositories of negative emotional associations and response sequences.

Safran and Greenberg (1987) illustrate how the emotional synthesis system functions. They consider a situation in which an individual is being criticized and feels threatened. This experience is synthesized from a series of facial/physiological perceptual-motor responses, a set of effectively laden schematic memories, which are activated and begin to direct attention, and a set of implicit rules, about being hurt or criticized, which are activated and begin to govern the expression or inhibition of the emotion. Concurrent with these processes, implicit meanings start being attached to the experience. These meanings in turn activate emotional schemas, which also direct attention and perceptual search activities, and evoke expressive-motor responses and sensory memories. A synthesis of this total process emerges into awareness as the momentary experience of feeling threatened.

Horowitz (1988) provides the idea of simultaneous rather than causative changes of the various aspects of an experience from a clinical perspective. He also stresses the dynamic changes of the different experiential components while internal congruence is maintained. He introduces the concept of states of mind to describe the relationship between experiential aspects in different mental conditions, especially in pathology. States of mind comprise emotions, thoughts, motives, action, and defense patterns, all of which act in a coordinated fashion. In a move from one conscious state to another, all the components are changed together. States of mind differ according to the degree of internal congruence of their components, or, in Horowitz's terms, the degree to which the states of mind are modulated.

Horowitz illustrates this by identifying several parallel states of mind in one of his patients, a woman who passed from one state of mind to another. He identified three states of mind which had a high degree of internal congruence and control. The first was 'the working woman,' in which the patient was active, could concentrate her efforts, felt some mild tension, and had the self-concept of a competent person. The second congruent, conscious state was 'the attacker,' characterized by her voice taking on a hard edge, by a scowling face, by feeling angry, and accusing others. The third state was that of 'the sparkling woman,' in which she was calm, lyrical, behaved openly, and felt creative. The different states of mind are activated by different circumstances, and represent distinct aspects of the self. When one state of mind turns into another, all aspects of the experience change accordingly.

The congruence—incongruence model of the unconscious maintains that perception (and memory), appraisal and emotion are the three basic elements which form an integrated experience. In a conscious state of mind there is a constant, coordinated flow of perceptions, interpretations, and emotions in harmony. From a phenomenological-subjective perspective it is difficult to define an experience composed only of thoughts, or only perceptions, or only emotions. Each aspect of an experience is always accompanied by the other two. When theorists such as Lazarus (1991) speak of perceptions as being appraised or interpreted, and eliciting emotions, they portray an artificial picture of the human subjective experience. Human beings simply do not undergo this fragmented development of experience, i.e., Perception (memory) ... Appraisal ... Emotion. An experience is immediately complete and integrated. Even Lazarus's concept of automatic appraisal does not resolve the artificiality of his portrayal of human experience. When an experience is felt as incomplete or fragmented, it is an indication of internal inconsistency or incongruence, eliciting further mental activity in order to achieve consistency or congruence.

Internal Congruence and Incongruence

The Gestalt approach can help us understand the meaning of internal congruence of experience. This approach describes the human organism's tendency to organize all stimuli into the best possible form. Form is judged according to degree of simplicity, orderliness, coordination, continuity, affinity of the elements, clarity, etc. When stimuli are only partially organized, in disarray, or uncoordinated, the organism naturally tends to arrange them in the best possible form, and to endow them with meaning accordingly. This corollary of the Gestalt provides a motivational-organismic flavor to the tendency to achieve inner harmony.

This view is echoed by Epstein (1983), who argues that humans have a natural tendency to assimilate different experience into a complete, harmonious, conceptual, and emotional system. Internal harmony is always the result of processes of assimilation (integration) and accommodation (differentiation). The end result of this process is not only inner harmony, but also greater enrichment. In conditions of internal incongruence, the processes of assimilation and accommodation are both absent. This theoretical concept will be clarified by the following clinical example which involves three components of the experience: emotion, meaning, and memory and perception.

A 50-year-old woman started undergoing psychotherapy to re-examine her relationships with the other members of her family. In one session, her relationship with her daughter came up. The mother suspected that the daughter was a lesbian, and was describing a situation in which the two embraced in reconciliation after quarreling. The mother recounted that she hugged her daughter with some reserve, saying to her, 'You're wonderful. I love you.' The daughter responded, 'No, it's you who are wonderful, and I love you,' and embraced her mother gently and warmly.

The client then described how she could not tolerate her daughter's hug — which had something erotic about it — and cut it short, as she was afraid that her daughter would interpret her discomfort as rejection. The woman was uneasy while describing this interaction. She then remembered and recounted an incident from her youth related to an erotic lesbian experience, stressing that she had not been embarrassed by the proposal made to her — to have sexual relations with another woman — and that she had rejected it without feeling anxiety or discomfort. Yet, the tension and unease which she felt during the session persisted. A little later she began talking about her relationship with her own mother: her mother's coldness, and her own yearning for a warm, loving embrace from her mother. She immediately continued, with a sense of insight, to the realization that she was not afraid of rejecting her daughter because of the eroticism of her embrace, but because if she surrendered herself to her warm hugs, her daughter might reject her in the same way that her mother had. The emotion accompanying this insight was one of relief and warmth toward her daughter.

An analysis of this therapeutic session enables us to understand an experience of internal congruence: the perception of the daughter's expression of affection was inconsistent with the client's feeling of discomfort, because, as she later realized, there was nothing sexual in the embrace. The resulting tension and feeling of discomfort during the recall led to continued attempts to achieve internal congruence — internal harmony. The tension prompted the memory of her yearning for love. This memory about fear of being rejected by her mother resulted in a change in the interpretation of her daughter's behavior. Consequently a change in emotion (from fear to rejecting the daughter's gesture on the basis of an erotic contact to fear of being rejected). This change led to a new feeling of warmth towards the daughter. The end result was the restoration of a relaxed feeling, replacing the uneasiness. The assimilation of the experience with the daughter into the schema of her experiences with her mother (integration) created a new congruence (differentiation), which took the form of awareness of her fear of being rejected by her daughter — a fear of which she had hitherto been unaware. This therapeutic incident helped the woman to begin to understand the nature of her relationship with her daughter, and to see it in a new light, and led to a desire to create a new and closer relationship with her.

This account highlights various processes: the tension of incongruence, the restoration of congruence, relief of the tension, and the creation of internal harmony.

Horowitz (1988) highlights the adaptive value of internal congruence. Internal incongruence prevents progress and change. Internal congruence, on the other hand, allows the individual to advance towards new meanings, new challenges, and to find solutions to old problems. Zajonc (1980) discusses the difference between 'hot cognitions' — those which are emotionally saturated — and 'cold cognitions' — which are devoid of emotions. He cites Hyde and Jenkins's study (1969) which examined the effect of different methods of teaching on the individual's ability to recall learned material. Participants in the study were divided into four groups. One group was asked to concentrate completely on the material learned; the second was asked to count the letters in the words learned; the third was asked to check whether a particular letter appeared in each word or not; and the fourth group was requested to arrange the words learned in order of pleasantness.

The fourth group succeeded in recalling the highest number of words. The researchers explained this result by claiming that rating the words according to their degree of pleasantness created a harmony between the emotional and the cognitive aspects. These endowed the words with a status of 'meaningful objects,' which triggered more associations and created an internal organization of associations which supported the memory structure. They concluded that the greater the degree of congruence that exists between emotion and cognition, the more organized and efficient functioning will be.

Some studies show that there is an almost spontaneous tendency to create harmony between different aspects of experiences. Teasdale and Fogarty (1979) manipulated subjects' feelings of depression or elation by getting them to repeat sentences in a sad or happy tone. They then asked the subjects to recall different events from their past. The depressed subjects remembered more sad than happy events, and vice versa. The intensity of the events also matched the degree of intensity of the appropriate mood — a correlation which was repeated with other measures of happiness and sadness.

Additional support for the adaptive value of internal congruence derives from an interesting study by Riskind (1984), who studied congruence between body posture and subjective experience. He suggests that when there is congruence between a certain experience, e.g., failure in a particular task, and body posture, the individual will experience less unpleasant emotions than when there is no such congruence. In other words, if in a situation of failure the body is stooped, the subject will feel less pronounced negative feelings than if his body were upright and erect. Riskind examined the effect of body posture on the extent of feelings of helplessness, depression, and apathy in situations of failure, and indeed his findings supported his hypothesis.

Riskind explains that congruence between mental and body posture draws individuals closer to authentic experience, thereby helping them to process their experiences and call upon appropriate adaptive reaction, e.g., lowering expectations, accepting failure, and replacing unsuccessful strategies of coping by new ones. On the other hand, the absence of accord between body posture and mental experience prevents correct handling of the failure, and creates competition between opposing patterns of action.

Bower (1981), in an eye-opening article, summarizes a large number of studies which support these findings. In one of the studies subjects were asked to keep a diary for one week. They were asked to record events that occurred during the week, to assess them as pleasant or unpleasant, and to grade the strength of the pleasantness or unpleasantness. In the second

At this stage it is important to define the internal congruence of experience by clarifying certain of its characteristics. The first is that it requires the existence of the three components of experience: perception-memory; meaning; and feeling. When individuals speak of a positive or negative emotion without being able to relate to it something real (event), internal or external, they are in a situation of incongruence. Likewise, if they relate to a positive occurrence, but the emotion is absent, or if they intellectualize an event, they are demonstrating an incongruent experience.

The second characteristic of internal congruence relates to the degree of harmony between the components. At its most superficial, internal harmony may relate, for example, to the perception of a happy event as positive, triggering feelings of happiness, and this feeling bringing to mind positive memories. When someone refers to a positive event, but the emotional reaction is one of indifference or even sadness, and the cognitive associations are negative and pessimistic, an internally incongruent experience is indicated. Examples of this may be found in daily life as well as in therapy, such as the patient who would burst out laughing when dealing with feelings of being insulted. When asked what she was feeling, she would reply, 'Nothing.' When asked what she was laughing at, she would answer, 'I don't know.' She claimed that the subject had an amusing side to it, but she was unable to identify it. When she examined the phenomenon, she explained that she laughed precisely when her feeling of embarrassment was growing, and was able to describe an experience in which embarrassment was related to being humiliated, and then she started to cry.

Another patient, on being asked about smiling inappropriately while talking about a particular unpleasant subject, spontaneously volunteered the information that her children, on seeing her smile, would ask if she was angry. They were accustomed to her reacting in this strange way when she felt anger. This is not a case of disguising one's feelings of anger or anxiety by means of a forced smile. The client described her response as uncontrollable, claiming that she did not feel the anger or anxiety itself.

The third characteristic of internal congruence relates to the number of internally congruent links — in other words, to a measure of its breadth and depth, i.e., its extent. Intensive internal congruence reflects many inner connections between emotions, cognitions, and memories. Experience automatically sets off a flow of associations between different components — perceptions, cognitions, and emotions. The network of these links is created on two levels, or planes: the breadth of congruence, which is the plane linking the three components (perception, cognition, and emotion) within a single experience; and its depth, which is the network of associations between other similar, and at times different, emotions, cognitions, and memories, of different layers of experience (present, past). The more connections of these types which an experience has, the higher the level of experiential awareness and consciousness. The greater the breadth and depth of an inner experience, the higher the level of self-differentiation.

Yet another aspect of inner congruence of an experience is the way in which such congruence is attained by means of change, either authentic or artificial. Following various other theorists (Greenwald, 1980; Epstein, 1983; Horowitz, 1988), we assume that internal congruence is achieved by means of authentic changes in emotion, thought, and memory, or by changes brought about by a defensive distortion, or denial. Authentic change generally results in inner harmony and adjustment. Artificial changes brought about by distortions of reality are considered to be distorting, defensive, and non-adaptive. Distortion of reality tends to drag in its wake further distortions, denials, and dissociations, which in turn result in greater incongruence.

The following clinical example will help to illustrate this point. A young patient tried to deal with the difficult problem of asserting her independence. She left home and tried to live by herself, but was unable to cope financially and was unsuccessful in her search for suitable employment. This situation caused great friction between her and her parents, which was exacerbated when her parents offered to help by contributing towards her rent. She reacted with anger (emotion) to her parents' offer of financial help by interpreting their offer as an attempt to increase her dependence on them (meaning). This is an example of a defensive attempt to create congruence. Yet when she related the story she felt sadness and not anger, indicating an incongruent experience. When she focused on her feeling of sadness, the forced congruence dissipated, as she acknowledged her authentic sense of dependence and her anxiety at moving away from home. This new meaning of her behavior helped her view her parents' offer differently. Sadness was an appropriate emotional response to her newly acknowledged weakness, and thus an inner experience of internal congruence was achieved. This congruence led to her first proper attempts to overcome her dependence. It released new mental strength to deal with the problem in a fresh, more effective way.

As hard as it is to come to grips with a difficult external or internal reality, assimilating it and working through the distressing emotions and meaning will result in a more harmonious and adaptive state of mind than a defensive distortion.

There are three main sources of experiential incongruence. First, when mental content is repressed or dissociated because it conflicts with personal constructs and beliefs; second, when mental content cannot be assimilated within the existing constructs, or when no appropriate construct exists to deal with specific contents or events; third, when content has been processed in pre-verbal form and therefore is not available to consciousness, yet still affects behavior (Epstein, 1983).

The emotional processes which are involved in creating internal splits are the best known: inner conflict and different types of trauma. These components stir up defensive mechanisms intended to restore congruence quickly, and usually in distorted form, including projection, excising the emotion, intellectualization, amnesia, selective attention, etc.

The second source of internal incongruence are experiences which cannot be assimilated because they do not suit any existing mental schema. This causes a confrontation with unusual experience or events which do not fit into one's established schemas.

The third process involved in creating experiential gaps is disharmony or incongruence in information processing. Information can be processed in more than one form. Kihlstrom (1984) and Neisser (1967), for example, formulate three forms of information processing: enactive, iconic, and symbolic. An experience or event which is generally worked through using only one form of processing is difficult to translate into another form. Van der Kolk and Ducey (1989) claim that an event, particularly a traumatic one, is usually experienced via the sensorimotoric sphere, and cannot easily be translated to the verbal sphere. The experience trapped in the sensorimotoric sphere can only find expression through sensory symptoms such as nightmares, delusions, and compulsive repetition of behavior from the time of the trauma. This difficulty in transformation is a source of splits and inner inconsistency.

Jacobs and Nadel (1985) claim that there are different brain structures for processing and storing different aspects of experience. The hippocampus registers and stores the contextual aspects of an experience, i.e., its space and time. This reaches maturity relatively late, usually at 3–4 years of age. On the other hand, cortical sub-systems responsible for processing and recording the qualitative aspects of an experience, such as feeling, sensation, sound, etc., mature earlier. As a result, there is a split between the processing of different aspects of an experience. During the first years the child can recall the qualitative aspects of experiences, but not the contextual ones. This may be the basis of childhood amnesia. Thus, a childhood experience which reaches awareness is incomplete and lack of internal congruence is almost inevitable. In maturity, too, situations occur in which a barrier appears within the processing continuum. The activity of the hippocampus is very sensitive and is easily damaged in situations of pressure; hence the ability to connect the qualitative with the contextual aspects is flawed. The experience therefore organizes itself on the sensorimotoric level, cannot be recalled verbally, and remains severed.

Thus, a traumatic-emotional kind of experience will have an inner experience break between its emotional aspect and its verbal-cognitive aspect. This makes remembering the experience difficult and causes a strong, uncontrolled emotional reaction. The trauma will remain 'undigested,' and will create a split within the experience.

A different measure of the experiential break arises from research on state-dependent learning. Learning of this sort illustrates even more clearly the point about discrepancies in the processing of information, and their influence on the unconscious and on psychopathology. This was studied by Bower (1981), who claims that learning and memory are situation dependent. In other words, learning and memory are at their most efficient specifically against the contextual background in which they were obtained. He gives an example of this process essentially in the area of recollection, showing that learning which takes place when one is in a particular mood is recalled best when in the same frame of mind. The closer the situational context of the recall to the original, the more efficient the recall. Bower's explanation for this is that the mood and the specific context in which the learning took place are integrated into the system of association of the material learned, and finding oneself in the same mood or in the same circumstances will itself elicit the material by means of association.

The same applies to different states of awareness: events which occurred while one was drunk are not remembered so clearly when one is sober, because of the different state of mind. Environmental or mental events experienced while under the influence of drugs cannot be recalled while not under that influence. Different forms of processing are also liable to integrate in situation-dependent learning.

In later articles Bower retracted a little from his stand on the efficiency of recall in situations of harmony between an emotional experience and remembered events (Bower and Meyer, 1985). Isen (1987) goes further and claims that remembering in congruent situations functions better with regard to positive emotions and events than negative ones. Nevertheless, the basic findings of improved memory in matching or congruent situations cannot be denied.

Isen offers an explanation for this phenomenon which is slightly different from Bower's. She maintains that the improvement in memory in congruent situations is not due to associative links between the emotion and the event which aroused it, as Bower suggests. The factor linking the event with the emotional situation at the time of recall is the similarity in significance between the original occurrence and the emotion at time of recall. Isen also holds that every emotion has not only a general physiological stimulation component, but also a meaning component. Different emotions such as sadness and fear also have different inherent significance. Contents and situations with similar meaning connect with the significance component of the emotion. The efficiency of recall in congruent situations is thus based on the similar meaning of the original recalled situation and its related emotion, and the meaning of the emotion in the recall situation. Therefore, behavior can be transformed unconsciously from a past situation to a situation in the present based on similarity in meaning rather than in a physical similarity.

Inner Congruence, Consciousness, and Unconsciousness

Consciousness may be regarded as a kaleidoscopic system which is in continuous flux, inventing ever-changing shapes, perspectives, and hues for memories and emotions.

As in a cog wheel system, the different elements of the experience activate each other, and movement of one of them activates all of the other elements. Each cog represents a perception, a particular meaning, or emotion. Moving one cog wheel automatically moves the others.

As conceived by the incongruence model, the unconscious does not relate to lack of knowledge, but rather to the quality of the knowledge or lack of knowledge. Consciousness or awareness is not intellectual knowledge. Consciousness is the internalization of knowledge and information regarding the self and the world with appropriate affect and meaning. This knowledge, vitalized with affect and meaning, creates the congruent experience, thus creating a different effect from intellectual knowledge. It transforms the individual's internal state of mind. The three elements are reciprocally influential. The information which is perceived is always interpreted according to the individual's emotional state at the given time. A particular meaning attributed to an item of knowledge may arouse specific feelings, while meaning and emotions may change concurrently in the light of additional information.

The three important ideas put forward by the internal congruence model are:

(a) There is inner harmony between the elements.
(b) Each element influences the mutual interaction of all of the elements.
(c) The flow of the experiential world is continuous.

It should be remembered that the influence of the mutual interaction of the experiential elements and the direction and intensity of the flow are monitored and controlled. The monitoring elements are the types of events to which individuals are exposed, their characteristic moods, their characteristic cognitive style, their inventory of meanings, and the specific individual's ability to create meanings. An example of a monitoring and regulating system for controlling the dimensions of change and the stability of the flow of experience may be found in Maddi (1980) and Horowitz (1988).

Lack of inner congruence was characterized earlier by incompleteness of the experience (a missing determinant), inappropriateness or lack of harmony between the determinants, generalized state of mind without inner differentiation and disconnectedness, and artificiality of the inner consistency. Each of these deficits limits one's awareness, both of self and of external reality. The young adolescent whose entire emotional world comes to be expressed by one dominant emotion, that of anger, is blind to a whole range of emotions, such as anxiety, frustration, fear of rejection, and more. Another adolescent who 'knows' that she is sad, but does not feel it misses the experience of what it is like to be sad, the meaning of the loss that made her sad, and the empathic understanding of sadness in others. A 'macho' male chauvinist has a very limited set of meaning as well as of interpersonal relationships. Restricting meaning imposes an experiential limitation, not only of external reality but of the self as well. The young woman who was angry at her parents for extending financial help to her obscured the real essence of her problem. Instead of handling her separation anxiety she 'coped' with her parents' attempt to restrict her independence, thereby limiting her own coping and problem-solving skills.

Often the incongruent experience in all its forms takes on characteristics of depersonalization and estrangement. At times in the clinical setting, clients refer to it symbolically as walking in a cloud, a monster, living in a black hole, or having the inexplicable feeling of constant danger. The transition from an incongruent, generalized, undifferentiated experience to a more harmonious, richer, and congruent one is of course not merely a matter of new informational enrichment or of acquiring new skills. It requires a working-through process which entails focusing on the experience, increasing differentiation, and integrating perception, emotions, and meaning through assimilation and accommodation.

The processes referred to can be seen in the following record of what was said (virtually a monologue) by a client, following a conversation about her plans to study social work.

CLIENT: It has made me very confused and afraid. I think I'm unsuited to this profession . . . it makes me panic inside. I felt the same when people asked me how come I haven't found a boyfriend yet, after I separated from my husband. I'm afraid that nobody will want me, and that I'll be rejected by everyone. Suddenly I was afraid that there was something wrong with me, that there's something going around inside me, leaving me confused and frightened.

THERAPIST: Frightened?

CLIENT: That everyone will keep away from me and no one will want me. I know that that's not true, and unrealistic, and yet it frightens me ...

THERAPIST: Tell me about the fear.

CLIENT: Sometimes I feel like a monster. There is some sort of wickedness, evil power in me ...

THERAPIST: Can you describe this monster?

CLIENT: I think that I possess a kind of destructive force which could seriously hurt people. I did it to my husband all the time. I was the one who started the arguments with him. When he lost his temper I would callously and cynically hit him below the belt. I would say something nasty, like: You really aren't normal, you're losing your self-control, you're behaving like a baby. (*Cries*) I'm really a monster. This evil can control me. I'm afraid it will come up with anyone I am in touch with.

THERAPIST: What did you feel during those arguments?

CLIENT: Sometimes he hurt me so much, and I was so humiliated by him, by his remarks, his violence. He made me feel dirty, unclean. I would feel so hurt, and then I would start to argue with him. When we quarreled I felt that I was stronger than him, until I saw him on his knees, and then I would feel sorry for him and would make up with him ... I basically used anger and cynicism to regain my self-respect. It was just like that with my father. (*Cries*) When we argued, we would clash over every stupid little thing. Whether my dress was nice, if my hairstyle suited me. I always felt that he wanted me to fall onto my knees, to admit that he was always right, to give in. I fought that with all my strength. I would hurt him in any way I could. He treated my mother the same way, and she didn't know how to fight back. She just kept quiet and gave in. It drove me crazy, and I would defend her and fight back for her. I can be a real monster if I want to.

THERAPIST: Carry on describing the monster.

CLIENT: I don't know, that's what bothers me. I'm scared to look at it. I think that I'm vulgar and I'm afraid that it will take over. It's something big; whenever I touch this big thing I feel that I'm lifting a huge stone, but then I close up again.

THERAPIST: What do you feel now?

CLIENT: Relief, a little relief. I think I'm not so bad after all. I can see what makes me so vulgar and aggressive sometimes. I am so scared of being humiliated, of giving in like my mother ... Right now I feel like in a cartoon, with a scary, monstrous character, and whenever it appears, everyone runs away. (*Tears*) But when I look at it, it's really not that frightening. It's even got a good heart, you can tickle it.

THERAPIST: You're making fun of your fears now.

CLIENT: Right, but it seems to me now that when it comes out, it won't be so terrible. I think that I know how to catch it.

The above excerpt from a therapy session illustrates the process of working through via assimilation and accommodation. The result of this is greater differentiation and internal enrichment, emotional relief, and new solutions. It also demonstrates clearly the creation of almost spontaneous connections between different emotions, meaning, and memories. The anxiety (emotion) aroused by the discussion about the choice of profession was linked to the sense of being a monster full of aggression (emotion). These were connected to the memory of arguments with the husband (memory). A self concept of a destructive, antisocial person, unable to establish relationships, who will always be lonely (meaning) emerged spontaneously.

Focusing on the feelings during the argument was initially linked to that of being hurt and this feeling stimulated new memories, new feelings of humiliation, vulnerability, and the struggle for respect. These feelings bring in their wake both new meaning and distant memories which support it: the memory of arguments with her father, the need to defend her mother. At this stage the client was able to interpret her behavior during arguments in a new light: it was not evil or a destructive power in her, but a defense against possible humiliation which brought out the monster. This interpretation led, in subsequent sessions, to the discovery of finer distinctions regarding humiliating situations and the meaning they carried for her. The process of working through provided emotional relief, reconciliation with the self, and self-forgiveness. The ultimate achievement of the process is no less important — the client's re-learning about herself, finer differentiation in her perception of something new about her method of coping with certain difficulties and relationships with others. This ultimately led to the conclusion that in contrast to her original view, she was in fact suited to social work.

The clinical vignette can also be analyzed from the perspective of assimilation and accommodation. The monstrous self described by the client represents the dissociative, disconnected part of the self of a primordial nature. By eventually identifying and defining the monstrous self, it was reduced and refined as a form of wickedness and argumentativeness. Then the wickedness took on the form of defensiveness against being hurt. At that stage, the monster became part of the self, while undergoing transformation. Simultaneously, the self also changed. By coming to accept the monster as part of herself, the client gained a new understanding of herself. She recognized her fear of being humiliated, her exaggerated defensiveness and the relevance of this tendency of hers to earlier, similar situations. The uncontrolled monster became a frightened, angry person who fears being humiliated. A new self-awareness was achieved which paved the way for her to adopt a new method for dealing with her fear of humiliation.

The described transformations are reminiscent of Neisser's (1967) theory of information processes, in which he describes six levels of information processing. The first is feeling, followed by perception, awareness, experience, introspection into the experience, and finally self-awareness. Each level refines the data more finely, on the one hand, while giving broader and more comprehensive significance to the perception of life and self, on the other.

It should be noted that the case described above started with an internally incongruent experience, which eventually became congruent. The patient started the session with a feeling of fear and rejection (emotion), that she was evil and violent (meaning). Yet she did not perceive actual rejection, and this provided the motivation for the processing which resulted in a more congruent experience, in which retrieved past memories, anger, and humiliation resulted in defensive behavior.

During the introspective search, her self-perception changed gradually, via a number of steps, from attacker to victim, anger to fear of humiliation, humiliation into pain, pain into sadness, sadness into self-acceptance and self-forgiveness. Similarly memories of arguments with her husband and of hurting him became memories of being hurt by him and by her father. It would thus seem that every imbalance, and subsequent regaining of balance, is accompanied by the activation of a new feeling, meaning, or memory. Each stage of establishing a new balance changes with other new feelings, meanings, and memories, until a more stable inner congruence is achieved.

The process of coordinated changes in the three components of experience can be seen and followed more clearly in the following case. A middle-aged woman came for help because of her inability to enjoy sex. Sex had always disturbed her, but only now had she decided that if she did not deal with the problem, she would never benefit from sexual relationships. In one session it was reflected to her that she was speaking about sex in a tone of bitter anger:

CLIENT: I don't want it. I'm not my husband's receptacle. He treats me as if I were a receptacle, and penetrates me mechanically, without passion ... I don't need it.
THERAPIST: You sound frightened.
CLIENT: Yes ... I don't know. I always feel this fear when sex comes up; it's as if I'm scared of being raped ... when I take a shower I close up the whole house, windows, doors, because I'm really afraid of being raped ... you know what I remember now? How my mother would always 'warn' me about my father. Once she actually said to me that I should be wary of him. When I was a child, whenever he would stroke

me, or sit me on his knee, or anything like that, she would always be right there. Once we went out for a walk, my father and I, and we were a bit late; my mother ran around looking for us, scared, and when she found us she started yelling at him, where had we been, and she asked me if I were okay ... To this day I am afraid to be alone with my father ... I get these strange feelings. Once, when I was about twenty, I was sick with high temperature; I opened my eyes and saw him bending over me to stroke me, and I got such a shock, as if he were about to rape me.

THERAPIST: Sex is frightening; it distances people instead of bringing them closer together.

CLIENT: Right, that's what happens with my husband, when he wants to make love. I always shudder and wish that he'd leave me alone. (*Pause*) But it's interesting, after he has finished, I actually feel free and calm, and then I can actually enjoy sex, and sometimes I start exciting him by doing a striptease (*laughs nervously*).

This session ended on a note of surprise — if sex arouses fear, is perceived as aggressive, as exploitation, and brings to mind memories of the mother warning her daughter against her father, what is the basis for her teasing her husband and behaving in this very seductive way after he has reached an orgasm? The answer came in the next session:

CLIENT: I'm tired ... I didn't want to come today ... I don't know what's wrong with me ... I feel this anxiety again ... I have a new grandson, my daughter had a son ... I suddenly had a terrible anxiety attack that something might happen to them, that they might die ... What strange thoughts I have ... I started eating and eating like crazy ... I'm trying to keep to a diet and I'm not managing ... I grab the food like I don't know what.

THERAPIST: You sound frightened, again. In panic.

CLIENT: Yes, I am frightened ... suddenly I'm afraid that I'll lose Atara [the daughter]. Suddenly I'm so afraid that something will happen to her ... I'm worried that now she won't have time for me ... the truth is, I'm afraid that she'll reject me now ... You know, recently we grew much closer than we ever were in the past. We started meeting more often and going out together. I went over to her quite often to play with her older son ... We went to a shop to try on some clothes, and she said, 'I don't want to buy anything for myself, I just came to be with you.' We really had a good time ... She gives herself to me, I'm afraid that it will change again and we'll lose this close tie ... You know, since I started talking about being afraid of rejection, it passed. I don't feel it anymore.

THERAPIST: But now you are still afraid of rejection.

CLIENT: I didn't think that I was so sensitive. It's funny what things I remember now. I've already told you about that young girl, my neighbor, who's fond of me, and I don't know why. Well, yesterday we met by chance at the supermarket, and she was so pleased to see me, she hugged and kissed me. I didn't know what to do with myself, I felt so uncomfortable. Afterwards I thought about it, and the thought went through my mind that when she really gets to know me, she'll simply change her mind and will reject me. That's exactly what happened two months ago, at the funeral of a soldier, our neighbor's son. I really wanted to share their grief. I wanted to go up to the mother and hug her, but I was afraid that she would just reject me, push me away from her ... If I'm afraid of being rejected, why is it so hard for me to lose weight? ... Why don't I lose weight ... Why do I want to be rejected? Why do I eat, eat, eat?

THERAPIST: Rejected? In what way?

CLIENT: Sexually ... Why do I do that? (*Starts shivering, puts on her coat*)

CLIENT: I'm cold, I'm shivering.

THERAPIST: What do you feel?

CLIENT: I don't know, I'm afraid of sex again ...

THERAPIST: Tell me about it.

CLIENT: Suddenly I'm afraid that I'll lose control. That if I let myself go, I won't be able to control it. That sexual desire will take over and I'll be really whorish ... I suddenly thought of *The Three Faces of Eve*, and that scares me. I know that there are different sides to me ... The side of the sexy, whorish, seductress Eve scares me ... I remember our last conversation about this, that I like to excite my husband after he has had an orgasm, when he's harmless ... Then I'm not afraid of that male mania ... but what scares me most with my husband is that I'll be really aroused, and I'll come onto him, and he won't want me, he'll simply reject me ... I can't believe the things that are coming into my head now. My mother, she's like that, she's a real sex maniac ... She talks about it all the time. To this day she flirts with men. I remember as a girl, when I came home from school, I would find them in bed. Not actually in the act, but I knew what they had done, and she really seemed like a prostitute to me ...

This excerpt provides the answer to the question raised in the previous session: What is the meaning of her seductive and provocative behavior towards her husband, at times when he was 'not dangerous'? The answer to the dilemma provided by the client was that her fear of sex was not just fear of potential male aggression, but was also a fear of her own sexual vulgarity, and even more, a fear of rejection.

At the end of the first session, the client had reached a congruent experience. She felt fear of sex to the point of panic (emotion). The fear awoke memories of her mother, who warned her against her father who can harm her sexually, and against men in general (memory — perception) which are considered sexually violent (interpretation — meaning). This is a congruent internal experience that enabled her to progress in a surprising direction: She recalled her experience as a seductress, albeit when she was safe from attack.

During the second session this experience switched into another, which also clarified her behavior as a temptress; this was the fear of rejection (emotion) related to her recollections of a sexually vulgar and provocative mother (memory — perception), and to her reaction to female sexuality as vulgar and repulsive (meaning). This experience is related to another kind of fear of rejection; i.e., in situations of intimacy and love, and also linked to the client's self perception as being repulsive. Fears and memories became linked in a chain, the fear of being rejected by her daughter, her neighbor, her young friend, and her husband. These led to the recall and recounting of repulsive memories of her father and mother. This chain of memories and feelings was also connected with interpretive associations: men lust for sex and are aggressive; women are vulgar and whorish; I am repulsive and rejected; my mother is a whore, etc.

The web of perceptions, meanings, and feelings displayed by this woman in the course of the sessions unfolded a changing inner world. It is easy to see the complex mental tapestry that develops and enters into the consciousness. During the process, the client discovered different, hitherto unknown, sides of herself. She discovered her internal richness, the continuum relating experiences from different areas, and the continuous internal change that occurs. While following this chain of associations, she assimilated every dissociated aspect and wove it into the rich, varied, and complex tapestry of experiences.

Through the movement from incongruent experiences to congruent ones she met a new desire for self-awareness and understanding: Am I really repulsive, do I really deserve to be rejected? Indeed, these questions were the main theme of subsequent sessions.

The experiential world is ever-changing, constantly assimilating and accommodating to new events, meanings, and emotions, creating new links, and moving from one incongruent or congruent experience to another. This changing stream of consciousness is a result of an ongoing working-through process resulting in inner differentiations and developments. The process is characterized by movements towards and away from inner changes. In the excerpt quoted below, one can clearly see the emotional fluctuations in the attempts to internalize, assimilate, and reach inner congruence, or come to terms with an experience which was difficult to integrate into the self.

The excerpt is from Dan Ben Ahmotz's book *To Remember and to Forget* (1980). It is well known that this novel is an emotional autobiography of the author, presenting his family history, the loss of his family in the Holocaust, and his own refuge in Israel. In the book the author returns to a past which he had tried to forget and excise from his awareness. The book thus presents a working-through process of assimilation of dissociative material. The story begins with the author's journey to Germany to receive financial compensation for his family's murder — a decision which causes great internal turmoil. While in Germany he meets a German girl, falls in love with her, and marries her, eventually bringing her back to Israel with him. These events elicited many mental machinations, moving back and forth with his plans, decisions, self-image, beliefs, attitudes, and feelings, trying to create an inner harmony between conflicting directions and finally achieving a new inner congruence.

The hero, Uri, is in the elevator on the way to the attorney's office to deal with the matter of compensation, and is accompanied by a young German girl; the lift gets stuck and he ends up in her apartment instead of in the attorney's office. The meeting and his attraction to the girl arouse a simultaneous conflicting movement, which takes the form of his refusal to speak German (in which he is fluent), and communicating with his lover in sign language. His avoidance of going to the attorney's office and its substitution by his attraction to the girl solved his internal dilemma over the compensation, at least for a while. However, falling in love with her created a new internal dilemma. The diversion of his anger against the language temporarily eases his emotional distress.

Eventually, Uri reveals that he can speak German and assimilates his feeling of love for a German, and in fact intends to marry her. This assimilation creates a new incongruence. He tries to cope with this incongruence by seeing Barbara, his lover, as a special person, exceptional, and different from all other Germans. This new meaning turns out to be only a partial solution, however, as it is followed by an outburst of intense anger at Barbara's parents' dog which he personalizes as a 'Nazi' and tries to kill it. The delicate balance which he has achieved is disturbed when Uri quite by chance meets an intensely anti-Nazi friend, who deepens his inner conflict. The friend, Martin, half drunk, starts virulent anti-Nazi monologues against those (Barbara?) who 'play the role of rebels disappointed in their parents. In the end they take over their father's business ... they "understand" their father, and the poison which they have been absorbing in minute quantities three times a day, begins to show itself' (Ben Ahmotz, 1980, p. 233).

Uri tries to calm the internal storm, but does not succeed. 'I listened to him, against my will. The confusion which weighed heavily on me made me bow my head. . . . He causes turmoil in my tidy room, I thought bitterly . . . all the suspicions which I placed on the shelf of the past, all the doubts which I packed away so carefully, all the apprehensions which I sorted and locked away in iron caskets are flying around and mixed up before my eyes in the draught he caused' (ibid., p. 234).

Uri again attempts to settle the inner confusion and goes to 'meet' his family by visiting his parents' house, which is still standing and now belongs to a German family. His attempt to impose his hatred on the new residents — his parents' killers and robbers of their property — in order to regain tranquility was unsuccessful, and instead new confusion was instilled in him. He hears from the occupants of the house that his brother, whom he had thought was dead, had apparently also visited the house some time previously, proving that not all the members of the family had perished, as he had thought. At this point Uri's shaky internal balance collapses. He tries to push the incident out of his mind and to sever himself from it. 'I want to forget and I hope that my brother has forgotten. I won't be able to take it, if he remembers and tries to remind me every day of the very things I'm trying to forget' (ibid., p. 260).

Uri tries to calm the disquiet by renewed anti-Nazi outbursts, in an attempt to make a distinction between Barbara, whom he is going to marry, and other Germans. The internal struggle, the move towards assimilation and the flight from it, reach a climax at the wedding. The meeting with Barbara's parents has a calming effect; he finds them to be nice people. This impression helps him temporarily to reconcile his inner turmoil of conflict. However, during the wedding his inner revolt and self-accusation manifest themselves in the form of a hallucination of his family, whom he imagines to be present at the wedding. The guilt feelings continue to intrude during the party which followed the wedding, and Uri, drunk, begins settling accounts with Barbara's father and his Nazi past, and with Barbara herself.

After the wedding, Uri rushes out in search for his brother as if making an attempt to atone for his having married Barbara. His search for his brother leads him to the Dachau concentration camp. When he arrives home, he tries to punish himself by having a cold bath, although it was mid-winter. The cold bath makes him ill, causing him to suffer more hallucinations when in a delirium.

Uri's inner conflict reaches a peak when he deliberately provokes Barbara in order to reveal her 'real' nature. After succeeding in fanning the flames of his inner battle, he devotes himself to fury: 'Who does she think she is? Does she expect me to take it lying down? She thinks that she can insult me and I'll bow my head in submission like a poor Jew who does what he's told. She doesn't know who she's dealing with. I won't swallow the insults silently. She'll feel the full weight of my pride. I'm an Israeli, and no German or anyone else is going to tell me what to do' (ibid., p. 252).

Barbara passes the test honorably and refuses to rise to the bait prepared for her by Uri's provocation. Uri is left with his dilemma. Although Barbara, the German, proves herself to be a fine, honorable person, an anti-Nazi, Uri's internal agitation, his guilt, his need to settle accounts with the Nazis before he is able to accept his wife completely, do not leave him. He renews his provocative behavior, appearing at a fancy-dress party in the guise of an orthodox Jew, and, together with his friend Martin, who is dressed up as an SS officer, enacts a confrontation between the Jewish victim and his Nazi tormentor. The guests (the Nazis) are astonished and in shock. Martin the 'Nazi' yells at him: 'Out, you damned Jew! Out, you swine, you.' Uri reacts by heading towards the exit, passing among the guests, with Martin following, shouting: 'Out, you Jewish shithead.' When they get outside, they hug each other and walk together, laughing so hard that tears are streaming from their eyes.

By this dramatization, Uri has succeeded in identifying totally with the Jewish victim in exorcising the Nazis and his hatred of Germans. Most important, he has completed the assimilation of the fact of his marriage and his love of a German by releasing her from Nazism, and that he was not able to accept her or able to make a distinction between a German of today and the Nazis of the past. From his own point of view, Uri has solved his problem and has completed the circle of assimilation— accommodation by working through his conflictual internal experiences.

This story also demonstrates how the honest confrontation with an inner incongruence, however frightening it may be, whatever meanings may arise, and whatever painful memories may be awakened, will eventually lead to emotional relief and to a softening of the mental anguish experienced. The descent to the 'bottom of the barrel' is always accompanied by a spontaneous emotional recovery, by creating inner harmony.

Having examined some clinical and literary examples, we may now summarize the complex and dynamic structure of inner harmony and congruence and how it relates to self-awareness and consciousness. This can be demonstrated with the help of Figure 6.1. In its most simple form, harmony within an experience as well as consciousness can be achieved by a congruent relationship between the three components of the experience: perception, meaning, and feeling. However, the internal diversity and wealth are achieved by a multi-complex system of inner associations.

Interrelationships can be of a different type, include different emotions combining with each other, different meanings which ally themselves, and

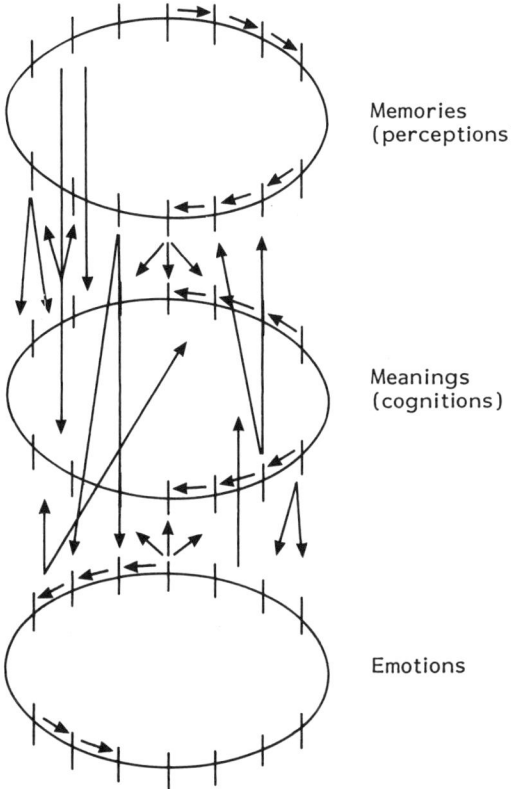

Memories
(perceptions)

Meanings
(cognitions)

Emotions

Figure 6.1 An example of a network of inner connections between the three aspects of the subjective experience

memories or perceptions of events which attach themselves together. The process may start at any one of the levels, and continue from it onto other levels and to new ranges of emotions, meanings, and memories. As can be seen in Figure 6.1, a number of emotions may join up with a single meaning or a single memory, and various meanings may connect with the same memory or the same feeling. Very often the links are spontaneous — when an emotion leads to a sequence of similar emotions, to memories, and to meanings; sometimes the relationships need to be actively initiated.

The web of relationships is a dynamic one, changing constantly. The consciousness's condition of awareness is changing all the time and an experience can do so too. A harmonious experience which has reached a stable, internal congruence may be reopened at a later stage in the light of new experiences. New events, changes in reality, the consolidation of neighboring experiences, a new memory, or a new meaning, may cause the experience to be reorganized. In this sense one can see the harmonization of the constant flow in an experience with the constant adaptation required by the changes taking place in reality and in the self.

Yet we must account, theoretically, for the control of two types of imbalance in the experiential flow. Namely, a total block in the flow and a total looseness in the flow. As mentioned earlier, we must assume the existence of a dynamic system monitoring the stability of congruence on one hand and for spontaneous change in the congruence experience on the other hand. In other words, we assume a control system responsible for the flexible stability in the experiential flow by which congruent experiences become incongruent to a certain degree and incongruent ones gain more congruence. It seems to us that Fisk and Maddi's account for this problem (see Maddi, 1980) discussed above is a good theoretical solution for this issue. As a general rule an incongruent experience creates a blockage in the experiential consciousness, whereas congruence sets the stream of consciousness into motion.

The present conceptualization of consciousness and unconsciousness by means of congruence and incongruence of the inner experience is supported by Bower's (1981, see also Yates and Nasby, 1993) associative network theory (ANT) and by Long's (1983, 1984) approach to emotional processing. Bower contends that the processing of memory and mood are viewed from the perspective of a united or node network. Each basic unit is a 'proposition,' namely the smallest unit of information or knowledge that can stand on its own as a separate assertion, and it is usually described as a sentence.

Propositions can be combined into groups and serve as conceptual or factual representations of events. When propositions or nodes are linked together they become associative structures forming a network. A proposition becomes associated with other encoded propositions active at the time of encoding. When nodes are stimulated they are activated above some threshold and become conscious. What is unique about Bower's approach is that he regards emotions to be structured as independent units or nodes, just like any other item of information capable of making associative links with other units. An emotion is a structural entity of readiness to react emotionally to specific events in an automatic way. Some of the basic emotions in the network are innate structures (see also Gilbert, 1989) and some are learned. Thus, specific events may form connections to emotional units within the associational network, acquire an emotional tone from these units, and remain organized in memory in the form thus acquired.

Long (1983, 1984) has elaborated even further Bower's associative network approach to memory and consciousness. He maintains that the basic emotional structures themselves include three principal elements:

1. Memory of the characteristics of the stimuli which aroused the emotional reaction.
2. Memory of the emotional reaction itself with its physiological and psychological characteristics (verbal and somatic relations).
3. The meaning component — the memory of the information which provided meaning to the arousal stimulus and to the emotional reaction itself.

The internal consistency—inconsistency approach to the unconscious fully concurs with Long's propositions. According to this model, the memory network is composed of three-part units comprising emotion, meaning, and memory. At times, all of the components of the units are congruent with one another, and at times elements are missing or incongruent. A rich network of connections between the units represents richly endowed and extensive consciousness, while an incongruent and impoverished network represents impoverished consciousness.

There is very little empirical evidence to support the notion of the unconscious as a lack of inner congruence. One exception is the research of Hansen and Hansen (1988) which supports some aspects of the model. Hansen and Hansen suggest that repression should not necessarily be manifested in blunting the intensity of the dominant emotion with which a memorial representation is tagged (e.g. fear in a fear-tagged memory), but in the dissociation between that emotion and other related, but non-dominant, emotions (sadness in a fear-tagged memory). They contend that repressors may engage in a less elaborative processing of emotional experience, and therefore the blends of non-dominant emotions with which a memorial representation is tagged may be simpler and less intense. Their data supported this prediction: While repressors and non-repressors did not differ in the reported intensity of dominant emotions, repressors reported less intense non-dominant emotions than did non-repressors. Hansen and Hansen concluded that repression is fundamentally a phenomenon of the relatively impoverished structure of the repressors' memory linked to the less elaborate, more discrete emotional tags with which the repressors' memorial representations are associated. Repression, they claim, is not simply an inaccessibility to unpleasant memories. Rather, the patterns of emotion associated with repressors' memories are different from those of non-repressors.

The explanation which Hansen and Hansen offer is exactly the approach presented here. The repressors have a poorer, simpler network of relationships between different emotions, as they do not process the dominant experience by linking it with other emotions. They are therefore unable to derive many secondary feelings. The non-repressors, on the other hand, who do not ignore the threat but work through it, thereby produce a more complex network. They are thus able to connect more emotions to a negative event and succeed in calling upon them when the need arises.

INCONGRUENCE, ANXIETY, AND PATHOLOGY

It should be emphasized that the model presented here offers lack of inner congruence as an important principle in viewing pathology, but it does not propose a new theory of pathology. We do not refer here to inner motives or to the development of pathology. Our viewpoint offers an additional dimension to the understanding of pathology but does not provide a revolutionary approach. The following examples and explanations only offer some principles and possibilities of viewing pathology as inflexible attempts to preserve an artificial inner congruence.

From the perspective of the present model, pathology is a maladaptive way of dealing with anxiety created by incongruence or threat of incongruence. There are three major forms of maladaptive attempts to create or restore inner congruence:

1. Artificially enforced congruence by means of distorting reality, denial, and rationalization.
2. Rigidity and extreme resistance to change.
3. Inner disconnections in the form of dissociations, splitting, distancing, and exclusion of some components of the inner experience (perception, meaning, or feelings).

The common feature of the three forms of maladaptive attempts is the inability to assimilate a major aspect of the self or of life events into existing congruent experiences without a major change. The denied or dissociated aspect threatens to create an inner imbalance. This is experienced as anxiety. At the same time maladaptive forms of inner congruence are in themselves a source for anxiety, as they are not sufficient to restore a stable inner balance.

Any pathological syndrome represents one type or another of inner discontinuity or the threat of such a discontinuity. Epstein (1983) exemplifies this idea by means of three different gulfs in three different pathologies: depression, paranoia, and schizophrenia. He views depression as the preservation of artificial inner balance at the cost of a change in self-evaluation. Depressives are prepared to sacrifice their self-evaluation in order to preserve their perception of the world. For example, they are ready to accept frustration and absorb insults, provided that they do not need to alter their view of their parents, their spouse, friends, etc.

Paranoiacs, with exalted, grandiose thoughts about themselves, maintain their self-image by sacrificing their perception of reality and accepting it as it is. Schizophrenics, according to Epstein, are expressing their surrender of a stable conceptual system of the world in order to preserve their self-image. All three pathologies result from the disturbance of inner balance and from different ways of achieving false congruity.

The incongruence model offers a slightly different analysis of maladaptive behavior than that of Epstein. Indeed, the different pathologies can be linked to different forms of inner experiential severance and different distortion in order to maintain inner congruence. In some of the pathologies, the main defensive approach is one of artificiality, distortion, and rigidity. In other pathologies the main defensive approach is based on exclusion of one important aspect of the experience. The first defensive approach can be observed in pathologies such as paranoia or schizophrenia. The second can be found in maladaptive behaviors such as hysterical and compulsive behavior, or individuals who use intellectualization as a main coping strategy.

Using an approach similar to Epstein's, we may link various forms of inner experiential severance with different expressions of pathology. The following examples do not represent the full range of pathology, but offer the possibility in principle of viewing pathological patterns as being caused by internal incongruence, and by inflexible attempts to preserve an artificial balance. The pathology simultaneously perpetuates the inner experiential gulf.

Paranoiacs can be described as those who grasp reality with a grain of truth, and can even react with emotions which are appropriate to the perception and meaning with which they relate to the world, but they nevertheless do this at the expense of distorting the realistic meaning. They distort meaning in order to keep it in harmony with their feelings of superiority or persecution, which is how they characteristically preserve their self-respect.

Schizophrenics, in contrast to paranoiacs, heavily distort reality itself (perception and memory), and react to it with emotion which matches the distortion, and even endow this reality with meaning which matches their emotions and perceptions. When a schizophrenic suffers a hallucination, say of seeing Satan, his or her emotional reaction, that of fear, is appropriate to this reality.

Hysterics show the dominance of emotional reaction, disconnected from memories or meaning. Intense emotions are expressed in a physical-motoric form, but cannot be related meaningfully to reality. Hysterics are fluid in their emotions and easily change mood and its intensity. There is no congruence between the intensity of the feeling and the perception of reality, either past or present. They find difficulty in explaining themselves rationally, and rely heavily on their sensations and intuitions, but find it difficult to relate these to reality. This approach represents hysterics' main line of defense against disturbing conflicts and their attempt to preserve their self-image.

Compulsive individuals, in contrast to hysterics, may be described as those whose inner experience is characterized by a lack of balance between emotional and cognitive processes owing to the dominance of the perceptible-tangible, and concentration on facts at the expense of emotional expression. Compulsives devote all their attention to detail, to analyzing events, to the search for harmony between different aspects of reality, with little attention to their inner realm of emotions.

Intellectualizing individuals put a major emphasis on explanation and rationalization. They switch from one set of meanings to another, yet they pay little attention to facts and to their feelings. They may be able to talk about their emotions and analyze these, as if they were just part of external reality, but not of inner experience. In this way such people try to avoid the feeling of anxiety and to preserve their self-esteem.

The above theoretical sketch and clinical examples provided some insights about pathology from the perspective of the congruence— incongruence model. As noted in the introduction to this section, the present model does not provide a complete theory of personality and development and, therefore, is insufficient to explain pathology. In so far as lack of self-awareness is believed to be one of the processes involved in pathological behavior, then the above theoretical sketch provides a general conceptual outline of the role of unconsciousness in pathology as viewed by the congruence—incongruence model.

The essence of the unconscious, according to the congruence— incongruence model, is not in repression of memories or in the absence of awareness, but rather in the inner discrepancy between various aspects of the subjective experience and between modes of experiencing. I believe that this model actually integrates many of the particularized concepts of other theories. Concepts such as repression, inhibition, splits, different levels of processing are all forms of inconsistencies and inner discrepancies. Similarly, striving for inner harmony through the elaboration of an associative network of information, cognition, and emotions, through bridging inner gaps, through increasing inner integration, is viewed as a basis for adaptive functioning in all approaches.

The unique contribution of the model presented here is in the assumption that there is a natural and consistent tendency towards seeking internal congruence and harmony, and that interruptions in achieving this goal create a state of mind of unconsciousness. The mind is conceived of as an ongoing stream of experience changing with the kaleidoscopic movement of its elements. There is a continual movement from congruent to incongruent positions and vice versa. Thus, being aware is not a result of using a technique or mechanism, but a result of ongoing effort to achieve a complex inner harmony.

CHAPTER 7

Incongruence: Principles of Therapy

Clearly, the unconscious is so central to the personality that discussion of its essential qualities and implications cannot remain detached from a broader theoretical framework, and must be related to a more comprehensive theory of personality. My personal conception of the personality and its development is based on my own interpretation of the interpersonal humanist approach, which emphasizes that the core of the phenomenological world is the dialectic between the self and others. The treatment approach to be discussed here is also based on the interpersonal humanistic approach. My approach also accords with modern cognitive-emotional information-processing theories relating to the functioning of mental processes. I do not intend to elaborate on this theoretical model of mental operations and treatment, but rather, as I indicated, to focus on the treatment of internal incongruence, which signals emotional distress. It should be remembered, therefore, that this presentation of the treatment approach is limited to the subject under discussion and is only one part of a broader theoretical and therapeutic approach.

CREATING A CONGRUENT EXPERIENCE: PRINCIPLES AND PROCESSES OF TREATMENT

If pathology is an expression of intra-experiential incongruence and incongruence between inter-experiential connections, treatment consists essentially of expanding consciousness by restoring intra-experiential congruence and augmenting the connections between the experiences. Creating inner experiential congruence includes disengaging artificial congruences, creating new congruences, and increasing the links between different experiences. Essentially, treatment focuses on the experience, seeking to understand the internal congruities and incongruities existing within its different forms and aspects. Some of these principles are not unique to the model presented here and are used in other therapeutic approaches which aim to achieve, in part, similar therapeutic goals. (See, for example, Safren and Greenberg, 1991; Greenberg, Rice and Elliot, 1993.)

First, I will describe three basic treatment principles and then some therapeutic processes that transpire in therapy when these principles are utilized. The principles include direct focus on the experience, engaging different aspects of the experience, and intensification of feelings and concretization. The use of these therapeutic principles helps set in motion five basic therapeutic processes:

- Creation of congruence by direct focus on the experience.
- Engaging the 'forgotten' aspects of the incongruent experience.
- Deepening and expanding the network of intra- and inter-experiential links.
- Long-term processing of the experiences — assimilation and accommodation.
- Construction of congruence through reconstructing memory.

Focus on the Experience

Direct focus on the experience is based principally on the approach of Sullivan (1956), who brought unconscious material into consciousness by helping the patient focus attention on material that was outside of awareness. His conception of unconscious processes was closer to the dissociative model than to the psychoanalytic model. Selective inattention, or the diversion of attention away from threatening material to another focus, is the principal mechanism engendering repression. This disregard of information was for Sullivan the essence of repression. Change required simply learning to pay attention to the rejected information.

A similar method of focusing attention is prescribed by the model of intra-experiential congruence. Focusing attention is obtained by asking questions relating to the 'what' and 'how' of the experience.

- 'What do you feel?'
- 'What does the subject or experience mean to you?'
- 'Does it remind you of something?'
- 'What other experiences come to mind?'
- 'How would you describe the feeling?'
- 'How did it happen?'
- 'What are you feeling now?'

Focusing attention is a fundamental technique for revealing the various elements which have been detached from the experience, which is a necessary initial step in the process of achieving congruence between the elements of the experience.

Greenberg, Rice and Elliot (1993) illustrate several instructive techniques for establishing direct focus on experience. The central difference between the approach presented here and the methods used by these authors is that they focus principally on the emotional aspect of the experience and less on the meaning and the reality. In addition, their approach does not focus directly on congruence itself, expecting this to evolve as a spontaneous reaction to the focus on the experience. Despite the occurrence of such a spontaneous reaction in many cases, specific treatment efforts must often be focused on creating congruence and removing the discrepancies within the experiences.

Engaging the Different Aspects of the Experience

As will be remembered, internal incongruence results, among other reasons, when certain elements of the experience are lacking or remain latent. According to this treatment principle, the missing experiential aspect is actively engaged by relating to it appropriately and asking pertinent questions about the present and past reality, the meaning, and the emotion. Engaging the different aspects of the experience requires knowledge of the way the specific patient typically organizes his or her experiences so that the missing element may be identified.

Intensification of Feelings and Concretization

Feeling is the dominant component of any experience. When an experience has been voided of its emotional aspects, bringing the feelings into awareness is the principal treatment aim. Relating to feeling is accomplished by focusing directly on the feeling itself. The most direct way to reach the emotional reactions is through questions such as, 'What are you feeling now?', or 'What did you feel then?', 'What are you feeling as we talk about this?'. Description of a particular event or predicament as tangibly and concretely as possible helps arouse the emotion felt. Gestalt techniques, such as role playing, psychodrama, imagery, reconstruction, and detailed description of events are established modes of making emotions palpable. Enriching the context with the original, realistic details, down to the last triviality, may help in reconstructing the entire experience and thus recreating its tone and emotional aura.

Speaking about an experience or its meaning in abstract phrases or over-generalizations causes the individual to lose touch with the feeling it

A young woman requested treatment for a feeling of unexplained misery that had existed for some time, but had recently become so unbearable that she sought relief. The experience was explored directly:

THERAPIST: Can you describe the misery?
CLIENT: It is hard to describe.
THERAPIST: What happens when you feel the misery?
CLIENT: (*Pause*) A kind of emptiness, like the discomfort of hunger . . . It's more like longing for something.
THERAPIST: Longing?
CLIENT: I don't know.
THERAPIST: Is this longing a familiar feeling?
CLIENT: I am homesick; I miss my parents.

This focus enabled the client to review with the therapist her leaving her childhood home, her difficulties in adjusting to the city and to her graduate school studies, the compromises she had to make, and then to discuss her relationship with her parents:

CLIENT: The first time in my life that I felt this kind of misery was when my parents separated and my father left home. I cannot remember that period. It's as though it simply disappeared from my mind.
THERAPIST: You first felt the misery when your father left?
CLIENT: Yes, I don't remember that I missed him, he simply wasn't there.
THERAPIST: What *did* you feel when he left?
CLIENT: I don't know exactly, but I do remember that I thought it seemed he didn't love us enough and that I didn't interest him enough.
THERAPIST: You didn't interest him enough?
CLIENT: No. That's a feeling I often have. Even with my mother that happens. I feel that maybe, when I come to visit her, I am not interesting enough for her. She was a social worker, and there were always people coming to the house to talk to her. When I was a child, I thought other people interested her more than I did. When my brother was born, I kept trying all the time to do things that would make her pay attention to me. I even hit my kindergarten teacher.
THERAPIST: The feeling that you are not interesting enough is a recurring one.
CLIENT: Yes. At school I'm afraid all the time that what I have to say isn't interesting.
THERAPIST: What happens when you feel that way?
CLIENT: There are times when it paralyzes me. I'm so pressured I avoid preparing some of my papers for fear that they are not interesting if they aren't perfect. I can't touch them. Then, suddenly, I get angry, feel

hateful. The anger isn't connected to anything specific; I hate the whole world, everything.

As the session continued, the patient connected her feelings of anger to the feeling that she is uninteresting, and to her strong need to interest people. Her dominant childhood memories related to her intense need to interest her mother, and the feeling that her father left because he was not interested in her.

Focus on the experience and on its different facets led to both an inner congruence and a web of associated feelings and memories. This further led the patient to focus on and to work through her feeling of being an uninteresting person, and her anxieties that people would shy away from her, abandoning her to loneliness. As this experience came to light, the feelings of misery slowly disappeared. Instead, she became aware of and focused on her value as a person to herself and to others, and on what she could give and receive in a mutually rewarding interpersonal relationship.

Engaging the 'Forgotten' Aspects of the Incongruent Experience

When the individual's internal world is based on a single aspect, his or her experiences are incomplete. At times, the inner world is based almost exclusively on one aspect, whether perception, meaning or feeling. The other facets of the experience remain latent. The primary goal of treatment is learning to find the missing determinant of experience. The following are some examples of therapeutic efforts to engage absent components so as to create the congruent experience.

Reality 'in Search of' Meaning and Feeling

As was demonstrated earlier, obsessive individuals do not have the means of connecting perceptions to feelings and meaning. Their internal world is nothing but a form of schematization of the external environment. Their experiences are barren, static, factual events.

David, a young man of 28, exemplifies a patient who experiences the world as a stream of factual perceptions of his surroundings. David came to treatment because he suffered difficulties in relating to women. Despite having had brief relationships, at the age of 28 he had begun to feel that he would never meet a woman who was 'his type.' Several times he managed to feel 'excited for a short time,' as he described his encounters with new acquaintances, but this passed quickly. He was greatly concerned that living together would interfere with his need for quiet and a good night's sleep, with his ability to commit himself to his other interests, and with his feeling of freedom. He repeatedly, but without elaboration, emphasized that one of his concerns was being trapped. 'At first she will do everything to please me, but later she will become a demanding monster.' He described his relationships with people — women, close friends and relatives, colleagues at work — and his life history as a series of dry facts.

Attempts to understand his internal world and to expand it beyond the bare facts were begun from two directions. One direction was the attempt to view the detached facts as part of a broader belief system, and the second was the effort to focus on feelings which these external events would normally arouse.

In one of the initial therapy sessions, David repeated things he had said a number of times previously, adding some similar experiences which occurred in the preceding few days. As the therapist attempted to find broader meaning in these life experiences, the interview developed in the following manner:

THERAPIST: I understand that you have some difficulties in committing yourself to a relationship with a woman, in spite of your wish to find a special person who could understand your needs.

DAVID: You're right. I want a relationship, but can't find anyone who fits what I want. I'm afraid it won't succeed.

THERAPIST: I guess that you are afraid that you won't find this special person who will understand and that makes you very cautious and suspicious and cools any excitement you might feel with a woman.

DAVID: Maybe. Maybe I am suspicious and maybe I'm afraid; but maybe I'm right that I simply can't find someone suitable, and if I find someone who's right for me, I won't be afraid.

THERAPIST: What does unsuitable mean — that she will be too demanding.

DAVID: Yes. That she won't let me sleep and so on.

THERAPIST: So, you must be very cautious with women.

DAVID: Yes.

THERAPIST: It seems to me that when you feel excitement, this indicates that something positive is happening; this happens to you sometimes, but does not last. What does this show?

DAVID: Maybe it shows that I like her at first and then later something happens that I don't like.

THERAPIST: Maybe then your caution and worry about falling into a trap makes you examine each woman's behavior very carefully. Any feeling of affection may make you lose interest.

DAVID: I think you're right. It could be that I really do something like that. I may be overly cautious; maybe I'm on guard and suspicious and that's what makes me fail.

THERAPIST: With this possibility in mind, let's talk about one of your dates and try to understand what happened.

At this stage, David seems to have been helped to connect the succession of recurring events and to conceptualize an internal principle which links them together in a meaningful fashion. An initial schema has been defined which helps the patient understand that an inner principle is guiding the events, rather than regarding them as simple, meaningless repetitions.

Theoretically, one could begin creating the internal experience from different aspects, such as, for instance, the experience of the fear or the worry about falling into a trap, the misgivings that his partner would be revealed as monstrous, or the need for special attention. With David, choosing one of these points of entry would have been ineffective because he blocks feeling, has few associations, resists general interpretations and rejects the idea that his body language reveals information in the interview. With a patient such as David, it is important to remain as close as possible to the facts as he presents them in order to arrive at their meaning. All-encompassing interpretations stemming from a conceptual system unknown to him should be avoided, as they could block his curiosity and openness and arouse resistance.

An opportunity to focus on David's feelings about an emotionally charged experience arose in relation to an experience of abandonment. When he was 15 years old his parents decided that he should go to a boarding school. After a short period there, during which he felt humiliated by the other boys in his room, he asked his parents' permission to return home and switch to another school. His parents vetoed his request to return home, maintaining that he was too dependent on them and had to learn to cope independently. I asked him to describe the conversation with his parents.

DAVID: I told them that I was having a difficult time, that I felt humiliated, that they were not considering my feelings, and that I would feel better living at home.
THERAPIST: Can you remember the situation? For instance, where did the conversation take place? With whom did you talk? Which of them was against your return, and any other detail?
DAVID: I don't remember exactly. I think my father was the one who said no. I don't remember exactly when, I think it was a Sabbath, I don't remember exactly.
[David's answer hinted that it was difficult to relate to this experience and to relive the experience. This is the reason that an indirect approach was taken which would be less emotionally threatening.]
THERAPIST: Can you think what a 15-year-old youth would feel, any 15-year-old who was suffering at boarding school and wanted to come

home, when his normally understanding parents refuse him permission?

DAVID: Anger ..., fear ..., anger at not being understood, not having his feelings considered. But I understood why they did it — they wanted to help me overcome my problem.

THERAPIST: Although their intentions were good, that would still arouse strong feelings. I wonder what you *felt*, even though you thought their refusal was justified.

DAVID: I was angry and in a panic, helpless and trapped. [David's face reddened and drops of sweat formed on his brow.]

THERAPIST: What are you feeling now?

DAVID: Nothing, a little excited ... don't know (*smile*).

THERAPIST: I believe that you felt a mixture of anger, fear and helplessness. When you talk about it, you seem to be feeling embarrassed and agitated.

DAVID: True. I was especially disappointed in my mother.

THERAPIST: You expected her, especially, to react differently.

DAVID: Yes.

THERAPIST: Tell me more about this.

DAVID: My father is more rigid, he has a goal and that's that.

THERAPIST: And your mother?

DAVID: More thoughtful.

THERAPIST: She is usually more thoughtful and empathic about your needs, but not at that time.

DAVID: Right.

[It was clear that at this point it would still be difficult to deal with his emotional experience fully. Instead, a more limited goal was established to help David approximate as congruent an experience as possible for him at this stage.]

Around the seventh session, David started to approach an inner congruence. He began the session almost as usual:

DAVID: (*Smiling*) I had a slightly difficult week. I had two dates and didn't feel anything toward either girl.

THERAPIST: It happened again.

DAVID: Yes.

THERAPIST: What made this time so difficult?

DAVID: I don't know what to do any more, I'm afraid it will stay this way.

THERAPIST: You're worried that you won't change and that you'll never be able to have a relationship?

DAVID: Right.

THERAPIST: You sound hopeless.

DAVID: Right.

THERAPIST: I would like you to talk about this feeling.

DAVID: Hopeless. That's it.

THERAPIST: Let's try to get beyond 'that's it.' You're concerned that something troublesome will happen to you if you fail to build a relationship with another person.

DAVID: Yes. I'll be alone.

THERAPIST: What will happen then?

DAVID: It's uncomfortable to be alone.

THERAPIST: Have you ever felt lonely before?

DAVID: At the boarding school.

THERAPIST: Tell me about what you felt.

DAVID: The most difficult feelings came at night. I was so homesick. I wanted so badly not to be there. I wanted to be somewhere warm. I was depressed, down. Sometimes I felt there was no point in living.

THERAPIST: Being at home meant having something to live for.

DAVID: As I went to sleep two days ago, I thought what would happen if, heaven forbid, my mother died, for whatever reason, and for the first time I felt that if that happened I would want to follow her.

THERAPIST: You would want to die too.

DAVID: Yes.

THERAPIST: You are saying that your life is connected to your mother's.

DAVID: Very much so. She's the only person, the most important to me.

THERAPIST: This is the most important relationship that you have and you don't want to lose it.

DAVID: Right.

THERAPIST: There is nobody else who can give you what your mother provides.

DAVID: Exactly.

THERAPIST: What are you feeling now?

DAVID: What I felt last night. Despair ... fear.

THERAPIST: Describe what happens to you when you feel this way.

DAVID: It's the same thing. I don't know ... it's hard, restlessness, despair. [David's face reddens.]

THERAPIST: What else happens?

DAVID: Sometimes I feel that I want to cry but no tears come. I feel restless.

THERAPIST: Describe it, please.

DAVID: It's like exploding. That's it.

THERAPIST: What's going on now? What are you feeling?

DAVID: I don't want to be so alone. But I can't build a relationship.

THERAPIST: Is this feeling familiar?

DAVID: I feel it all the time now.

As the therapy session continued, David repeatedly talked about these feelings. The forming of a congruent experience has begun in these expressions of the strong attachment to his mother and the belief that she is the person who means the most to him, the fear of losing her, the sense of despair and loneliness, and in the reliving of the experience of loneliness at night. His difficulty in creating a congruent experience, especially in allowing himself to feel, is expressed in his attempts to stop the process of raising his feelings to consciousness by saying 'that's it.' This expression serves as a signal that, in his internal experience of that moment, his feelings are so overwhelming that he cannot tolerate them and he wants to stop and control the process.

An interpretation pointing out the relationship between his difficulty in separating from his mother and his lack of readiness for a relationship with a partner seems imperative, but such an interpretation would be pointless, or, worse, block the development of experiential flow. Eventually, the connection will become apparent spontaneously. Creation of a rich and congruent internal experience affects the core of the problem by providing an opportunity for the first time to cope with it through focusing on what he felt during the experience. Needless to say, this interview did not lead immediately to similar experiences in the succeeding sessions, but it did provide an example which facilitated further attempts to create congruent experiences.

Meaning 'in Search of' Reality and Feelings

Rina, a woman about 40 years old, is an example of an intellectualizer who processes information from both external and internal sources by attributing almost mystical meanings to her experiences. She speaks of her feelings as general, unfocused and artificial sensations. Her presenting problem was general dissatisfaction with life. The same pattern appeared in all of her first therapy sessions. The following is a session that is typical of the first few weeks of treatment.

RINA: I don't know what is happening to me lately. I feel like I'm standing at the edge of a void, everything is passing me by. I feel a kind of heaviness. My life is heavy. Everything seems a waste. My marriage seems like an inflated balloon that is going to explode at any moment.
[In spite of these emotional expressions, Rina is incapable at this stage of relating to specific feelings.]
THERAPIST: I hear that you are flooded by so many feelings that you are on the verge of exploding.
RINA: I can't stand it any more.
THERAPIST: What is it like to feel like this?

RINA: Actually, right now I feel detached, I'm only telling you about it. I feel closed off. This is how I feel most of the time. It's connected to the way I live. I want to love Jacob [her husband], but can't get close to him. It's the same with my girlfriends. I get very attached to the people around me, but can't always find things in common . . . I aspire to something spiritual, but feel so mundane. The only thing that lifts my spirits is music. Some form of spiritual aesthetics. But even listening to music I feel detached, kind of 'down.'

Rina sounds as though she is in an intensely emotional state. This state of mind, however, is very general and Rina cannot relate it to any specific moment or event. She is also unaware of emotional changes that are occurring in her. The therapeutic approach adopted to create a congruent experience involved exploring the minute, simple details of her everyday life, and only after this focusing on her feelings. Emphasis was placed on reviewing events in detail while examining the changes in expressions of feeling during the review. This principle is illustrated in the following interview.

THERAPIST: When did this bad mood take over?
RINA: For example, it happened two days ago while I was visiting a friend. I felt good when I went to her home. We spent several hours together. But when I left, I felt these feelings.
THERAPIST: What feelings?
RINA: Detachment, heaviness, emptiness, nervousness. It's hard to define.
THERAPIST: Let's go back to what you did that day. What did you actually do?
RINA: We had lunch together. We talked about our husbands. We talked a lot about drawing. We are studying drawing at the same studio. I felt pretty good while we talked — close to her.
THERAPIST: You say you felt nervous when you left. Exactly when did your mood change?
RINA: Something happened. The phone rang and she talked in such a friendly fashion with someone; she laughed and it was so clear she enjoyed the conversation that then I wanted to leave.
THERAPIST: You felt that you don't want to be there after she enjoyed herself so much with another friend.
RINA: I had a strange feeling for a moment, that she sounds that way when she talks to me on the telephone, and then I had a kind of disappointment that I am not the only one she talks to that way.
THERAPIST: You were disappointed that you are not the only one and wanted to leave.

RINA: I'm embarrassed even to talk about it.
THERAPIST: What are you feeling now?
RINA: Anger. I feel as though she betrayed me.
THERAPIST: Yes.
RINA: It's anger at betrayal, at being abandoned.
THERAPIST: You felt she was disloyal and deserted you, so you became
    angry and then deserted her. [Rina blushed, her eyes clouded, and a
    tear ran down her cheek.] What's happening, what are you feeling now?
RINA: I am remembering my brother's wedding. I was thirteen years old.
    I was terribly nervous and felt awful during the wedding. I had been so
    close to him. In the middle of the wedding, I went mad and ran to him
    yelling, 'don't leave me' in front of all of the guests. [Rina was openly
    crying now.]

After relating this memory and feelings, Rina spoke of her attachment to
her brother, her jealousy of his wife, and of feeling that he had betrayed
her, and her disappointment when he did not take her side during conflicts
with her sister-in-law over the years.

   At the end of this session, Rina was able to grasp the specific meaning of
her friend's telephone conversation, and the meaning of her intense need
for a total, harmonious relationship. This understanding was very different
from her usual tendency to intellectualize in vague terms. The specific
focus on the most minute details of the events brings the accompanying
feelings into awareness spontaneously and the generalized intellectualized
meanings are thus transformed into specific meanings within a congruent
experience.

Feelings 'in Search of' Meaning and Reality

Another important factor interfering with creating congruence in an
experience is undeviating focus on floating feelings unconnected to reality
and meaning. These feelings are usually experienced intensely, but are
unstable and unfocused. Metaphorically, these feelings may be thought of
as 'seeking' anchorage.

   Ilana, a woman of 45, a high-powered, functioning person, sought
treatment for depression that followed her discovery that her husband had
been involved in an extra-marital affair with his secretary. She was
especially offended because she supported him in his grief over the death
of his beloved father while he was planning and enjoying a week's trip to
Paris, the city of romance, with his lover. When she found a hotel bill in the
names of Mr. and Mrs. X, Ilana felt like a discarded old shoe. The internal
incongruence in this experience surfaced immediately, however, when

Ilana repeatedly maintained that she had never loved her husband, that she herself had had a few extra-marital affairs, and that she was continuously on the verge of leaving him. Attempts to work on Ilana's distress through focus on experiences of jealousy, exploitation, deception, and anxieties about ageing did not bring about any relief. Ilana's principal difficulty in creating internal congruence was finding the meaning of the betrayal and of the family's disintegration.

In the first sessions, Ilana spent much time speaking of feelings of nervousness, depression, and restlessness. She was also continually picking at the wound by talking about her husband's affair. One of the goals of treatment was, therefore, to try to discover the hidden meaning of the reality of her life and her feelings. In the initial session, the work focused on encouraging her to question the discrepant rationalizations about her life events, while listening attentively for the development of her feelings. In the fifth session, there was a breakthrough.

ILANA: Nothing has changed. I'm stuck. I don't feel any better. This whole story haunts me and I can't understand why. I keep asking myself why I am so involved in this; after all, I did the same thing to him. I'm so nervous, restless, I feel out of control.

THERAPIST: In spite of what you say to yourself and despite telling me that you don't love your husband and wanted to leave him, your feelings are saying that when he did the same thing, it did not seem the same to you. [This was an attempt to detect new directions in the search for meaning.]

ILANA: I don't know. I keep searching and getting lost. I hate myself for what I'm doing. I've become an angry, nasty bitch. Kind of nosey; I hate that so much.

THERAPIST: Hate?

ILANA: That nosiness. I check phone bills every day, look into his wallet and his diary all the time, and at the bills from Paris that he didn't bother to hide.

THERAPIST: What are you looking for in all those places?

ILANA: I don't know. Maybe to find out if he's lying to me again. An answer to why I'm so bothered about whether he's still trying to put one over on me. What they did in Paris.

THERAPIST: Maybe you're looking in the wrong place?

ILANA: I don't understand.

THERAPIST: The answer is probably in you. I suggest you take a fantasy trip to Paris. Try to reconstruct their trip.

ILANA: ... I can see them getting off the plane, giggling and hugging each other, arriving at their hotel in a taxi ... going to their room ... apparently doing something before they go downstairs for coffee.

THERAPIST: What are they doing?

ILANA: Getting undressed and making love. Later he goes over to the telephone to call me, and she's probably sitting on his lap and they're hugging. I see him treating her like a queen. [Here her feeling tone changed significantly into something akin to excitement, and she began to clear her throat as though she felt choked.] He never treated me that way. That's what's bothering me. I don't care so much about his having an affair or sleeping with her, but I think he did things for her he never did for me. [The feeling is beginning to take on a new meaning.]

THERAPIST: What are you feeling now?

ILANA: Frightened and choked. As though I'm in a panic.

THERAPIST: What does that tell you?

ILANA: That this is terribly important to me ... I want him to treat me that way. I never thought I needed that from him. I was always the queen at home. My mother loved me very much. Everything I did was fine with her. So why do I suddenly feel this way? [Ilana is trying to reject the new meaning, intellectualizing her needs as being exaggerated, and to evade her feelings of neediness.]

THERAPIST: Did your mother really accept everything you did? [The therapist questions Ilana's perception of the past.]

ILANA: Everything. Except when I felt hurt. I could not be hurt or dissatisfied. I had to be OK all the time. I still can't talk to her about what is happening to me. She immediately has loads of advice about what to do, how to get rid of the problem and feel better. She can't be with me in my pain for a single moment.

THERAPIST: Who is available for you when you feel pain?

ILANA: [Long silence — Ilana is struggling not to cry.] My brother [who is deceased]. His eyes would glow when he saw me. I would run to him whenever I had trouble at school. [Here, while connecting feelings and crying, Ilana reconstructs some memories of her brother defending her in school, talking to the parents of children who hit her, comforting her when she failed.]

ILANA: ... I felt I always came first to my brother.

THERAPIST: You lost both first place and your comforter when your brother died.

ILANA: (Silence) That's what I am looking for in my husband's wallet. How stupid. When I think about it now I see that I didn't calm down when he told me that the affair blew up and that he doesn't want to separate and that we are both guilty of contributing to what happened. I think that what I want to hear is that he is sorry for what happened. I want to hear him say, 'If I had known how hurt you would be, I wouldn't have done it.' But he didn't say that. He's never really said he wants me.

THERAPIST: That's what you are looking for in his wallet?

This session opened many new channels for working through Ilana's experience: loss of her brother, her relationship with her mother and her brother, her own contribution to her alienation from her needs and pain, and many other issues. Moreover, the new congruent experience also required much work, although the most important sign that Ilana had succeeded in initiating the process of creating new congruence during this session was her report of feeling relief. For the first time in the long months that had transpired since she learned of her husband's affair, she was able to mobilize the flow of inner experience, break out of her inertia, and stop searching compulsively in her husband's wallet.

Deepening and Expanding the Network of Intra- and Inter-experiential Connections

One of the primary goals of creating internal congruence is to deepen and expand the network of associations within and between experiences. Deepening and expanding the network refer to creating a multitude of connections between different feelings, different meanings, and different perceptions and memories. In this process, a continuous flow of experiences is created and, as the components change, the quality of the experiences changes unceasingly. An important outcome of the flow and variation of experiences is new awareness of self and of reality, which creates internal wealth.

One of the ways to create intra-experiential congruence is by bringing about transitions in the state of mind through transitions in time, between past, present, and fantasied future. This is achieved by asking questions about what the client is experiencing or feeling at the moment, whether he or she has experienced such sensations previously, etc. Another way to mobilize a flow is through transitions in feelings and thoughts. This is elicited by questions about what else the client thinks or feels, what the event or feeling means today, and what it meant in the past, and other questions in this vein. The transitions in the dimension of time are effective principally when the client is 'stuck' in a particular incongruity. The meaning of a specific present feeling may have originated in a similar feeling or situation which occurred in the past. This is also true regarding the meaning of events in the client's life. When an experiential change occurs in a certain aspect, the network may be enriched by focus on the other aspects of the experience.

Another method of expanding the experiential network is by deepening and differentiating. Repeated questions, such as what the client is feeling now, what it feels like, and what else he or she felt in that situation, what other thoughts come to mind, encourage expansion of the network. Often they lead to more discriminating differentiation of the superficial experience and sometimes to deepening the experience.

The reframing of meaning and the relabeling of feeling by the therapist in response to the client's veiled hints is a more active means of expanding the experiential network. Feedback that what the client defines as anger sounds like fright, or that a marital partner sounds demanding rather than responsible, helps clients orient themselves anew to their experience and re-examine their feelings and the meaning of the experience.

Expansion of the network of experiences has consequences that extend beyond expanding consciousness. Enriched and expanded internal congruence moderates feelings of pain and other negative emotions, engendering compensation, and self healing. When the different aspects of the experience of pain are processed and emotional and cognitive associations are raised, the experience of the pain or the painful event is spread out among many more feelings. This dispersal moderates and subdues the pain itself, in that the experience is not composed of one feeling, but rather anchored in a number of feelings with different highlights. The diversity creates mediating processes that moderate between the painful event itself and the experience of the pain, thus alleviating the pain. If the feelings of helplessness and fear experienced during sexual exploitation at an early age by a family member are dispersed among additional feelings of anger, vengeance, pity for the family member, pride at the ability to survive such an experience, and other feelings, the traumatic experience is ameliorated. These diverse emotions and meanings are absorbed more easily and may also be attached to (relatively) more positive experiences related to the trauma.

Examination of the trauma from different perspectives generates this mediation by a variety of emotions and moderates the suffering. The pride, for example, at being able to survive and the meaning of the trauma as an event that can be instructive compensate the individual for his or her terrible pain. The diversification of the reaction to the trauma into many emotions and various meanings facilitates a richer variety of activities and solutions related to the trauma. Hansen and Hansen (1991) expressed similar ideas after performing studies of memory, in which they found that 'repressors' had limited emotional memories as opposed to those who are not 'repressors', whose emotional memories are complex.

Some of the above-mentioned processes are exemplified in a vignette from treatment of Dina, a woman who was seriously suicidal. Dina remembered a very traumatic incident in which she, as a child, deliberately and coldly choked baby chicks to death. The chicks had been a present from her parents. This experience became connected with the no less traumatic event of her husband's suicide. When she learned of his death, the first thought she had was 'Finally, what a relief.' In treatment, she undertook the difficult task of working through her guilt and the fear of her murderous aggression. The treatment session to be described began with her experiences after the previous session in which she had reacted with anger toward the therapist.

DINA: I felt I was awful. I felt as though I was bad and you would never want to see me again. That you'd throw me out of therapy.

THERAPIST: I didn't see your reaction as 'bad.' I felt that you were angry and that you were expressing it directly. [Dina rubbed her hands together, with greater and greater agitation.] I see that you're wringing your hands. What's happening to you now? [Dina remains quiet.] Something important is happening to you.

DINA: (*In a shaky voice*) I'm remembering now ... something awful ... (*long silence*).

THERAPIST: I'd like you to share it with me.

DINA: When I was about twelve years old ... I asked my parents for a dog ... but they always refused ... finally they agreed to buy me chicks ... I was very happy ... and then one day, I don't know why ... I sat down and choked them one by one ... in cold blood ...

THERAPIST: What made you do it?

DINA: I don't remember ... I just remember that I was very angry with a kind of bad anger ... awful.

THERAPIST: Do you remember when and where it happened?

DINA: Can't remember.

THERAPIST: What are you feeling now?

DINA: Awful.

THERAPIST: What else are you feeling?

DINA: That I'm a monster.

THERAPIST: You believe that you're a monster because you killed those chicks, but what are you feeling?

DINA: Bad, guilt.

THERAPIST: What other feelings?

DINA: I'm remembering now how I told you that I was happy about my husband's suicide and how I felt relieved.

THERAPIST: And what is happening to you now as you remember that?

DINA: I'm thinking what a monster I am.

THERAPIST: And what do you feel toward that monster?

DINA: Angry ... afraid.

THERAPIST: Angry and afraid, what else?

DINA: Shame, guilt.

. . .

THERAPIST: Anger, fear, shame, guilt. This monster is apparently very complicated. Let's get to know it better. Describe it to me.

DINA: It's my evil. My anger ... It's the fear that I'll lose control and what I am capable of doing, if I could kill those chicks. It's also guilt that maybe it *is* my fault my husband committed suicide, if I could feel such relief that he did it. Maybe I have something murderous in me.

THERAPIST: This murderous monster feels both fear and guilt.

DINA: The monster is wickedness.

THERAPIST: And the fear and the guilt?

DINA: No, that's not the monster. That's me, I'm afraid and feel guilty. The monster is the murderous anger.

THERAPIST: Where else did you get to know this murderous anger?

DINA: I can't remember ... All my life, my mother told me I was bad. I remember that once my uncle was playing with me on his lap and I think he was touching me in all sorts of places and suddenly my mother came in and said, 'What's this? Put her down right now.' He left the room and she slapped me and called me a little whore.

. . .

THERAPIST: What are you feeling now?

DINA: Angry. [She's again rubbing her hands together.]

THERAPIST: What else is going on in you?

DINA: I'm afraid, afraid of the anger ... afraid I won't be able to control it.

THERAPIST: What does that mean to you?

DINA: That my anger is so great that I won't be able to control it. [She is shaking and again rubbing her hands together.]

THERAPIST: When you have such great anger with no way to let it out, you become afraid that you won't be able to control it.

DINA: Look what I did. How I killed the chicks.

THERAPIST: What else does that mean to you?

DINA: I let my anger out on the chicks.

THERAPIST: Who else were you allowed to take your anger out on?

DINA: No one. Ever.

THERAPIST: Your anger killed the chicks you loved so much.

DINA: I was furious.

THERAPIST: What about?

DINA: Being humiliated, getting beaten, being treated with contempt, like their punching bag.

THERAPIST: It's becoming apparent that your place in this story is unclear. It's not clear whether you were the victim or the aggressor.

DINA: As a child I was a victim. All my life I've been a victim.

THERAPIST: What are you feeling now?

DINA: Rage, anger, rebellion. It's not fair. (*Rubbing her hands*) I think I did to the chicks exactly what my parents did to me.

THERAPIST: So you hurt the very thing you loved, you hurt yourself.

DINA: I feel such anger now, they can go to hell.

THERAPIST: Stay with this anger.

DINA: I feel like screaming. I feel like cursing.

THERAPIST: Say what you feel like saying to them.

DINA: Why did you do that to me? Why did you torture me? I didn't deserve it. What did I do to you? Go to hell ... Why did you put me down so much? What did I do to you? (*Silence*).

THERAPIST: What else?

DINA: I feel like breaking something.

THERAPIST: What do you want to break?

DINA: I simply want to be able to be angry and to throw it back at them. I never dared to be angry at them.

THERAPIST: You're still afraid to be angry, even though you want to let it out.

DINA: Yes.

. . .

THERAPIST: What else are you afraid of?

DINA: From here, too. I get angry and don't dare ... am afraid and embarrassed.

THERAPIST: What is fearful and embarrassing about anger?

DINA: You might make fun of me or laugh at me like they did. They never took me seriously. They always made fun of me when I was angry. They punished me too. [At this point, Dina related another incident from the past in which she experienced anger.]

THERAPIST: And you feel that the fear and the shame take over when you get angry, here too. That is your experience here, feeling ashamed and afraid.

DINA: Not now.

THERAPIST: What are you feeling now?

DINA: Rebellion, relief and also victory.

THERAPIST: What do you mean?

DINA: Simple. I was a better mother. In spite of everything they did to me, I simply did better than my mother did. I never did such things to my children.

THERAPIST: I hear a tinge of pride in your voice.

DINA: Yes, about this, yes. On this issue I dared to rebel against my parents and stand up for myself. I raised my children the way I wanted to.

This segment is only a portion of this difficult session, and, as is true of the other examples, some of the material required many additional sessions of processing. But even in this short segment, one can see how the internal experience which begins with fear of the anger, fear of losing control, feelings of being evil and murderous, becomes a more variegated and congruent experience which has gained many facets by the working-through process. Rebellion, liberated anger, and pride all appeared alongside the guilty anger, shame, and fear. The experiences of the anger shifted from the murder of the chicks to the husband who committed suicide, to her parents, and to the therapist. The meanings changed from perception of self as an evil monster, to self-perception as a victim and also as a victor. This example provides only a partial demonstration of the process of expanding the experiential network and the results of doing so.

One of the paradoxes that becomes evident when focusing on the inner traumatic experience (pain, fear, 'meeting with the monster') is the surprising fact that uncompromising focus on the painful experience terminates in relief and change. Staying with the difficult emotion to the end creates processes which expand the experiential network and thereby mitigate the difficulty of the experience. This effect, in itself, provides relief and changes the person's state of mind. The symbolization of feeling facilitates clarifying it, focusing and defining the global but unclear feeling experience, reducing its dimensions and delimiting it.

Establishing boundaries for the experience allows room for additional emotions to enter awareness and assists in organizing the incongruent experience internally. Expanding the specific context by creating a congruent experience and by connecting the experience to other experiences furthers more refined differentiation. Differentiation and integration transform the traumatic experience and reduce its magnitude. In this fashion, Dina's monstrous evil became a smaller part of her personality by comparison with other parts. From a theoretical viewpoint, this process demonstrates an important adaptive function. Individuals' basic wish to eliminate painful emotions motivates them to search repeatedly for an avenue to release the painful experience. This powerful motivation leads the individual to review the experience constantly, eliciting a vast stream of associations in a search for an outlet and resolution. This is the power that enables and propels the working through of the experience, expediting the search for new meanings, bringing new emotions and realities into awareness in the attempt to attain relief.

Long-term Processing of the Experience: Assimilation and Accommodation

In the previous chapter, the assimilation—accommodation process was described as a process of gradual change of experiences and schemas. This process was described as a system of forward and backward movements, disengagement of previous links between the various aspects within the experience, changes in meanings and in perceptions of reality, retrieval of new memories more appropriate to these changes, and evoking new emotions. In the wake of these changes, the entire experience is transformed. From the perspective of the congruence or incongruence of an experience, assimilation—accommodation is a series of transitions from congruent or incongruent experiences to a new congruent experience. The latter is disrupted again by additional perceptions of reality, new meanings, or the appearance of new emotions.

Obviously, this new congruence creates its own changes. From the long-range perspective, the treatment process may be considered as movement from a situation of incongruent experience to a high level of congruence and integration. The processing of experiences by means of assimilation and accommodation was illustrated in the preceding chapter through the story by Don Ben Ahmotz, *To Remember and Forget*. Now the same process will be described within the context of treatment, with emphasis on the changes which occur during this long process.

The transformations of experiences between incongruence and congruence in a specific aspect of a client's life will be described, rather than the details of the entire therapeutic process. It should be noted that the changes in the structure and organization of the experience do not occur exclusively in the clinic. The effects of the therapeutic work or changes in realities of the client's life may spontaneously generate additional new experiences.

Gill, a married woman about 35 years old, came for treatment of a clinical depression, with presenting symptoms of depression in the form of apathy, insomnia, nightmares, and compulsive thoughts of death. At the beginning of therapy, she immediately presented a more focused problem. In spite of loving her husband and feeling very attached to him, she also felt intense rejection toward him. Although Gill considered him handsome, she claimed she did not feel attracted to him because he was relatively short in stature. Gill maintained that this interfered with spiritual closeness and full harmony in their relationship. She often found herself attracted to other men, especially those who reflected a spiritual authority.

This focused problem indicated discrepancies among her emotions, and incongruence between her tendency to idealize her husband and her actual feelings toward him. Her description of his thoughtfulness and kindness toward her was also incongruent with her feelings of rejection and wish to divorce him.

The initial step to delimit the inner incongruence was attempted through a role play of the inner drama of loving and rejecting. The loving Gill spoke of her husband's thoughtfulness, his reliability, his strength and integrity, and his patience. The rejecting Gill focused mostly on feeling ashamed that her husband is not tall enough for her taste, and that she recoils from physical contact with him. When role playing the rejecting Gill, she sounded angry, and she subsequently described feeling pressured in his presence. The rejecting Gill expressed a wish that her husband's plans to go abroad for a few weeks would be implemented quickly so that she could rest and think about their relationship quietly.

When Gill's husband did go abroad on business, her depression was not alleviated entirely, but she did feel greatly relieved. Yet, she maintained close contact with him by telephone and daily faxes. She brought all problems to his attention. Although she did not feel she missed him, she did look forward to his return. During this period, Gill spoke of how helpless she was and how her husband was her own private savior. As more time elapsed, Gill saw more and more of her husband's positive attributes. Then, as his return from abroad became imminent, she again began to feel repelled by him. Gill could distinguish between feelings she felt when her husband was close to her physically and when he was far away from her, but the nature of the conflict was still a mystery.

When her husband returned from his trip, Gill again felt the conflict in all its intensity. Her husband demanded that she decide about their future. Gill began to feel that this was a heavy burden on her. She then discovered another paradox in her relationship with her husband. He placed the entire weight of the decision regarding their future on her without his taking a clear stand on the issue. Despite his giving her much power, she experienced herself as helpless about making the smallest decisions. Thus, her husband gave Gill a free hand in making 'the big decisions,' while all of the daily 'little decisions' were his entirely to initiate, so that he seemed to be a savior.

Gill was beginning to clarify some of the discomfort she felt in her married life. She started to realize that her contradictory feelings were strongly linked to her husband's double bind messages, which conveyed many demands yet made her feel totally helpless. Her new perception of the reality of her life and the meaning of this reality as confusing and containing contradictory messages were congruent with her contradictory and inconsistent feelings toward her husband.

Objectively, the partial equilibrium that Gill attained in her experience was somewhat artificial at this point, and it was not clear that Gill's condition was entirely a direct result of her husband's behavior. What is described here is the evolution of her inner incongruence into phenomenologically more congruent experiences during her inner searching.

The first drastic change in Gill's experience occurred in the wake of an apparently insignificant evening when she went with her husband to a concert in a community center. At the end of the concert, an announcement was made about the next cultural event. As the details were unclear, Gill's husband asked her to go over and clarify them. When she did not come back with a clear answer, her husband gave her a piercing look. That night, Gill did not let her husband touch her, but she could not understand why. In the treatment session, I asked Gill to describe the experience in detail as though it were occurring at that moment.

GILL: I went back and told Jack [her husband] that I still didn't understand what they meant. Jack gave me a kind of angry look and asked why I can't get a clear answer to something so simple? And I felt confused and that he was right.

THERAPIST: Let's go back to the moment that Jack said what he said. What are you feeling?

GILL: Kind of uncomfortable. I want to shake myself out of it, I feel restless.

THERAPIST: What else?

GILL: Anger. I'm really angry. When I think about it now, he was really putting me down.

THERAPIST: You were angry at the way he related to you.

GILL: Now that I think about it, why didn't he go to ask the chairman himself? Why does he use me and then insult me?

In her anger following her interpretation of her husband's behavior as insulting, Gill achieved a new, congruent experience. The confusing conflict about him gave way to a clear emotion. Apparently for the first time, Gill formed and assimilated a new, clear feeling toward her husband. She was not, as yet, able to accommodate the new feeling to her basic experiences of helplessness and of aspiring for spiritual experiences and harmony. In the session which followed, Gill reported that her depression and thoughts of death had worsened. It gradually became evident that Gill regarded anger as frightening, hurtful, destructive, even murderous. Gill could not assimilate — accommodate the experience of being an angry person and tried to deny it. When she was asked whether she had ever experienced such an emotion, she remembered that when she was first married, she felt angry when her husband hurt her; but she never expressed the anger and quickly succeeded in overcoming it. Gill was attempting to achieve the unattainable goal of going through life and its frustrations without ever feeling anger. In her inner world, there was no room for anger.

In one of the following sessions, Gill expressed her reawakened misery about deciding whether or not to stay in her marriage. Her voice carried a tone of despair and pleading. When I showed her that she was asking me to save her from her misery, Gill agreed and emphasized that indeed she is totally helpless, and that this problem was too heavy a burden for her. When I continued to show interest in these feelings instead of offering advice about a solution, she reacted with annoyance. When asked about her feelings, she answered that she is angry, that she is not getting help, and that she does not know if there is any point in continuing therapy.

Beginnings of anger reappeared about my unhelpful response when, as her therapist, she thought I should be responding to her request to be guided out of her misery. Surprisingly, she opened the next session by declaring that the previous session had done her good. 'For two days I was angry at you,' she said, 'but then I noticed that instead of feeling depressed and despairing, I was feeling angry. I slowly understood that I am not so weak, nor so depressed, and anger can give me strength and power. By the way, after that realization, I started driving again.'

In Gill's eyes, the meaning of anger was transformed from destruction and death to strength and power. My inability to provide her with the requested help aroused her frustration and anger. During the days after that session, the anger led her to a new interpretation of her behavior and feelings. Anger and the ability to feel angry were now interpreted and experienced as self-assertion and strength. On this occasion, the assimilation of the anger was more complete and balanced and led to accommodation, that is, internal change. Following this new congruent experience, Gill viewed her relationship with her husband in a new way. She was gradually able, with continued work in therapy, to identify her needs to be saved and merge harmoniously into total dependency. Gill was also able to cope with her husband's encouragement of her dependency on him, and to recognize that this encouragement reflected both her husband's needs as well as her wish to be dependent on him.

This anecdote schematically illustrates the process of assimilation and accommodation through a series of movements from one incongruent inner experience to another, until a more stable and coherent congruent experience was achieved. Gill experienced an inner incongruence when unable to tolerate a conflict about her unsatisfying relationship with her husband. Love meant dependency; anger meant destructiveness. Her husband was perceived as savior and feelings of anger about him were suppressed. Gradually, she started to acknowledge her anger and express it toward both her husband and the therapist. Simultaneously, the meaning of anger changed from being a destructive force to an expression of assertiveness. These transformations were also associated with changes in the perspective of her husband and of her self-image as a weak and helpless person.

CONSTRUCTING CONGRUENCE BY RECONSTRUCTING MEMORY

The importance of memory has been discussed in previous sections of this chapter and in the previous one. A significant number of theoreticians and researchers investigating perception and memory have established that memory is a process of construction – reconstruction, not a photograph of reality. Bartlett (1932) maintains that memory reflects one's position in relation to reality rather than reproducing actual traces of reality. Moreover, reconstruction of memory is intended to justify the individual's present position regarding the reality and not necessarily to reproduce facts.

Neisser (1967) is even more radical in describing memory as a process of reconstructing ever-changing reality in the light of current circumstances. Changes and distortions of reconstructed memories also do not maintain their initial form, but are always in flux. On the basis of this view, the process of reconstructing memory could be described as playing with a kaleidoscope, in which a change in its position results in reorganization of the structures and the picture obtained. The different components are in fact the same, but the different combination brings about drastic changes. This is also true of memory: when the components of memory are reorganized, a new reality is created.

Research findings support these ideas, as we have seen (Bower, 1981, Conway and Ross, 1984, and Isen, 1987). Greenwald (1980) also believes that the self is a totalitarian entity who will subjugate past and present information to protect its own image from unwanted change, just as Orwell's 'big brother' controlled information distribution. All individuals, according to Greenwald, use their history for their own present needs and continually rewrite it in order to protect their positive self-image or for other similar purposes. Elizabeth and Geoffrey Loftus (1980), who also rely on a long list of research studies, maintain that it is possible to change an accurate version of the past into a distorted version. They claim that sometimes this process is irreversible, in that the original version cannot be recalled accurately. They hypothesize that memory is usually organized into parallel versions rather than only one version, so that mistaken memories of the past can easily be induced.

The following anecdote from an article by the Israeli writer Yitzhak Auerbach Orpaz in the newspaper *Yediot Aharonot* (16 April 1984) tells of the manner in which an author may exploit reality events and transform them into the materials of his creation. The anecdote, which is connected to his book *The Dowager*, clearly and persuasively illustrates the way in which opinion, belief, feeling, and memory intervene with each other so the author may meet his own needs and exploit reality for the sake of the story, without being at all aware of the process.

The Dowager begins with a somewhat traumatic occurrence. The protagonist, deeply engrossed in his dream and his research into feminine archetypes, gets up from his work desk and goes over to his window to relax and feast his eyes on the poplar tree outside his window. He opens the shutter, and — the tree is gone. It transpires that the downstairs neighbors have cut it down, and our aging hero feels as though he has been struck down in his prime. This feeling will remain with him during the entire story.

And in reality: Outside the window of my fourth floor apartment, there is a poplar tree. It is the only tree, and, aside from it, all that graces the view from my window are bare roofs accommodating solar water heaters and antennas. The tree, obviously, is intact, available for my contented viewing. Am I anxious that it may be cut down one day? Apparently. There is a residents' committee and a gardener and there are the city workers' electric saws — you can never be sure. I told the member representing the residents' committee that I hoped the gardener would not suddenly decide to 'take care of' the tree, and the man reassured me, 'What do you mean, Mr. Orpaz? We would never touch your tree.' I did not understand why he said 'your' — after all, the tree belongs to all the neighbors. Anyway, I felt reassured.

In the story, the tree was truncated. In reality, it remained intact. In the story, the tree is an object of identification and anxiety. In reality, perhaps there was a basis for concern, but after clarifying the situation, I could relax: there was no rational reason to worry. In this way, a suitable balance was established between facts and emotions, and I could maintain a reasonable emotional distance from the story of my biographical poplar tree.

And then, a peculiar thing happened. Walking home from a literary evening devoted to *The Dowager*, in which I told of my biographical tree versus the tree in the book and of my reassuring conversation with the man from the residents' committee, I suddenly stopped, dumbfounded. 'Wow,' I said to myself, 'Are you sure you didn't make up this whole thing about the residents' committee?' The next day, when I asked the man from the residents' committee whether we had held such a conversation, he looked wonderingly at me and said, 'What happened to you? We don't need a gardener. There's no garden here, just the weeds we burn once a year.' And for the first time I thought, 'what a shrewd and devious manipulator exists inside me. It sold me this story in order to neutralize my real anxiety, the deep one, that my tree would be cut down, the tree I am so accustomed to that I identify with it, so that the more I accrue years and loneliness, my identification with it grows deeper — and it changed the facts in front of my eyes (on the subject of a garden and gardener which never existed in my neglected yard) and filtered the story of talking to the member of the residents' committee into my consciousness — and all this for one purpose and one purpose only: to enable the storyteller within me to treat emotionally charged, threatening material as though they were cold building materials — stones and gravel.'

Another anecdote from the newspaper *Yediot Aharonot* was told during an interview of Yuval Neria by Yaron London, when Neria's book *Fire*, about the Yom Kippur War, was published.

> Yuval Neria chose to write his book in the form of fiction. In the introduction to the book, he avers that, 'All the characters are composites.' Why does he need such disguise? 'This made it easy for me, since until now I have not been able to remember the facts. I simply did not believe that faithful, accurate documentation could be achieved. I'll give you an example: At the beginning of the book, there is a description of the parade in Jerusalem just before the war. Do you know when I remembered that it took place? Only after I had given the publisher the first handwritten draft of the book.
> 'That is incredible. There was nothing traumatic about the parade that would make me erase it from my memory. So why did I forget it? Maybe because of the contrast between the orderly, safe parade and what came afterwards.'
> He was right. Literature is always more faithful than documentation, which is deceptive.   *Yediot Aharonot*, 22 September 1989

This perspective of memory justifies Janet's revising the hypnotized patient's memory to erase the traces of the traumatic experience, and thus eradicate the various symptoms that plagued her as a result of the trauma. A similar therapeutic principle was utilized by the late psychiatrist, Yehudah Fried (see Levi, 1992). He established therapeutic 'trials' of paranoid patients who suffered from strong, irrational guilt feelings. The 'punishment' meted out by the 'judge' relieved the guilt. Fried's use of this technique affirmed his willingness to distort reality to achieve the therapeutic goal of reducing suffering.

When we return to the perspective of inner experiential congruence, it may be fruitful to examine, use, and stimulate various versions of memory to create inner experiential harmony and sometimes to disrupt artificial, rigid harmony to create a more harmonious organization in the future. If the memory is, in fact, enlisted in the service of maintaining existing positions and emotions, it is likely that the client can be helped to find other perspectives than those which he or she is striving to obtain.

CONCLUSION

The main objective of the therapeutic approach as suggested by the inner congruence – incongruence model is the restoration of internal congruence within the subjective experience. For this purpose, various therapeutic principles are employed, including focusing on the experience, engaging different aspects of the experience and intensification of feelings. This therapeutic approach is similar in many ways to techniques which focus on emotional working through and emotional processing. But it is distinct from these techniques by its balanced focus on emotion, meaning, and perception of reality. The main objective is integration and inner harmony between the three aspects of the experience, with equal weight given to each aspect. As demonstrated in these chapters, therapy is a voyage to the inner subjective experience of the troubled mind. When successful, it results in an inner harmony, inner expansion, and richer awareness, all of which are different facets of consciousness. The outcome of this expansion is relief, inner integration, and self-expansion.

CHAPTER 8

Relationships Between the Different Theoretical Models

Five theoretical models representing different conceptualizations of the unconscious have been discussed in this book, as well as the implications of these varying conceptualizations for pathology and therapy. Now, the following four theoretical alternatives regarding the relationships between these approaches will be examined:

1. These five models present different theories, each of which explains the unconscious in a different way.
2. Although the differing theories utilize different terminology, they actually offer identical explanations of the same phenomena.
3. The different approaches represent different unconscious processes, which are related to different problems. A specific problem activates a specific unconscious process, and different processes occur in parallel fashion in the same person if he or she suffers from more than one form of problem.
4. The different models reflect the unconscious processes of different personality structures. One type of unconscious may be more characteristic of a certain type of personality than of another type.

The first possibility assumes that each of these five models is different from the others and provides a unique perspective of the unconscious. As described in this book, the unconscious is qualitatively different in each of the theories. The psychoanalytic model views substitution as the essential process; the humanist model regards inhibition as the principal process; the dissociative model views split and lack of control as the main characteristics; the internal homeostasis model defines internal incongruence as the heart of the unconscious; while the cognitive model emphasizes subliminal information processing and hidden schemas as the essence of the unconscious.

Differences between the various theories may be highlighted by the different explanations they provide for a specific phenomenon. This is demonstrated in the different possible interpretations of Judd's behavior in *Compulsion* (see Chapter 2). Although the events in the book are described from a psychoanalytic point of view, and distinguishing between the facts and the theoretical interpretations is sometimes difficult, Judd's behavior will have different meanings in the light of the different perspectives of the various theoretical orientations.

Psychoanalysis regards Judd's unconscious behavior as a substitute expression of a dual wish: to die and be reborn as a girl.

The humanist inhibition model emphasizes the inhibition of true self-expression, leading to formation of a false self-representation which protects the true self but diminishes the self's resources and limits it to a rigid way of life. This process definitely characterizes Judd, whose personal and sexual identity were not only inhibited — they were cruelly attacked and negated by sending him to a girls' school, disguised as a girl, for several years. Rejection of his sexual identity could hardly be more extreme! This is the background for his becoming dependent on Arty, who seemed to represent a loving and accepting figure, and for his adopting the false identity of paranoid superiority to defend himself from feeling his true, injured self. The aggressive act may be regarded as an expression of anger at the rejection of his identity and love, and also as seeking inner awakening, excitement and life.

In the multiple control centers version of neo-dissociation, the events of Judd's childhood, attendance at a girls' school, sexual stimulation by the maid, and his mother's death, can be regarded as traumas causing dissociative reactions. Undoubtedly, Judd would have experienced attending a girls' school at a young age as a violent mental trauma arousing feelings of helplessness, but also tremendous aggression and anger. The school experience, helplessness, and anger were split off from the central control systems and functioned as the nucleus of a separate, dissociated personality. Because this encapsulated nucleus gained control of his life, Judd attached himself to a dominating, aggressive personality, and eventually released the murderous aggression which emanated from his dissociated personality nucleus. Judd's behavior glaringly demonstrates lack of executive control, especially in relation to aggression.

The lack of inner congruence model focuses on internal discrepancies and achievement of false harmony as unconscious processes. Judd's internal experiential world is comprised of many incongruities which originated in problems of sexual identity development and early sexual experiences. The incongruity between his feelings of anger and frustration in reaction to his parents' humiliating and unjust treatment, and his courteous and obedient 'good boy' behavior, is the deepest expression of this. According to this model, Judd felt tremendous aggression, unconnected to meaning which would have clarified it for him and enabled him to establish internal congruence between that meaning and the other aspects of his experiences. In all of his relationships, Judd behaved like the good child — to his mother, father, and to his good friend, Arty. Even when he felt anger and jealousy about Arty's flirting with girls, Judd overtly remained the courteous and well-behaved friend. Judd's active participation in the crime, which is so contradictory to the image of the good boy, only strengthens the hypothesis that there is a vast discrepancy between his different feelings. It is unlikely that Judd connected his tremendous aggressive feelings with memories of his mother's unjust behavior toward him. Finally, through his relationship with Arty, Judd established artificial harmony between his angry feelings and the philosophy of the superior being by which he justified acting out his aggression toward innocent people.

Cognitive theory, which is based on thought and information processing, would seek understanding of Judd's unconscious processes by defining the hidden schemas which cause him to act without awareness. Several different schemas may be identified, such as those relating to hostility and grandiose hatred, but probably the most relevant schema for Judd is that which depersonalizes human relationships. In this schema, people are objects to be manipulated. The only two ways of relating to people are either to manipulate them or be manipulated by them. The strong and talented people manipulate the others, and the weak are manipulated. There is no middle ground, nor are there limits to exploiting others for one's own ends; even murder is permissible. This schema would be appropriate to someone like Judd, who was himself manipulated and exploited by his parents as a helpless child, and later to some extent by his good friend. His attachment to Arty, a genius at manipulation, helped transform Judd from a passive, helpless, manipulated person into a murderous manipulator himself. All of this transpired outside Judd's awareness of the principles and rules governing his behavior.

Conceptual analysis and comparison of the different models may enhance our understanding of the relationship between them. In comparing the psychoanalytic model with the cognitive model, Eagle (1987) notes that both models include several similar principles. These consist of the following: unconscious contents may influence behavior; conscious information processing and thought patterns are different from those which are unconscious; various and contradictory unconscious contents may exist simultaneously, whereas in consciousness the contents are organized around only one central idea at a time; and the unconscious is inferred from its effects rather than being overtly perceptible.

Eagle indicates two principal differences between the psychoanalytic and the cognitive views of the unconscious. In the psychoanalytic model, the unconscious is dynamic; it functions on the basis of conflicts, anxieties, defenses, and energy. In the cognitive model, the unconscious is a result of thought processes and information processing. The relationship between conscious and unconscious is created by the form of the information processing. Thus, for example, unconscious contents may be determined by the amount of information flowing into awareness at one time, by the intensity of the stimuli, concentration, attention, and/or the level of skill in performing the behavior — but not necessarily by anxiety.

A second principal difference is the quality of the unconscious contents which are retrieved and appear in consciousness. According to Eagle (1987), Freud assumes that unconscious contents are identical to the conscious material that has been retrieved from the unconscious. In other words, the unconscious contents do not undergo any basic changes within the unconscious, although they may be organized differently in the unconscious to the conscious. When repression is lifted, the original contents are simply exposed. By contrast, the cognitive model emphasizes that retrieval itself is information processing. Because the retrieved contents are not passively stored in the unconscious, but undergo reconstructive processes which change their meaning according to their context and processing, they are not identical to conscious material.

Spiegel et al. (1988) differentiate between the dissociation model and the psychoanalytic repression model. Repression is the result of developmental difficulties, conflicts, and internal processes, such as instinctual desires which arouse anxiety. In contrast, the dissociative model is based on the interrelationship between humans and their environment. As opposed to repression, dissociation occurs under conditions of traun'a and experienced helplessness, lack of control, exploitation, and humiliation. The situation itself is one of lack of control, and the experience of internal lack of control is a mirror image of the reality situation. The dissociative split is an attempt to split off and distance the experience of humiliation and helplessness.

Hilgard (1986) also compares his dissociative model with classical psychoanalytic theory, but his comparison differs from that of Spiegel et al. Hilgard agrees that dissociation occurs in reality situations that are traumatic or arouse conflict, and that the experience which is split off is usually connected with a specific event or tangible experience which can be reconstructed. By contrast, repression reflects an experiential entity which cannot be reconstructed, but only built through interpretations based on inferences and conjecture.

The unconscious, conceptualized as based on repression, 'contains' early childhood experiences, instinctual activities and processes, and primary mental activities, similar to primary process thinking. These do not reflect tangible occurrences, but rather mental activities which cannot be expressed in words. The earliest of childhood experiences are also repressed; these occur and are repressed at a pre-verbal stage before the child has developed the ability to formulate events as they occur, to organize them, and to store them as memories of concrete events. Repression, therefore, involves difficulty in identifying and reconstructing primitive mental processes, which transpire without involvement of cognitive-linguistic mechanisms. The psychoanalytic work of removing repression is merely the work of reconstruction and interpretation with the help of an *a priori*, hypothetical conceptual system which may not reflect reality.

Hilgard presents a clinical example which illustrates the essential difference between repression and dissociation. A man came to the hospital seeking treatment for a limp which he had developed suddenly. When a physiological examination revealed no pathology, the doctors decided to attempt hypnotic treatment. Under hypnosis, the man reconstructed the experience of a conflict with his employer, during which he felt a strong urge, which he suppressed, to kick the employer. His limp appeared immediately after this incident. The treatment, still using hypnosis, was specific and focused on the phenomenon itself; reconstruction and understanding of the experience cured him. Apparently, the patient's wish to suppress the kick caused his functional inability to move his leg properly, and led to splitting off of the entire experience by his losing control of his leg and forgetting the incident. Treatment of the dissociation was sufficient to remove the symptom. A psychodynamic interpretation, Hilgard maintains, would infer a conflict from childhood in relation to his authoritarian father deep within the patient's personality; if conceptualized as repression, this would belong to the level of the unconscious. Dissociation and repression, therefore, relate to different levels of the personality, to different aspects of time, and to external reality as opposed to internal motivations.

Comparison of the dissociative and the cognitive models reveals significant similarities and differences between them. The dissociative model links dissociative splits to a traumatic experience. This model asserts that certain external experience cannot be integrated with existing structures, which is the reason for its pathological splitting off through dissociation. As was demonstrated, the cognitive model does not require the existence of a trauma or threat to stimulate unconscious processes; these are ordinary elements of cognitive activity.

On several issues, these two models concur. First, the cognitive model and the dissociative models agree in concluding that the lack of an appropriate schema for integrating information or an experience creates difficulties in perceiving the information or digesting the experience.

Conceptually, a traumatic situation or internal threat are similar conditions. In both cases an appropriate schema to perceive the stimulus or experience is missing. Secondly, the two models seem to argue that during information processing, any experience or information which relates to the 'self' becomes conscious, whereas information which is perceived as distant or irrelevant to the 'self' is processed out of awareness, or unconsciously. Hence, trauma on one hand and irrelevant information on the other are involved in unconscious information processing (see Kihlstrom, 1984).

The dissociation and the incongruence models differ principally in postulating splitting as opposed to internal disharmony as the central process of the unconscious. In contrast to the dissociation model, the incongruence model does regard splitting as only one specific case of unconscious processes. Furthermore the incongruence model focuses on the subjective phenomenological experience, whereas the lack of control version focuses on personality systems, such as the executive or monitoring systems.

The inhibition model has many obvious differences from most of the others. Its uniqueness lies in regarding unconscious contents as positive potentials which have not been actualized, rather than reflections of problems or difficulties. Moreover, the unconscious process is not an actual process in the form of repression, splitting off, or information processing, but rather a situation of absence, lack of actualization, or a potential that could come into being.

The second alternative regarding the relationships between the various models is that these models all relate to the same processes and differ only in terminology and conceptualization of phenomena. Eagle (1984) concurs with this approach. He contends that all of the models consist of purely theoretical concepts which facilitate organizing observation and understanding of human behavior. According to this view, psychological theory is not a reflection of truth, but only serves as a framework for understanding human behavior and internal world. The same would apply to the unconscious; the various models of the unconscious also do not represent truth, but rather are convenient concepts for understanding humankind. Eagle concludes, as is logical from this viewpoint, that a therapist and his or her client may choose any of these models, accommodate the model of choice to the particular person, and utilize it to achieve change.

The third possibility is to regard these different models as conceptualizations of different constellations of human problems. The models are not mutually exclusive alternatives, but rather conceptual representations of a variety of personal and life problems. If so, several different unconscious processes might occur simultaneously within the same individual. Hilgard (1986) suggests such a viewpoint in his comparison between the repression and dissociation models. This view seems to assume that repression relates essentially to early and long-term conflict situations and to early developmental problems; inhibition is related to inhibiting, restrictive and rigid life conditions and to series of deficiencies in actualizing potentials; the dissociation model describes reactions to sudden and overwhelming traumatic situations; the incongruence model is related to situations causing internal discrepancies, behavior which is not congruent with a value system, inconsistency, or other incongruities. The cognitive model does not relate to specific life problems, but to a specific aspect or process existing in the situations represented in each of the theoretical models. In this case, the specific unconscious cognition could be a determinant of repression, inhibition, or dissociation.

Finally, there is a fourth possibility: the hypothesis that the diverse models do not represent differing theories or problems, but rather different unconscious processes within different people. In other words, each model could represent a set of processes which occur in a specific personality, according to the character and structure of the personality. According to this view, each person utilizes a specific process. Not everyone will repress or dissociate mental material; some will use inhibition exclusively, whereas others' characters and customary patterns of activity will engender repression but not dissociation.

A detailed examination of this hypothesis is in order. Repression is appropriate to the hysterical character, because of such people's emotional constitution and unique cognitive style. The hysterical character, as described by Shapiro (1965), lacks focus and usually perceives in generalized fashion. As their strong emotional reactions often interfere with their objectivity, they are likely to deny, forget, change their mind, and become involved in one problematic situation after another. Their characteristic defenses, in addition to repression, are denial, reaction formation, displacement and considerable exaggeration. To such a person, whose cognitive style consists of generalizing and obscuring, it is 'easier' to forget, to repress, to change reality, and exchange one feeling for another or one object for another. Thus, it seems reasonable that the hysterical person would be inclined to cope with stress by using repression as a means of removing contents from awareness.

By comparison, the analytic or intellectualizing person, who normally perceives acutely, clearly and precisely, sensitively observing each detail and minute distinction, will be unable to repress, forget, or deny material which he or she has cognitively organized so clearly. Such people tend to focus on the source of their problems rather than denying them. Their principal defenses are rationalization and intellectualization, which naturally sharpen perception rather than blurring it. Intellectualizers tend to create splits between the various elements of their experience. It is true that they will focus on the cognitive aspects of their experience, but they may split off and ignore the feeling aspects of the experience, using mechanisms of isolation, which separate feeling from cognition. This type of person may feel most comfortable coping with unpleasant experiences by creating internal incongruence or false congruence, rather than using repression.

The obsessive-compulsive person is similar to the intellectualizer, combining the intellectualizer's style with difficulty controlling his or her internal world. This type of person behaves in a strange fashion, using ritualistic behaviors and extreme organization and order, in an attempt to preserve internal control or the illusion of such control. People of this personality type seek external power, in the form of an authority, law, ideal, value, or norm, to help them control themselves, make choices, or decide between alternatives. It might be assumed that such people would react by dissociating their behavior from the control of the executive control system through the use of automation and ritualization.

The restrained and introverted person, who tends to focus on his or her internal world, is inclined to react to external threat or conflict by 'backing off' or turning inward. Their typical defenses might be inhibition, regression, turning against the self, and limiting the ego's development, all of which are appropriate to their general tendency to introversion. It may be assumed that people with these tendencies will cope with difficulties by inhibiting expression of their inner potentials.

AN ATTEMPT AT THEORETICAL INTEGRATION

The psychoanalytic substitution model is no longer the only model of unconscious processes. Today, dissociation, actualizing potentials, unconscious information processing, and subliminal perception are all regarded as processes involved in the formation of the unconscious. It is acknowledged that the mechanisms which 'send' the contents to the unconscious are not exclusively repression and forgetting, but also loss of control, splitting, inhibition, and receipt of information from the external world in a manner that circumvents consciousness. Moreover, the unconscious entities are not necessarily related to a threat and anxiety, but also may be expressions of an essential reservoir of positive contents and processes that contribute to positive adjustment. The unconscious world, with its processes, is apparently richer than that portrayed by the psychoanalytic model.

Many of the revisions in the picture of the unconscious are due to changed perceptions of the essence of humankind. Freud determined that the truth (instincts and childhood experiences) is innate, and that coping with this truth frees us from suffering (in the broad sense of the word). By contrast, the cognitive approach, and to a certain extent the other approaches as well, maintain that 'truth' must be constructed. It is not innate. We are not composed of a true essence, or at least we do not have one exclusive essence. We construct our truth through interaction with the world or from virtually endless internal potentials. The cognitive and humanist theoreticians replaced determinism with reconstructionism.

This transition from determinism to attempting continually to understand fluctuating external and internal worlds points the way to totally different methods of coping with suffering and anxiety. According to psychoanalysis, redemption will be attained only through revelation of the truth. All of the defenses are forms of denying truth, and denial is disastrous. People must reveal the true roots of their anxiety and suffering rather than denying these truths, in psychoanalytic theory. Reconstructionism changes this view regarding the truth and leads to the belief that, just as we have understood and built suffering on the basis of perceptions and convictions we adopted, we can shape and build happiness.

Past and present are interdependent, and each may influence the other. I am reminded again of a patient who spent many therapy hours talking about his miserable childhood, but when he brought some family photographs from the past, he suddenly discovered his rejecting mother hugging him. He remarked that perhaps it had not been so terrible and that his bad relationship with his mother may have been an exaggeration or a fantasy. He illustrated that the truth is more malleable than previously thought; it is not always uni-directional nor deterministic.

Rather than seeking the truth in therapy, perhaps it is more efficacious to search for and create meaning. Any fact may have many meanings. A young woman complained that her life was wasted. She came from a rich, licentious home where she was both neglected and rejected, and at the age of 18 required hospitalization in a mental hospital. When she discovered that her psychotic episode was basically a disturbance of identity, which reflected her inability and unwillingness to identify with what she regarded as her parents' immorality, she realized that her suffering was not in vain and felt relief. Had she identified with them, she might have avoided her psychotic episodes, but she would have resembled her parents. Is this the truth? I am convinced that this is one of the possible meanings, not the Truth. This constructed meaning opened the door to a more meaningful life. We are capable of building variegated structures which augment and multiply possible meanings in life. Theoretically, this multiplicity of meanings engenders a different life approach from that generated by the psychoanalytic concept of fixation on an unconscious problem. The question of how to choose between the various meanings is not for discussion here. But the idea that we provide flexibility and meaning to our behavior and to our environment as well as to our past clearly leads to the concept of an unconscious which is transfigured by these different meanings.

Cognitive research surprised us by revealing that the unconscious is sophisticated and intelligent, capable of accommodating multiple meanings, of perceiving subliminally with great precision, and of learning an abundant variety of material. These findings contrast to some extent with the Freudian unconscious, in which perception is subordinate to the instincts.

It seems to me that the concept of internal incongruence may serve to integrate the apparently different approaches to the unconscious, and contribute to a more encompassing and productive theoretical understanding of the concept of the unconscious.

According to this approach, the essence of the unconscious lies not in lack of knowledge or forgetting, but rather in inner discrepancy and in the quality of the knowledge. The concept of discrepancy is a general one, which may contain the more particularized concepts from the other theories that have been discussed in this book. Repression, inhibition, inner split, dissociation, dissonance — all of these are examples of discrepancies. It would seem, therefore, that the concept of incongruence is more general and encompassing than the other concepts of the unconscious.

The concept of internal congruence or incongruence also relates to the ramifications of the connections between the various components of the experience. The harmonious, congruent experience contains many internal connections. Events become associated with other events which are similar (from the perspective of meaning), specific feelings arouse other feelings and particular meanings arouse associations to other similar meanings, and all of these create a rich and polychromatic network of experiences, which expands awareness and consciousness. Internal disharmony may be created when one of the components does not appear at all in the experience. In other words, the lack of one of the hypothesized components of experience expresses both internal disharmony and dearth of internal connections. As mentioned earlier, consciousness may be regarded as a continually moving kaleidoscopic system, taking on and divesting itself of different forms and viewpoints, as well as a variety of feelings and memories. Clearly, there are some regulatory systems which maintain a balance between consistency and change preventing extreme rigidity or extreme instability.

Using the metaphor of cog wheels again, the different components of an experience activate each other: moving one of them causes the others to move. Perhaps it is here that we can find an explanation for the fact that these diverse approaches, each of which emphasizes a different feature, arrive at similar results despite their differences. Metaphorically, each theory represents a different cog wheel. When one wheel is set in motion it mobilizes all the other wheels (different theoretical aspects). It follows that each treatment method launches a similar process, regardless of the particular point of origin.

The concept of multiple internal links, as a reflection of expanded awareness or consciousness, is a concept which integrates concepts from different and opposing theories into one unified theory. The psychoanalytic theory of associations, the theory of the relation between the real and the phenomenological self (Rogers), theories of dissociation and parallel distribution processes (PDP), and the cognitive theoreticians' associative network theory (ANT) may all coexist within it without conflicting with one another.

'Psychoanalytic' stream of associations is a process which is designed to bridge the gap between the conscious and the unconscious. Integrating the real and phenomenological self is intended to expand the self by actualizing potentials and to resolve contradictions between different parts of the personality. Mending the dissociative splits will integrate the different parts of the personality whose independent functioning or internal contradictoriness is creating problems. ANT is a theoretical model of information processing conceptualizing connections between different areas of functioning, such as cognition and emotion, and different categories of information which contain similarities.

All of these processes are represented by theories that understand behavior in different ways, but all of the theories relate to the attempt to attain harmonious activity and greater integration among the various parts of the personality, through bridging discrepancies and contradictions. The theoretical assumption which is common to these processes is that the personality's harmonious and integrative functioning engenders greater richness of experiences and expansion of awareness, which eventuate in more adaptive behavior.

It should be emphasized that there is a basic difference of opinion between the proponents of internal congruence and the cognitive theoreticians in their general outlook on behavior, and specifically their outlook on the unconscious. The cognitive approaches regard the relations between the aspects of experience as a uni-directional system, in which interpretations of perceived reality fit into pre-conceived internal schemata and these interpretations generate feelings accordingly. In other words, an emotional reaction cannot occur unless it is based on a definitive interpretation of reality, which may be conscious or unconscious. The internal congruence model postulates a multi-directional flow of the various components of experience. Reality may be interpreted in a unique fashion because the individual is in a unique emotional state at a given time; and vice versa, feeling may be changed by a surprising, enlightening interpretation (Bower, 1981).

One does not have to assume any longer that feeling precedes or succeeds cognitive interpretations of feeling. The internal congruence model assumes the existence of mutual, multi-directional influences. Internal harmony may originate from any of the elements of experience. (See Pascual-Leone, 1991.)

The different models discussed in this book, together with the hypotheses about the possible relationships between them, do not represent final conclusions. However, it is hoped that their presentation here will lead to new hypotheses concerning the theoretical, clinical and methodological study of the unconscious.

Bibliography

Allport, G. W. (1937). *Personality: A psychological interpretation*. New York: Holt.

Allport, G. (1955). *Becoming*. New Haven: Yale University Press.

Allport, G. (1961). *Patterns and Growth in Personality*. New York: Holt, Rinehart and Winston.

Almgren, D. E. (1971). Relationship between perceptual defense, defined by the Meta Contrast Technique and adaptive behavior in two serial behavior tests. *Psychological Research Bulletin*, Lund University, Sweden, **XI**, 3–19.

Archard, D. (1984). *Consciousness and the Unconscious*. La Salle, IL: Open Court Publishing.

Ariam, S. and Siller, J. (1982). Effects of subliminal oneness stimuli in Hebrew on academic performance of Israeli high school students: Further evidence on the adaptation-enhancing effects of symbiotic fantasies in another culture and another language. *Journal of Abnormal Psychology*, **91**(5), 343–9.

Arnold, M. B. (1960). *Emotional Personality*. New York: Columbia University Press.

Bartlett, F. C. (1932). *Remembering: A study in experimental and social psychology*. Cambridge, England: Cambridge University Press.

Bateson, G., Jackson, D. D., Haley, J. and Weakland, J. (1965). Toward a theory of schizophrenia. *Behavioral Science*, **I**, 251–64.

Beck, A. T. (1976). *Cognitive Therapy and the Emotional Disorders*. New York: International Universities Press.

Becker, E. (1973). *The Birth and Death of Meaning*. New York: The Free Press.

Ben Ahmotz, D. (1980). *To Remember and to Forget*. Tel-Aviv: Metziut.

Berlyne, D. E. (1960). Novelty and curiosity as determinants of explorative behavior. *British Journal of Psychology*, **41**, 68–80.

Bonanno, G. A., Davis, J. P., Singer, J. L. and Schwartz, G. E. (1991). The repressor personality and avoidant information processing: A dichotic listening study. *Journal of Research in Personality*, **25**, 386–401.

Bornstein, N. and Rodin, G. C. (1983) An experimental study of schizophrenic man. *Psychotherapy: Theory, Research and Practice*, **20**, 384–416.

Bower, G. H. (1981). Mood and memory. *American Psychologist*, **36**, 129–48.

Bower, G. H. and Meyer, D. (1985). Failure to replicate mood dependent retrieval. *Bulletin of the Psychonomic Society*, **23**, 39–42.

Bowers, K. S. (1984). On being unconsciously influenced and informed. In S. Bowers & D. Meichenbaum (Eds), *The Unconscious Reconsidered*. New York: Wiley.

Bowers, K. S. (1987). Revisioning the unconscious. *Canadian Psychology*, **28**, 93–104.

PART II: DEVELOPING STEAM CLASSROOMS

PART III: MAKING STEAM WORK

Bowers, K. S. (1989). Unconscious influence and hypnosis. In J. L. Singer (Ed.), *Repression and Dissociation*. Chicago: The University of Chicago Press.

Breuer, J. and Freud, S. (1893). The psychical mechanism of hysterical phenomena: Preliminary communication. In J. Strachey (Ed. and Trans.), *The Standard Edition of the Complete Psychological Works of Sigmund Freud (Vol. 2)*. London: Hogarth Press, 1955.

Bryant-Tuckett, R. and Silverman, L. H. (1984). Effects of subliminal stimulation of symbiotic fantasies on the academic performance of emotionally handicapped students. *Journal of Counseling Psychology*, **31**, 295–305.

Buckhout, R., Eugenio, P., Licita, T., Oliver, L. and Kramer, T. H. (1981). Memory hypnosis and evidence: Research on eyewitness. *Social Action and the Law*, **7**, 67–72.

Cameron, N. (1963) *Personality Development and Psychotherapy: A dynamic approach*. Boston: Houghton Mifflin.

Carroll, R. I. (1979). Neurophysiological and psychological mediators of response to subliminal perception: The influence of hemisphericity and defensive style on susceptibility to subliminally presented conflict-laden stimuli. Unpublished doctoral dissertation, St. John's University.

Chapnik-Smith, M. (1983). Hypnotic memory enhancement of witnesses: Does it work? *Psychological Bulletin*, **94**(3), 387–407.

Condon, J. J. and Allen, G. J. (1980). The role of psychoanalytic merging fantasies in systematic desensitization: A rigorous methodological examination. *Journal of Abnormal Psychology*, **89**, 437–43.

Conway, M. and Ross, M. (1984). Getting what you want by changing what you had. *Journal of Personality and Social Psychology*, **47**, 738–48.

Davis, J. P. (1987). Repression and the inaccessibility of affective memories. *Journal of Personality and Social Psychology*, **53**, 585–93.

Davis, J. P. and Schwartz, G. E. (1987). Repression and the inaccessibility of affective memories. *Journal of Personality and Social Psychology*, **52**, 155–62.

Decharms, R. S. (1968). *Personal Causation*. New York: Academic Press.

Dixon, N. F. (1981). *Preconscious Processing*. New York: Wiley.

Dollard, J. and Miller, N. E. (1950). *Personality and Psychotherapy*. New York: McGraw-Hill.

Eagle, M. (1984). *Recent Developments in Psychoanalysis: A critical evaluation*. Cambridge, MA: Harvard University Press.

Eagle, M. (1987). The psychoanalytic and the cognitive unconscious. In R. Stern (Ed.), *Theories of the Unconscious and Theories of the Self*. Hillsdale, NJ: The Analytic Press.

Ekman, P. (1992). An argument for basic emotions. *Cognition and Emotion*, **6**, 169–200.

Epstein, S. (1983). The unconscious, the preconscious, and the self concept. In J. Suls and A. Greenwald (Eds), *Psychological Perspectives of the Self*. Hillsdale, NJ: Erlbaum.

Erdelyi, M. H. (1985). *Psychoanalysis: Freud's Cognitive Psychology*. New York: Freeman.

Erdelyi, M. H. and Goldberg, B. (1979). Let's not sweep repression under the rug: Toward a cognitive psychology of repression. In J. F. Kihlstrom and F. J. Evans (Eds), *Functional Disorders of Memory*. Hillsdale, NJ: Erlbaum.

Erickson, M., Rossi, E. L. and Rossi, I. S. (1976). *Hypnotic Realities*. New York: Irvington Publishers.

Faught, W. S., Colby, K. M. and Parkinson, R. C. (1977). Inferences, affects, and intentions in a model of paranoia. *Cognitive Psychology*, **9**, 153–87.

Feffer, M. (1970). Symptom expression as a form of primitive decentering. Unpublished manuscript, Yeshiva University.

Festinger, L. (1957). *A Theory of Cognitive Dissonance*. Evanston, IL: Row Peterson.

Forster, P. M. and Govier, E. (1978). Discrimination without awareness. *Quarterly Journal of Experimental Psychology*, **30**, 282–95.

Frank, A. (1969). The unremembered and the unforgettable: Passive primal repression. *Psychoanalytic Study of the Child*, **24**, 48–77.

Frank, A. (1984). History and screen memories. *International Journal of Psychoanalysis*, **65**, 85–8.

Frankel, F. H. (1976). *Hypnosis: Trance as a coping mechanism*. New York: Plenum Medical Book Co.

Freud, S. (1900). The interpretation of dreams. In J. Strachey (Ed. and Trans.) *The Standard Edition of the Complete Psychological Works of Sigmund Freud (Vols. 4 and 5)*. London: Hogarth Press, 1953.

Freud, S. (1901). The psychopathology of everyday life. In J. Strachey (Ed.) and A. Tyson (Trans.) *The Standard Edition of the Complete Psychological Works of Sigmund Freud (Vol. 6)*. London: Hogarth Press, 1960.

Freud, S. (1909). Notes upon a case of obsessional neurosis. In J. Strachey (Ed. and Trans.) and A. Strachey (Trans.) *The Standard Edition of the Complete Psychological Works of Sigmund Freud (Vol. 10)*. London: Hogarth Press, 1955.

Freud, S. (1911). Psychoanalytic notes upon an autobiographical account of a case of paranoia (dementia paranoides). In J. Strachey (Ed. and Trans.) and A. Strachey (Trans.) *The Standard Edition of the Complete Works of Sigmund Freud (Vol. 12)*. London: Hogarth Press, 1958.

Freud, S. (1915a). Instincts and their vicissitudes. In J. Strachey (Ed. and Trans.) *The Standard Edition of the Complete Psychological Works of Sigmund Freud (Vol. 15)*. London: Hogarth Press, 1957.

Freud, S. (1915b). Repression. In J. Strachey (Ed. and Trans.) and C. M. Baines (Trans.) *The Standard Edition of the Complete Psychological Works of Sigmund Freud (Vol. 14)*. London: Hogarth Press, 1957.

Freud, S. (1915c). The unconscious. In J. Strachey (Ed. and Trans.) and C. M. Baines (Trans.) *The Standard Edition of the Complete Psychological Works of Sigmund Freud (Vol. 14)*. London: Hogarth Press, 1957.

Freud, S. (1917). Introductory lectures on psychoanalysis. In J. Strachey (Ed. and Trans.) *The Standard Edition of the Complete Psychological Works of Sigmund Freud (Vols. 15 and 16)*. London: Hogarth Press, 1961 and 1963.

Freud, S. (1918). From the history of an infantile neurosis. In J. Strachey (Ed. and Trans.) and A. Strachey (Trans.) *The Standard Edition of the Complete Psychological Works of Sigmund Freud (Vol. 17)*. London: Hogarth Press, 1958.

Freud, S. (1923). The ego and the id. J. Riviere (Trans.) In J. Strachey (Ed. and Trans.) *The Standard Edition of the Complete Psychological Works of Sigmund Freud (Vol. 19)*. London: Hogarth Press, 1961.

Freud, S. (1926). Inhibitions, symptoms and anxiety. In J. Strachey (Ed. and Trans.) and A. Strachey (Trans.) *The Standard Edition of the Complete Psychological Works of Sigmund Freud (Vol. 20)*. London: Hogarth Press, 1959.

Fribourg, A. (1981). Ego pathology in schizophrenia and fantasies of merging with the good mother. *Journal of Nervous and Mental Disease*, **1969**, 337–47.

Fromm, E. (1941). *Escape from Freedom*. New York: Farrar and Rinehart.

Fromm, E. (1955). *The Sane Society*. New York: Rinehart and Company.

Fromm, E., et al. (1968). The Oedipus complex: Comments on the case of Little

Hans. *Contemporary Psychoanalysis*, 4(2), 178–88.

Gazzaniga, M. S. (1985). *The Social Brain: Discovering the networks of the mind*. New York: Basic Books.

Geisler, C. (1986). The use of subliminal psychodynamic activation in the study of repression. *Journal of Personality and Social Psychology*, 57, 844–51.

Gilbert, P. (1989). *Human Nature and Suffering*. Hove, East Sussex: Erlbaum.

Giora, Z. (1988). *The Unconscious and Psychoneurosis*. Tel-Aviv: Zmora Bitan (Hebrew).

Greenberg, L. S. and Safran, J. D. (1984). Integrating affect and cognition: A perspective on the process of therapeutic change. *Cognitive Therapy and Research*, 8(6), 578–99.

Greenberg, L. S. and Safran, J. D. (1989). Emotion in psychotherapy. *American Psychologist*, 44, 19–29.

Greenberg, L. S., Rice, L. N. and Elliot, R. (1993). *Facilitating Emotional Change*. New York: Guilford Press.

Greenwald, A. C. (1980). The totalitarian ego: Fabrication and revision of personal history. *American Psychologist*, 35, 603–18.

Groeger, J. A. (1984). Evidence of unconscious semantic processing from a forced-error situation. *British Journal of Psychology*, 75, 305–14.

Groeger, J. A. (1988). Qualitatively different effects of undetected and unidentified auditory primes. *Quarterly Journal of Experimental Psychology*, 40, 323–39.

Gudgonsson, G. H. (1981). Self-reported emotional disturbance and its relation to electrodermal reactivity, defensiveness, and trait anxiety. *Personality and Individual Differences*, 2, 47–52.

Haley, J. (1973). *Uncommon Therapy*. New York: W. W. Norton.

Hansen, R. D. and Hansen, C. H. (1988). Repression of emotionally tagged memories: The architecture of less complex emotions. *Journal of Personality and Social Psychology*, 55, 811–18.

Harlow, H. F. and Meyer, D. R. (1950). Learning motivated by a manipulation motive. *Journal of Experimental Psychology*, 40, 228–34.

Haspel, R. C. and Harris, R. S. (1982). Effects of tachistoscopic stimulation to subconscious Oedipal wishes on competitive performance: A failure to replicate. *Journal of Abnormal Psychology*, 91, 437–44.

Hastie, R., Landsman, R. and Loftus, E. F. (1978). Eyewitness testimony: The danger of guessing. *Jurimetrics Journal*, 19, 1–18.

Heilbrun, K. (1980). Silverman's subliminal psychodynamic activation: A failure to replicate. *Journal of Abnormal Psychology*, 89, 560–66.

Heise, D. (1977). Social action and control of affect. *Behavioral Science*, 22, 163–77.

Higgins, E. T. (1987). Discrepancy: A theory relating self and affect. *Psychological Review*, 94, 319–40.

Hilgard, E. R. (1986). *Divided Consciousness: Multiple control in human thought and action*. New York: Wiley.

Horowitz, M. J. (1981). Psychological processes induced by illness, injury and loss. In T. Millon, C. Green and R. Meagher (Eds.), *Handbook of Clinical Health Psychology*. New York: Plenum Press.

Horowitz, M. J. (1988). *Introduction to Psychodynamics: A new synthesis*. New York: Routledge.

Horowitz, S. L. (1970). Strategies within hypnosis for reducing phobic behavior. *Journal of Abnormal Psychology*, 75, 104–12.

Hyde, T. W. and Jenkins, J. J. (1969). The differential effects of incidental tasks on the organization of recall of a list of highly associated words. *Journal of*

Experimental Psychology, **82**, 472 — 81.

Isen, A. I. (1987). Positive affect, cognitive processes and social behavior. *Advances in Experimental Psychology*, **82**, 472 — 81.

Izard, C. E. (1984). Emotion-cognition relationship and human development. In C. E. Izard, J. Kagan and R. B. Zajonc (Eds.), *Emotions, Cognitions and Behavior*. New York: Cambridge University Press.

Izard, C. E. (1991). *The Psychology of Emotions*. New York: Plenum Press.

Izard, C. E. (1992). Basic emotions, relations among emotions, and emotion-cognition relations. *Psychological Review*, **99**, 561 — 5.

Jackson, J. (1983). The effects of subliminally activated fantasies of merger with each parent on the pathology of male and female schizophrenics. *Journal of Nervous and Mental Disease*, **1971**, 280 — 89.

Jacobs, S. W. J. and Nadel, L. (1985). Stress-induced recovery of fears and phobias. *Psychological Review*, **92**, 512 — 31.

Jacoby, L. L., Walshyn, V. and Kelly, C. M. (1989). Becoming famous without being recognized: Unconscious influence of memory produced by divided attention. *Journal of Experimental Psychology: General*, **118**, 119 — 25.

Janet, P. (1889). *L'automatisme Psychologique: Essai de psychologie experimentale sur les formes inférieures de l'activité humaine*. Paris: Felix Aléan. Reprint Société Pierre Janet/Payot, Paris, 1973.

Janet, P. (1911). *L'état Mental des Hysteriques (édition seconde)*. Paris: Aléan.

Jelicic, M., De Rode, A., Bovill, J. G. and Bonke, B. (in press). Unconscious learning established under anaesthesia. *Anaesthesia*.

Jennis, J. L. (1986). The forgotten distinction between psychology and phenomenology. *American Psychologist*, **4**, 1231 — 40.

Johnson-Laird, P. N. and Oatley, K. (1989). The language of emotions: An analysis of a semantic field. *Cognition and Emotion*, **3**, 81 — 123.

Johnson-Laird, P. N. and Oatley, K. (1992). Basic emotions, rationality, and folk theory. *Cognition and Emotion*, **6**, 201 — 23.

Kelly, G. A. (1955). *The Psychology of the Personal Construct*. New York: W. W. Norton.

Kihlstrom, J. F. (1977). Models of hypnotic amnesia. *Annals of the New York Academy of Sciences*.

Kihlstrom, J. F. (1984). Conscious, subconscious, unconscious: A cognitive perspective. In K. S. Bowers & D. Meichenbaum (Eds.), *Unconscious Reconsidered*. New York: Wiley.

Kihlstrom, J. F. and Evans, F. J. (1976). Recovery of memory after posthypnotic amnesia. *Journal of Abnormal Psychology*, **85**, 558 — 63.

Kinston, W. and Cohen, J. (1986). Primal repression: Clinical and theoretical aspects. *International Journal of Psychoanalysis*, **67**, 337 — 55.

Kissin, B. (1986). *Conscious and Unconscious Programs in the Brain*. New York: Plenum Medical Book Company.

Klein, D. B. (1977). *The Unconscious: Invention or discovery*. Santa Monica, CA: Goodyear.

Kluft, R. P. (1984). Treatment of multiple personality disorder. *Clinics of North America*, 7(1), 9 — 29.

Kotze, H. F. and Moller, A. (1990). Effects of auditory subliminal stimulation on GSR. *Psychological Reports*, **67**, 931 — 4.

Kroger, W. S. and Douce, R. G. (1979). Hypnosis in criminal investigation. *International Journal of Clinical and Experimental Hypnosis*, **27**, 358 — 74.

Lacan, J. (1966). *Ecrits: A selection*. A. Sheridan (Trans.). New York: Norton, 1977.

Lacan, J. (1973). *The Four Fundamental Concepts of Psychoanalysis*. J.-A. Miller (Ed.) and A. Sheridan (Trans.). New York: Norton, 1978.

Laing, R. D. (1966). *The Divided Self*. New York: Penguin Books.

Laing, R. D. (1969). *Self and Others*. New York: Pantheon Books.

Laing, R. D. (1970). *Knots*. New York: Pantheon Books.

Langner, S. K. (1967). *Mind: An essay on human feeling (Vol. 1)*. Baltimore, MD: Johns Hopkins University Press.

Lazarus, R. (1982). Thoughts on the relations between emotion and cognition. *American Psychologist*, **37**, 1019−24.

Lazarus, R. S. (1991). Cognition and motivation in emotion. *American Psychologist*, **46**, 352−67.

Lecky, P. (1945). *Self-consistency: A theory of personality*. New York: The Shoe String Press.

LeDoux, J. E. (in press). Sensory systems and emotions: A model of affective processing. *Integrative Psychiatry*.

Leiter, E. (1982). The effects of subliminal activation of aggressive and merging fantasies in differentiated and non- differentiated schizophrenics. *Psychological Research Bulletin*, **22**, 1−21.

Leventhal, H. (1979). A perceptual motor processing model of emotion. In P. Pliner, K. R. Blankstein and I. M. Spigel (Eds.), *Advances in the Study of Communication and Affect (Vol. 5): Perception of emotions in the self and others*. New York: Plenum.

Levi, A. (1992). Paranoia: A psycholinguistic approach. *Sihot*, **6**(1), 52−7 (Hebrew).

Levin, I. (1958). *Compulsion*. Tel-Aviv: Idit (Hebrew).

Loftus, E. F. and Loftus, G. R. (1980). On the permanence of stored information in the human brain. *American Psychologist*, **35**, 409−20.

Lomanzino, L. (1969). The depiction of subliminally and superaminally presented aggressive stimuli and its effect on the cognitive functioning of schizophrenics. Unpublished doctoral dissertation, Fordham University, New York.

Long, P. J. (1983). Cognition in emotion: Concept and action. In C. Izard, J. Kagan and R. Zajonc (Eds.), *Emotion, Cognition and Behavior*. New York: Cambridge University Press.

Long, P. (1984). The cognitive psychophysiology of emotions: Fears and anxiety. In A. H. Tuma and J. D. Maser (Eds.), *Anxiety and the Anxiety Disorders*. Hillsdale, NJ: Erlbaum.

Ludwig, A. M. (1983). The psychobiological functions of dissociation. *American Journal of Clinical Hypnosis*, **26**, 93−9.

MacKay, D. (1973). Aspects of the theory of comprehension, memory and attention. *Quarterly Journal of Experimental Psychology*, **25**, 22−40.

MacKinnon, D. W. and Dukes, W. (1964). Repression. In L. Postman (Ed.), *Psychology in the Making*. New York: Alfred A. Knopf.

Maddi, S. (1980). *Personality Theories: A comparative analysis (4th edn)*. Homewood, IL: Dorsey Press.

Madison, P. (1961). *Freud's Concept of Repression and Defense: Its theoretical and observational language*. Minneapolis: University of Minnesota Press.

Marcel, A. J. (1980). Conscious and preconscious recognition of polysemous words: Locating the selective effects of prior context. In R. S. Nickerson (Ed.), *Attention and Performance*. Hillsdale, NJ: Erlbaum.

Marcel, A. J. (1983). Conscious and unconscious perception: An approach to the relations between phenomenal experiences and perceptual process. *Cognitive Psychology*, **15**, 298−300.

Markus, H. and Nuris, P. (1986). 'Possible selves.' *American Psychologist*, **51**, 858–66.

Markus, H. and Wurf, E. (1987). The dynamic self-concept: Asocial psychological perspective. *Annual Review of Psychology*, **38**, 299–337.

Masling, K. M., Bornstein, R. F., Poynton, F. G., Reed, S. and Katkin, E. S. (1991). Perception without awareness and electrodermal responding: A strong test of subliminal psychodynamic activation effects. *The Journal of Mind & Behavior*, **12**, 11–48.

Matte-Blanco, I. (1975). *The Unconscious as Infinite Sets*. London: Duckworth.

Meichenbaum, D. A. (1977). *Cognitive-behavior Modification: An integrative approach*. New York: Plenum.

Meichenbaum, D. and Gilmore, B. (1984). The nature of unconscious processes: A cognitive perspective. In K. S. Bowers and D. Meichenbaum (Eds.), *The Unconscious Reconsidered*. New York: Wiley.

Merleau-Ponty, M. (1962). *The Phenomenology of Perception*. New York: Humanities Press.

Miller, N. E. (1950). Learnable drives and rewards. In S. Stevens (Ed.), *Handbook of Experimental Psychology*. New York: Wiley.

Minsky, M. R. (1980). K-lines: A theory of memory. *Cognitive Science*, **4**, 117–33.

Murphy, G. (1958). *Human Potentialities*. New York: Basic Books.

Myers, F. W. H. (1892). The subliminal consciousness. *Proceedings of the Society for Psychic Research*, **VII**, 298–355.

Myers, L. B. and Brewin, C. R. (1994). Recall of early experiences and the repressive coping style. *Journal of Abnormal Psychology*, **103**, 288–92.

Neisser, U. (1967). *Cognitive Psychology*. New York: Appleton-Century-Crofts.

Nemiah, J. C. (1984). The unconscious and psychopathology. In K. S. Bowers and D. Meichenbaum (Eds.), *The Unconscious Reconsidered*. New York: Wiley.

Nichols, M. P. and Efran, J. (1985). Catharsis in psychotherapy: A new perspective. *Psychotherapy*, **22**(1), 46–58.

Nisbett, R. E. and Wilson, T. D. (1977). Telling more than we know: Verbal reports on mental processes. *Psychological Review*, **84**, 231–59.

Novaco, R. W. (1975). *Anger control: The development and evaluation of an experimental treatment*. Lexington, MA: Lexington.

Noyes, R., Hoenk, P. R., Kuperman, S. and Slymen, D. (1977). Depersonalization in accident victims and psychiatric patients. *Journal of Nervous and Mental Disease*.

Noyes, R. and Kletti, R. (1976). Depersonalization in the face of life-threatening danger: A description. *Psychiatry*, **39**, 19–26.

Oatley, K. (1988). Gaps in consciousness, emotion and memory in psychoanalysis. *Cognition and Emotion*, **2**, 29–50.

Oatley, K. and Johnson Laird, P. N. (1987). Towards a cognitive theory of emotions. *Cognition and Emotion*, **1**, 29–50.

Orbach, I. (1989). Intrafamilial and intrapsychic splits in suicidal adolescents. *American Journal of Psychotherapy*, **XLIII**, 356–67.

Orbach, I. and Bar-Joseph, H. (1990). Styles of problem solving in suicidal individuals. *Suicide and Life-Threatening Behavior*, **20**, 56–64.

Orbach, I., Shopen-Kofman, R. and Mikulincer, M. (1994) The impact of subliminal symbiotic vs. identification messages in reducing anxiety. *Journal of Research in Personality*, **28**, 492–504.

Orni, M. T. (1972). On the simulating subject as a quasi- control group in hypnosis research: What, why and how? In E. Fromm and R. E. Shor (Eds.), *Hypnosis: Research development and perspectives*. Chicago: Aldine Atherton.

Ortony, A. and Turner, T. J. (1990). What's basic about basic emotions? *Psychological Review*, **97**, 315–31.

Packer, S. (1984). Subliminal activation of unconscious fantasies as an adjunct in behavior assertiveness training. Paper presented at the meeting of the American Psychological Association, Toronto, Canada, August.

Palmatier, J. R. and Bornstein, P. H. (1980). The effects of subliminal stimulation of symbiotic merging fantasies on behavioral treatment of smokers. *Journal of Nervous and Mental Disease*, **168**, 715–20.

Panksepp, J. (1989). The neurobiology of emotions of animal brains and human feelings. In H. Wagner & A. Manstead (Eds.), *Handbook of Social Psychophysiology*. New York: Wiley.

Panksepp, J. (1992). A critical role for 'affective neuroscience' in resolving what is basic about basic emotions. *Psychological Review*, **99**, 554–60.

Pascual-Leone, J. (1991). Emotions, development and psychotherapy: A dialectical-constructivist perspective. In J. D. Safran and L. S. Greenberg (Eds.), *Emotions, Psychotherapy and Change*. New York: Guilford.

Pawer, M. and Brewin, C. R. (1991). From Freud to cognitive science: A contemporary account of the unconscious. *British Journal of Clinical Psychology*, **30**, 1–22.

Perls, F. (1969). *Gestalt Therapy Verbatim*. Lafayette, CA: Real People Press.

Piaget, J. (1951). *Play Dreams and Imitation*. London: Routledge & Paul.

Piaget, J. (1968). *Le Structuralisme*. Paris: Presses Universitares de France.

Piaget, J. (1986). *Six Essays on Mental Development*. Tel-Aviv: Sifriat Poalim.

Pitman, R. K. (1987). Pierre Janet on obsessive-compulsive disordered (1903). *Archives of General Psychiatry*, **44**, 226–32.

Plutchik, R. (1968). The evolutionary basis of emotional behavior. In M. B. Arnold (Ed.), *The Nature of Emotion*. New York: Penguin.

Plutchik, R. (1989). Measuring emotions and their derivations. In R. Plutchik and H. Kellerman (Eds), *The Measurement of Emotions (Vol. 4)*. San Diego, CA: Academic Press.

Plutchik, R. and Kellerman, H. (Eds.). (1989). *Emotion, Theory, Research and Experience (Vol. 4): The measurement of emotions*. New York: Academic Press.

Porterfield, A. L. and Golding, S. L. (1985). A failure to find an effect of subliminal psychodynamic activation upon cognitive measures of pathology in schizophrenia. *Journal of Abnormal Psychology*, **94**, 630–39.

Putnam, F. W., Guroff, J. J., Silberman, E. K., Barban, S. and Post, R. M. (1986). The clinical phenomenology of multiple personality disorder: Review of 100 recent cases. *Journal of Clinical Psychiatry*, **47**(6), 285–93.

Rachman, E. E. S. and Lopatka, C. (1990). Affect, pain and autobiographical memory. *Journal of Abnormal Psychology*, **99**, 174–78.

Rapaport, D. (1967). The scientific methodology of psychoanalysis. In M. M. Gill (Ed.), *The Collective Papers of David Rapaport*. New York: Basic Books.

Reber, A. S. (1976). Implicit learning of artificial grammar. *Journal of Verbal Learning and Verbal Behavior*, **6**, 855–63.

Riskind, J. H. (1984). They stoop to conquer: Guiding the self-regulatory functions of physical posture after success and failure. *Journal of Personality and Social Psychology*, **47**, 479–93.

Rogers, C. (1961). *On Becoming a Person*. Boston: Houghton Mifflin.

Rumelhart, D. E. and McClelland, J. L. (Eds.). (1986). *Parallel Distributing Processes*. Cambridge, MA: MIT Press.

Rutstein, E. H. and Goldberg, L. (1973). The effects of aggressive stimulation on suicidal patients: An experimental study of the psychoanalytic theory of suicide.

In I. Rubinstein (Ed.), *Psychoanalysis and Contemporary Science (Vol. 2)*. New York: Macmillan.

Rychlak, J. F. (1973). *Introduction to Personality and Psychopathology*. Boston: Houghton Mifflin.

Safran, J. D. and Greenberg, L. S. (1987). Affect and the unconscious: A cognitive perspective. In R. Stern (Ed.), *Theories of the Unconscious and the Theories of the Self*. Hillsdale, NJ: The Analytic Press.

Safran, J. D. and Greenberg, L. S. (1991). Affective change processes: A synthesis and critical analysis. In J. D. Safran and L. S. Greenberg (Eds), *Emotion, Psychotherapy and Change*. New York: Guilford.

Sartre, J. P. (1943). *Being and Nothingness: An essay on phenomenological ontology*. H. E. Barnes (Trans.). London, 1957.

Shapiro, D. (1965). *Neurotic Styles*. New York: Basic Books.

Shapiro, D. (1981). *Autonomy and Rigid Character*. New York: Basic Books.

Sharansky, N. (1989). *I Shall Not Fear Evil*. Tel-Aviv: Idanim (Hebrew).

Shavit, D. (1989). *A Poet who Intends to Commit Suicide*. Tel-Aviv: Hakibbutz Hameuhad (Hebrew).

Shevrin, H. S. and Dickman, S. (1980). The psychological unconscious. *American Psychologist*, **35**, 421–34.

Shevrin, H., Smith, W. H. and Fritzler, D. E. (1971). Average evoked response and verbal correlates of unconscious mental processes. *Psychophysiology*, **8**, 149–162.

Shneidman, E. (1982). *Voices of Death*. New York: Harper & Row.

Shor, R. E. (1970). The three factor theory of hypnosis as applied to the book reading fantasy and the concept of suggestion. *International Journal of Clinical and Experimental Psychology*, **28**, 89–98.

Silverman, L. H. (1976). Psychoanalytic theory: The reports of my death are greatly exaggerated. *American Psychologist*, **September**, 621–36.

Silverman, L. H. (1982). A comment on two subliminal psychodynamic activation studies. *Journal of Abnormal Psychology*. **91**, 621–37.

Silverman, L. H., Borenstein, A. and Mendelson, E. (1976). The Fertler use of the subliminal psychodynamic activation method for the experimental study of the clinical theory of psychoanalysis: On the specificity of relationships between manifest psychopathology and unconscious conflicts. *Psychotherapy: Theory, Research and Practice*, **13**, 2–16.

Silverman, L. H., Lachman, F. and Milich, R. (1982). *The Search for Oneness*. New York: International Universities Press.

Silverman, L. H., Ross, D. L., Adler, J. M. and Lusting, D. (1978). Simple research paradigm for demonstrating subliminal dynamic activation: Effects of Oedipal stimuli on dart throwing accuracy in college males. *Journal of Abnormal Psychology*, **87**, 341–57.

Singer, E. (1970). *Key Concepts in Psychotherapy*. New York: Basic Books.

Smith, S. M. (1979). Remembering in and out of context. *Journal of Experimental Psychology: Human Learning and Memory*, **5**, 460–71.

Somekh, D. E. and Wilding, J. M. (1973). Perception without awareness in a dichotic viewing situation. *British Journal of Psychology*, **64**, 339–49.

Spanos, P. N. and Hewitt, E. C. (1980). The hidden observer in hypnotic analgesia: Discovery or experimental creation? *Journal of Personality and Social Psychology*, **39**, 1201–14.

Spiegel, D. (1989). Hypnosis, dissociation and trauma: Hidden and overt observers. In J. L. Singer (Ed.), *Repression and Dissociation*. Chicago: The University of Chicago Press, pp. 121–147.

Spiegel, D., Hunt, T. and Donershine, H. E. (1988) Dissociation and hypnotability in posttraumatic stress disorder. *American Journal of Psychiatry*. **145**, 301−5.

Stagner, R. (1961). *The Psychology of Personality*. New York: McGraw-Hill.

Stein, N. L. and Trabasso, T. (1992). An organization of emotional experience: Creating links among emotion, thinking, language, and intentional action. *Cognition and Emotion*, **6**, 225−44.

Stevenson, J. H. (1976). The effects of posthypnotic dissociation on the performance of interfering tasks. *Journal of Abnormal Psychology*, **85**, 398−407.

Stewart, W. D. (1982). Jacques Lacan and the language of the unconscious. *Bulletin of the Menninger Clinic*, **47**(1), 53−9.

Stewart, W. D. (1986). Lacan's linguistic unconscious and the language of desire. *Psychoanalytic Review*, **73**(1), 17−29.

Strauman, T. J. and Higgins, E. T. (1987). Automatic activation of self-discrepancies and emotional syndromes: When cognitive structures influence affect. *Journal of Personality and Social Psychology*, **53**(6), 1004−14.

Sullivan, H. S. (1956). Clinical studies in psychiatry. In *The Collected Works of Henry Stach Sullivan (Vol. II)*. New York: Norton.

Teasdale, J. D. and Fogarty, S. J. (1979). Differential effects of induced mood on retrieval of pleasant and unpleasant events from episodic memory. *Journal of Abnormal Psychology*, **88**, 248−57.

Tellegen, A. and Atkinson, G. (1974). Openness to absorbing and self-altering experiences (absorption): A trait related to hypnotic susceptibility. *Journal of Abnormal Psychology*, **83**, 268−77.

Van der Kolk, B. A. (1987). *Psychological Trauma*. Washington, DC: American Psychiatric Press.

Van der Kolk, B. A. and Ducey, C. R. (1989). The psychological processing of traumatic experience: Rorschach patterns in PTSD. *Journal of Traumatic Stress*, **2**, 259−274.

Van der Kolk, B. A. and Van der Hart, O. (1989). Pierre Janet and the breakdown of adaptation in psychological trauma. *American Journal of Psychiatry*, **146**, 1530−40.

Warrington, E. K. (1971). Neurological disorders of memory. *British Medical Bulletin*, **27**, 243−7.

Watzlawick, P., Weakland, J. H. and Fisch, R. (1979). *Change: Principles of problem formation and problem solving*. Palo Alto, CA: Mental Research Institute.

Weakland, J. H. (1960). The double-bind hypothesis of schizophrenia and three-way party interaction. In D. D. Jackson (Ed.), *The Etiology of Schizophrenia*. New York: Basic Books.

Weinberger, D. A. (1990). The constructive validity of the repressive coping style. In J. L. Singer (Ed.), *Repression and Dissociation*. New York: University of Chicago Press.

Weinberger, D. A., Schwartz, G. E. and Davidson, R. J. (1979). Low anxious, high anxious, and repressive coping styles: Psychometric patterns and behavioral and physiological responses to stress. *Journal of Abnormal Psychology*, **88**, 369−80.

Wortman, C. B. and Loftus, E. F. (1988). *Psychology*. New York: Alfred A. Knopf.

Yager, K. E. (1987). Subliminal therapy: Utilizing the unconscious mind. *Medical Hypnosis Journal*, **2**(4), 138−47.

Yalom, D. (1980). *Existential Psychotherapy*. New York: Basic Books.

Yates, J. L. and Nasby, W. (1993). Dissociating, affect and network models of memory: An integrative proposal. *Journal of Traumatic Stress*, **6**, 305−26.

Zajonc, R. B. (1980). Feeling and thinking: Preferences need no inferences. *American Psychologist*, **35**, 151−75.

Zelig, M. and Beidleman, W. B. (1981). The investigative use of hypnosis: A word of caution. *International Journal of Clinical and Experimental Hypnosis*, **29**(4), 401−12.

Author Index

Subject Index

aroused. The opposite is also true; the more the memory or the circumstance are described in tangible terms, the stronger will be the emotional overtones aroused by the description.

This was illustrated in the treatment of a woman who sought help after repeated failures to establish relationships with men. In the first stages of therapy, she spoke generally and with emotional distance of her difficulties with men: 'They're all wrong for me. I don't have anything in common with any of them.' Later, she phrased her feelings more specifically: 'I'm really frightened that I won't get along with them. Whenever I find someone, I think I'm losing someone else.' Finally, when she was even more specific and spoke of feelings in more tangible fashion, her description of the experience became charged with feeling: 'I get nervous each time the subject of love comes up. I feel kind of restless and want to run away.' This concrete description of her feelings carried a strong emotional charge. 'When I go to bed with Jack (whom she likes), I actually get nauseous. I want to throw up and I have to stop what we are doing.' Despite the fact that all of these statements relate to the same problem, the very general and emotionally distant phrasing achieved little effect, while the last description freed the feelings that had been restrained earlier.

Feelings are engaged more effectively when they are described concretely. This is congruent with Neisser's (1967) hypotheses about the stages of information processing, which begin with general and vague primary processing and progress to more specific and detailed secondary processing.

Intensification of feeling may be achieved by utilizing the more extreme techniques of exposure and flooding. These techniques create an extreme reaction. For example, a phobic patient is purposely exposed to the anxiety-provoking object. At first, the patient becomes extremely anxious in response to the exposure, but remaining in the continued presence of the feared object leads to gradual reduction of anxiety. This technique functions by arousing and releasing maximum feeling, rather than creating a harmonious experience. From the standpoint of the internal congruence model, release of feeling is only partially effective if the release does not affect the other dimensions of the experience.

PROCESSES THAT ESTABLISH INTRA-EXPERIENTIAL CONGRUENCE

Creation of Congruence through Direct Focus on the Experience

Focus on the experience means what it says — looking at the experience presented by the patient from all possible angles. The following is an example of focusing treatment on the experience.

Related titles of interest from Wiley...